Meaning in Western Architecture

Meaning in Western Architecture

Christian Norberg-Schulz

RIZZOLI
NEW YORK

This revised edition published in the United
States of America in 1980 by:

RIZZOLI INTERNATIONAL PUBLICATIONS, INC.
712 Fifth Avenue/New York 10019

Second impression, 1981
Third impression, 1983
Originally published in Italy under the title
Significato nell'architettura occidentale
by Electa Editrice
© 1974 by Electa Editrice, Milano,
English translation © 1975 by Praeger Publishers, Inc.
First published in Great Britain in 1975

ISBN 0-8478-0319-8
LC 80-51173

Printed in Italy

Contents

Preface

This is a book about architecture.
Architecture is a concrete phenomenon.
It comprises landscapes and settlements,
buildings and characterizing articulation.
Therefore it is a living reality.
Since remote times architecture has helped man
in making his existence meaningful.
With the aid of architecture he has gained
a foothold in space and time.
Architecture is therefore concerned with something more
than practical needs and economy.
It is concerned with existential meanings.
Existential meanings are derived
from natural, human and spiritual phenomena,
and are experienced as order and character.
Architecture translates these meanings
into spatial forms.
Spatial forms in architecture are
neither Euclidean nor Einsteinian.
In architecture spatial form means
place, path and domain,
that is, the concrete structure of man's environment.
Therefore architecture cannot be satisfactorily described
by means of geometrical or semiological concepts.
Architecture ought to be understood
in terms of meaningful (symbolic) forms.
As such it is part of the history of existential meanings.
Today man feels an urgent need
for a reconquest of architecture
as a concrete phenomenon.
The present book is intended as a contribution
to gain this end.[*]

Christian Norberg-Schultz

Oslo, January, 1974

[*] The theory of space which is applied in the present book is discussed in the author's *Existence, Space and Architecture* (London and New York, 1971). For a general theory of architectural symbolism, see the author's *Intentions in Architecture* (London and Cambridge, Mass., 1963).

1. Egyptian Architecture

1.   *Giza. From left to right: pyramids of My-cerinus, Chephren and Cheops. Fourth Dynasty (2723-2563 BC).*

2.   *Abusir. Fifth Dynasty (2563-2423 BC). Aerial view.*

(1)   G.Kaschnitz von Weinberg, *Mittelmeer-ische Kunst* (Berlin, 1965), p. 168.

(2)   Mesopotamian architecture did not arrive at an analogous level of abstraction, and the characterizing detail remained a mere application. See, for instance, the articulation of the Kassite Temple of Karaindash from Warka (about 1440 BC). H. Frankfort, *The Art and Architecture of the Ancient Orient* (Harmondsworth, 1954; and Baltimore, 1959), p. 63.

(3)   H. Schäfer, *Weltge-bäude der Alten Ägypter* (Berlin, 1928), pp. 89 ff. I may also point out that the Egyptians substituted for "south" and "north" "up the river" and "down the river." They characterized the Euphrates as "the preposterous water which flows down when it goes up."

(4)   "The whole symbolism rests on the accepted correspondence of things, on an intuitively conceived and perceived connexion between microcosm and macrocosm." M. Lurker, *Symbole der alten Ägypter* (Weilheim, 1964), p. 9.

Introduction

The buildings of ancient Egypt may still be counted among the most impressive constructions in the history of architecture. Megalithic masses and precision of form give them a singular strength and power. Simple stereometric shapes and strict geometric organization prevail, and, although it is possible to see a certain historical development in Egyptian architecture, the basic intentions seem to have been constant during the course of almost three thousand years. These intentions are most convincingly represented by the pyramid, which is generally regarded as the typical manifestation of Egyptian architecture. Its balanced form, appearing as a synthesis of vertical and horizontal forces, and its incomparably massive and solid construction seem to embody a constant, eternal order.

In fact "order" and "constancy" well indicate the basic aim of Egyptian architecture. Stone was selected for its hardness and resistance to decay, and its natural character is enhanced through the contrasts of smooth surfaces and sharp edges. Mass and weight are thereby abstracted so as to become part of a general system of symbolic organization, in which the vertical and horizontal are unified to form an orthogonal space which is basically the same throughout. We may call this "absolute space," and the single building acts as a materialization of it.[1] In achieving this, Egyptian architecture arrived at a level of abstraction which was not attempted by other early Mediterranean civilizations, and it may be considered the first integrated architectural symbol system in the history of mankind.[2] As such, however, it seems to have had a relatively narrow range of expressive possibilities.

It would be wrong to describe Egyptian space as no more than the static orthogonal coordinate system it might appear to be. A closer look at the monuments shows that as a rule they are axially disposed. Axiality, then, becomes another distinguishing phenomenon in Egyptian architecture. It is particularly evident in the great temples of the

3. *Plan of the Egyptian pyramids of the Fourth Dynasty of the Ancient Reign.*

4. *Tell el-Amarna. Eighteenth Dynasty (1580-1314 BC). Reconstruction of the central quarter.*

New Kingdom, but the pyramids of the Old Kingdom also formed part of a spatial sequence. Although it implies a direction, Egyptian axiality, however, is always enclosed. It does not symbolize a dynamic occupation of the surroundings, but rather seems to represent an eternal state of affairs. Orthogonal and axial organization therefore fulfill the same purpose: the creation of a constant, eternally valid environment.

This general intention, however, did not prevent a considerable variety and richness in articulation and detailing. It is certainly true that Egyptian decoration never threatens the integrity of the general form, and usually it enhances the crystalline quality of the plastic elements, but it may also give the individual building a certain particular flavour. The great themes of the main building tasks could be interpreted anew over and over again, and we may distinguish changes in taste and artistic intent over the long history of Egyptian culture. In fact, it is possible to talk about a *history* of Egyptian architecture because a level of abstraction had been reached which allowed for the concretization of general existential meanings. But rather than manifesting a wish for experiment the development involved was an ever more systematic working-out of the same basic intentions.

Landscape and Settlement

The Egyptian landscape offers a first clue to a better understanding of the basic phenomena indicated above. Hardly any other country has a geographical structure of such simplicity and regularity. On both sides of the long and narrow Nile valley are deserts which put clearly defined limits to man's space. Egypt can therefore be described as a longitudinal oasis with a relatively uniform character throughout. Its climate is dry and stable, and together with the regular flooding of the Nile, it seems to manifest an eternal natural order. Together the basic elements of nature establish a simple spatial structure, with the Nile flowing from south to north and the sun rising in the east and setting in the west. These simple bearings are represented in the

hieroglyph for "world": a section through a valley with the sky above and the transversely moving sun inscribed.[3]

The fields on either side of the Nile were divided to form an orthogonal coordinate system with the river acting as a longitudinal axis. In Upper Egypt this pattern is confined by ranges of mountains, as indicated in the world hieroglyph. In Lower Egypt the transition between oasis and desert is more gradual, although clearly defined. Here we find the great pyramids which were placed to form a long row of artificial mountains parallel to the Nile. From the pyramids long causeways led approximately at right angles down to the river. Even in Thebes the temples form a similar row along the range of mountains, although there are no pyramids but tombs in the mountain itself. We see, thus, how planning and architecture were employed to complete and articulate the natural structure of the country. The purpose was to make visible the spatial structure which gave Egyptian man his sense of existential identity and security.

Within this general structure those places having a special, individual character were from early times ascribed local gods. These gods only played a subordinate role in Egyptian mythology; the primary characters were derived from the more general aspects of nature and human life. Although they have a distinct character, the Egyptian gods were not motivated by individual wishes and caprices, but formed part of an integrated mythological system where each is functionally and symbolically dependent upon the others.[4] Analogously, the natural elements were conceived as general characters rather than individual places. For instance, the concepts of "earth" and "desert" were abstractions, denoted respectively by the colours black and red.

Thus Egypt's simple geographical structure provided a basis for symbolizing basic existential meanings. In the physical environment these were concretized as axially organized and orthogonally structured enclosures, which were disposed in accordance with the great longitudinal space of the Nile valley. This also holds true for the layout of settlements and towns.

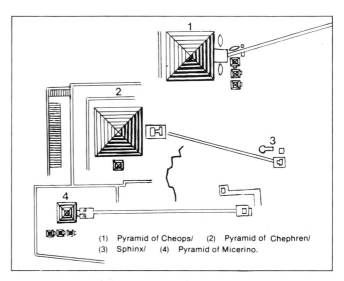

(1) Pyramid of Cheops/   (2) Pyramid of Chephren/
(3) Sphinx/   (4) Pyramid of Micerino.

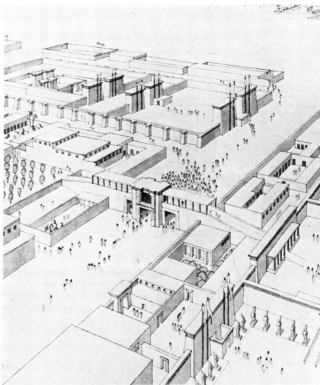

5. *Temple of Amon, Karnak. Nineteenth Dynasty (1314-1200 BC). Isometric detail of the hypostyle hall.*

6. *Giza.*
(1) terrace of the Sphinx (2) temple of Amenhotep II (3) rock tomb (4) temple of Harmachis (5) valley temple of Chephren.

7. *Temple of Amon, Karnak. Nineteenth Dynasty (1314-1200 BC). Reconstruction and ground plan.*

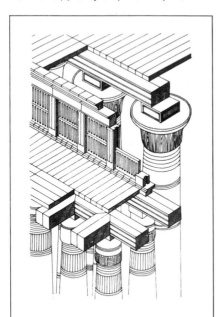

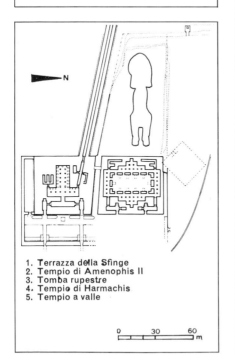

1. Terrazza della Sfinge
2. Tempio di Amenophis II
3. Tomba rupestre
4. Tempio di Harmachis
5. Tempio a valle

0   30   60
m.

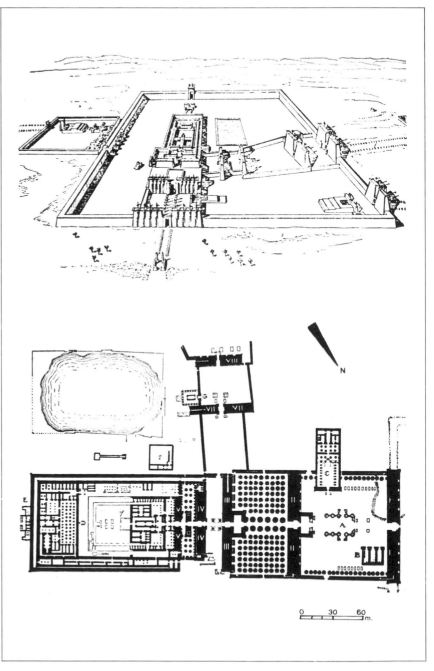

0   30   60
m.

8. *Administrative building of Lower Egypt, Saqqara. Third Dynasty (2778-2723 BC).*

9. *Valley temple of Chephren, Giza. Fourth Dynasty (2723-2563 BC). T-shaped passageway to the hypostyle hall.*

10. *"White Chapel," pavilion of Sesostris I, Karnak. 1971-1928 BC.*

11. *Temple of Amon, Karnak. Nineteenth Dynasty (1314-1200 BC). Columns of the hypostyle hall.*

Building

The wish to present an eternal order in symbolic form implies a necessity to demonstrate the continuation of life after death. Tombs and mortuary temples, that is "houses of eternity," were therefore the primary building tasks of ancient Egypt. We have already seen that the vital order to be concretized was closely related to the structure of Egyptian nature and landscape. The temple repeats the same structure on a smaller scale. As an axially organized and orthogonally structured oasis, it was obviously intended as a direct representation of the Egyptian cosmos. This becomes still more evident in an examination of its monumental gateway—the pylon. The pylon consists of two massive towers with inclined walls, united by a tall door. Over this door, between the towers, is a representation of the sun. The relationship with the hieroglyph for world is evident. As the temples were generally oriented towards the east, the rising sun was seen from the inside between the two halves of the pylon, and the door became the "gate of heaven" through which emerged the shining sun-god and his representative, the Pharaoh.

Basically the plan of the temple consists of three parts—a colonnaded courtyard, a hypostyle hall and a sanctuary—arranged along an axis. In the larger temples there may be two courtyards and two or more halls. Whereas the court is open to the sky and the sun, the halls are covered by ceilings decorated with painted stars. The arrangement of the temple is symbolic. The main hall functioned as a Hall of Appearances where the dweller in the temple-palace came forth among his court. It was usually lit from a central clerestory.[5] Penetrating into the building the spaces become gradually smaller. The floor rises and the ceiling drops down. Finally, the sanctuary appears as an enclosed cell at the end of the axis, which disappears into a symbolic false door carved in the west wall. We can read this as a representation of the path of life, whose end is not monumental space but rather an eternal return to the origin.

The systematic layout of the great temples of the New Kingdom was prefigured in the pyramid complexes of the Old Kingdom. Here the tomb proper, the pyramid, is preceded by a mortuary temple at its foot, containing a hall, a courtyard and a sanctuary with a false door in the west wall. Towards the east a long, straight causeway leads down to the vestibule or "valley temple" on the Nile.[6] This is another interpretation of the path with the static and absolute mass of the pyramid as the goal. The pyramid may be understood as a monumentalized version of the simpler and more ancient mastaba tomb, which again stems from the more primitive earthen tumulus. In this continuous process of abstraction, the original spontaneous experience of a powerful and durable mass has been symbolized in terms of absolute stereometric relationships.

In general, Egyptian buildings represent a synthesis of four fundamental intentions: the enclosed "oasis," the durable, megalithic mass, the orthogonal order and the path or axis. All these are presented symbolically in Egyptian architecture and together constitute a convincing representation of the Egyptian cosmos. Other buildings, such as dwellings, make use of the same basic forms, although they are applied with less rigour than in the great public tasks.

Articulation

Characteristic means of architectural articulation developed naturally from the wish to represent a highly organized cosmos. Whereas the spatial organization described above symbolizes the general properties of the Egyptian world, other means were used to show that organic and human life also belong to this cosmos. In particular, even from the first dynasties stone architecture is embellished with plant motifs or forms borrowed from lighter wooden constructions.[7] Two intentions must be distinguished in this connection. As wooden structures usually have a skeletal character, they form an important source of inspiration for the articulation of the originally amorphous mass of clay or stone buildings, and the wish to concretize an orthogonal space must have made an articulation of this kind necessary. But plant motifs were also used because of the wish to give every aspect of life an absolute, eternal form.

(5) The most grandiose example is the great hypostyle hall at Karnak built during the reigns of Ramses I, Sethos I and Ramses II (Nineteenth Dynasty), which measures 103 by 52 metres (338 by 171 feet) and contains 140 columns.

(6) The disposition is well illustrated by the pyramid group at Abusir from the Fifth Dynasty.

(7) E. Baldwin Smith, *Egyptian Architecture as Cultural Expression* (New York and London, 1938), first two chapters.

(8) *Ibid.*, p. 249.

12. *Relief sculpture from an obelisk, Karnak.*

13. *Temple of Amon, Luxor. 1478-1372 BC. Colonnade of the court of Amenhotep III.*

Articulation in general consists in a simultaneous dividing and linking of parts. Any articulate totality has to consist of parts which have a different function within the whole, but which are interdependent rather than independent. Egyptian architecture provides the first conscious and systematic attempt at an articulation of this kind. The different exterior or interior walls of the buildings are separated by mouldings which form a continuous frame, as is well exemplified in the pavilions of Sesostris I and Amenhotep I at Karnak. Here the roof is also interpreted as a separate part by means of a deep cavetto. Although these means of articulation are derived from primitive structures in wood, they have a formal function which goes beyond the simple wish to give them permanence.

Artists of the Old Kingdom developed representative surface reliefs whose aim was to make the actions of men and gods appear as expressions of an absolute, divine order. We might say that the figures do not act on the basis of an individual will, but rather participate in scenes which have a universal, normative character. These reliefs also play a general formal role in the whole. As they always leave the frontal plane intact, a textural effect is obtained which enhances the comprehensive orthogonal structure, rather than dissolving it into a play of light and shadow. Originally the effect was strengthened by the use of colour.

However, the most conspicuous expression of the Egyptian wish for articulation is found in the rich variety of columns. Mostly they are derived from plant forms; there are closed and open versions of papyrus and lotus columns as well as palm columns. Although they played a role as structural members, the columns were primarily "fertility emblems, symbols of the land and of sacred plants which rose out of the fertilized soil to bring protection, permanence and sustenance to the land and its people." [8] This symbolic meaning was combined with the conception of mass, solidity and size as an expression of durability. In certain buildings there are also simpler structural members, such as pillars or proto-Doric columns, which mainly contribute to make the orthogonal space visible.

14. *Mortuary complex of Zoser, Saqqara. Third Dynasty (2778-2723 BC). Reconstruction.*

15. *Mortuary complex of Zoser, Saqqara.*

16. *Heb-Sed court and pyramid of Zoser, Saqqara.*

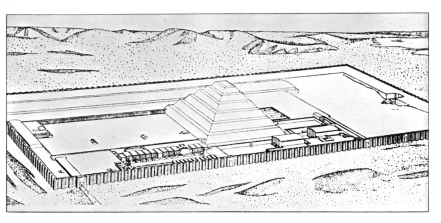

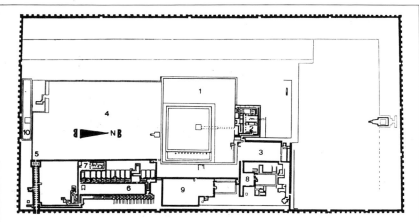

(1) step pyramid derived from mastaba tombs with quadrangular ground plan (2) mortuary temple of Zoser (3) court with serdab (chamber for statue of the deceased) (4) main court with altar and two B-shaped stones (5) entrance portico (6) Heb-Sed court (7) small temple (8) court in front of the southern palace (10) southern tomb.

Whereas more primitive architectures reveal an immature relationship between the different formal levels such as a mere application of characterizing detail, the Egyptian language of architectural forms possesses a logical coherence from the most comprehensive level down to the articulating details. This coherence is very simple and consists in the general validity of the orthogonal order.

Saqqara

The great stone architecture of Egypt was born at Saqqara, south of Cairo, where the impressive remains of King Zoser's large mortuary complex from the Third Dynasty (2778–2723 BC) can be found. We even know the name of its builder, Imhotep, who may be considered the first architect in history. But Imhotep was more than an architect; he also was "high priest," "grand vizier," "chief judge," "overseer of the King's records," "bearer of the Royal seal," "chief of all the works of the King," "supervisor of that which Heaven brings, the earth creates and the Nile gives," "supervisor of everything in this entire land," and after his death he was raised to the stature of a god.[9] Imhotep's position indicates his success in embodying the Egyptian world view in his architecture, as well as showing the importance of the creative individual in history.

The complex at Saqqara consists of an enclosed rectangle measuring 545 by 278 metres (1788 by 912 feet), surrounded by a 10-metre-high (32.8 feet) wall of limestone. Within the precinct there is a rectangular step pyramid, over 60 metres (197 feet) high, and several smaller structures around a number of courtyards. The entrance is situated near the southeastern corner. It leads into a long processional hall flanked by 6-metre-high (19.7 feet) engaged columns. At the end of the hall there is a great court which contains a main altar at the foot of the pyramid. From the processional hall a narrow corridor also leads into the smaller Heb-Sed court which is flanked by rows of dummy chapels. Towards the northeast is situated a "double palace," with two dummy buildings and courtyards in front of them. On the northern side of the pyramid, finally,

(9) S. Giedion, *The Beginnings of Architecture* (New York, 1964), p. 269.

17. Heb-Sed court, Saqqara. Dummy chapel.

18. Processional hall, mortuary complex of Zoser, Saqqara.

(10) Ibid., p. 267.

stands the mortuary temple of King Zoser as well as the small *serdab* chamber which contained his *Ka* statue. The general layout is strictly orthogonal, but it is not organized by means of axial symmetry.

Throughout the complex at Saqqara an abundance of interesting details and attempts at formal articulation can be found. The exterior wall shows a system of major and minor recesses as well as a series of irregularly disposed bastions, which imitate towered gateways with closed, double doors carved on them. The columns of the processional hall resemble bundled reeds and consist of a multitude of convex shafts. In the small temple "T" and the façade of the northern palace, however, we find true fluting. The small temple also has torus mouldings on both corners and a kind of cavetto cornice. The façades of the dummy chapels and palaces are articulated by means of slender engaged columns with papyrus and lotus capitals.

The use of dummy structures indicates the symbolic character of the Zoser complex. The outer walls were probably copies of the brick walls which King Menes of the First Dynasty built around his capital, Memphis, and the two dummy palaces represented the Pharaoh's White House as king of Upper Egypt, as well as the Red House as king of Lower Egypt. Dummy chapels represented the provinces *(nomes)* of the two lands, and were used in connection with the Heb-Sed ceremony which renovated the vital force, or *Ka,* of the King and thus "all those beneficial relations between heaven and earth which the throne controls."[10] Finally the pyramid, as a momumentalized version of the mastaba tomb, made the eternal presence of his *Ka* visible. All the articulating details gave the representations a concrete, pictographic character.

The basic structure of the complex at Saqqara is then a symbolic concretization of the Egyptian cosmos, which through the use of durable stone and orthogonal organization was given "eternal" validity. In addition to this, Saqqara is important to us in that it initiated the history of architecture as the conquest and use of meaningful forms. Here the enclosure, the axial corridor, the vertically oriented mass and the articulated wall

19. Giza. Fourth Dynasty (2723-2563 BC).
Ground plan.

20. Pyramid of Cheops, Giza.

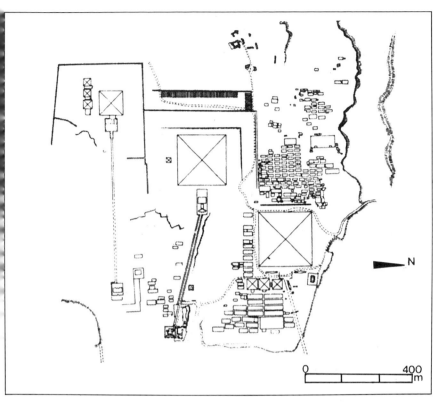

became generalized concepts which could be used anew in a variety of situations.

Giza

With a group of royal tombs at Giza from the Fourth Dynasty (2723–2563 BC), Egyptian intentions were given their most direct and impressive realization.[11] After the somewhat hesitant introduction of the pyramid motif at Saqqara, at Giza there appear the first full-fledged pyramids where the vertical and horizontal directions are unified to form a true synthesis. The three great pyramids of Cheops, Chephren and Mycerinus state and emphasize a fully developed "theme," and the smaller structures which accompany them show the same wish for unequivocal and elementary, stereometric form.

In general the complex at Giza consists of three similar units which are placed next to each other and with the same orientation. Each of them consists of a pyramid which was the tomb proper, a mortuary temple at its foot which served for veneration and offerings to the dead, and a long causeway leading down to a "valley temple" on the river, where the corpse was received for purification and mummification. The causeways are not parallel, and the causeway repeats the direction of the pyramid itself only on the Mycerinus complex. A city of mastabas is orthogonally disposed around the main units, together with other structures which served for the priests and as storehouses.

The Cheops pyramid is the largest mass of stone ever erected by man. It originally measured 230 by 230 metres (755 feet) and rose to a height of 146.6 metres (475 feet). Today it is somewhat smaller, as the outer casing, which was highly polished and reflected the rays of the sun, has disappeared. The Chephren pyramid measured 215 by 215 metres (705 feet) and rose to a height of 143.5 metres (471 feet). At its top a large fragment of the casing is still intact, which gives a vivid impression of the original megalithic power of the pyramids. The Mycerinus pyramid is considerably smaller than the other two.[12]

The mortuary temples have come down to us in a ruined state, but their plans may be

(11) "... in the powerful buildings of the Fourth Dynasty we experience the sudden breakthrough of the megalithic idea, the complete transfer of the orthogonal spatial structure to the technique of hewn and polished stone." Kaschnitz von Weinberg, op. cit., p. 141.

(12) For a detailed discussion of the pyramids see I. E. S. Edwards, The Pyramids of Egypt (Harmondsworth and Baltimore, 1961).

21. *Mortuary temple of Hatshepsut, Deir el-Bahari. 1511-1480 BC. Reconstruction and ground plan.*

22. *Mortuary temple of Hatshepsut, Deir el-Bahari.*

reconstructed. They all show an axial layout with a pillared court at the core. In the Chephren temple this court is preceded by a T-shaped hall, and between the court and the pyramid are five parallel sanctuaries. In the Mycerinus temple there is only one deep sanctuary, preceded by a wider pillared portico which serves as a transition from the transversal courtyard to the longitudinal sanctuary. A certain historical development is indicated by the decrease in size of the pyramid from Cheops to Mycerinus and a complementary increase in the relative size of the temple, at the same time as the spatial disposition becomes more systematic.

The complexes at Giza are characterized by an unsurpassed wish for pure and simple form. Articulating details and decoration are abolished to strengthen the effect of the smooth surfaces and stereometric shapes. This is still evident in the well-preserved valley temple of Chephren, where a T-shaped hypostyle hall is constructed of monolithic pillars, lintels and slabs. This is the first fully mature orthogonal space-structure of Egyptian architecture. But the primordial mass is still more important; the spaces at Giza appear as if they were excavated within large masses of stone, and the pyramid may in fact be considered the culmination of massive building.

The development from Saqqara to Giza may be described as an abandoning of pictographic motifs, a further systematization of space, and an increasing abstraction which stresses the basic themes of orthogonal organization and axial path. Nevertheless, the essential form is still the overpowering semiconcrete symbol of a pyramid which unifies the primordial mountain with the radiant sun and represents the King as the son of Ra. Its synthesis of elementary megalithic power and eternal stereometry still conveys a human message of archetypal significance.

Deir el-Bahari

A thousand years passed between the completion of the buildings at Giza and the construction of the funerary temple of Queen Hatshepsut at Deir el-Bahari during the Eighteenth Dynasty (1511–1480 BC). Now a tra-

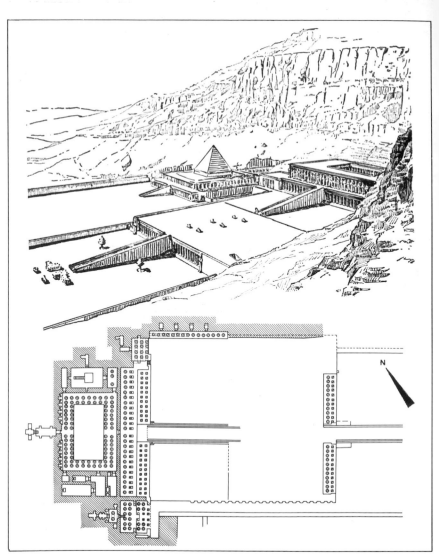

23. *Mortuary temple of Hatshepsut, Deir el-Bahari. Proto-Doric cloumns on the middle terrace.*
24. *Mortuary temple of Hatshepsut, Deir el-Bahari.*

23. *Mortuary temple of Hatshepsut, Deir el-Bahari. Proto-Doric cloumns on the middle terrace.*

24. *Mortuary temple of Hatshepsut, Deir el-Bahari.*

beated system of construction has replaced the megalithic mass. Important steps in the intervening development are represented by the mortuary temple of Mentuhotep at Deir el-Bahari (Eleventh Dynasty, 2133–1992 BC) and the small processional pavilion of Sesostris I at Karnak (Twelfth Dynasty, 1991–1928 BC). In the mortuary temple an emblematic pyramid is placed within a great hypostyle hall and penetrates above it. This main unit was raised upon a terrace, and both storeys were accompanied by exterior, trabeated porticoes. A trabeated portico has become the constituent theme for the pavilion of Sesostris I. The pyramid disappears altogether in the temple of Queen Hatshepsut and a series of porticoed terraces rises instead in front of the great western mountain.

We know the name of the architect of Queen Hatshepsut, Senmut, who had a social position and an architectural talent comparable to those of his great predecessor Imhotep. Again, close collaboration between a ruler and a man of genius produced a fundamental advance in the development of architecture as a symbol system. This advance was a full materialization of axially organized, orthogonal space. The orthogonal system is no longer drawn on the surfaces of megalithic masses or excavated within them, but is realized as an open repetition of posts and beams. Existential security, thus, is no longer symbolized by means of indestructible masses, but in terms of a repetitive abstract order. "Like the monotonous reiteration of long and formalized prayers for the dead . . . the Egyptian iteration of architectural units was all a part of the same, fearful quest for certainty."[13]

The mortuary temple of Queen Hatshepsut is organized along a longitudinal axis which continues the main axis of the great Amon Temple at Karnak on the other side of the Nile.[14] A wall originally defined the precinct which consists of three terraces connected by long centrally placed ramps. The fronts of the second and third terraces are formed by regular rows of pillars, and on the third terrace the remains of the temple proper can still be seen, containing a transverse courtyard and a longitudinal funerary chapel hewn into the cliff wall. The disposition is clearly derived from the pyramid temples of the Old Kingdom, with the mountain taking over the

(13) Baldwin Smith, *op. cit.*, p. 246.

(14) "Every year the small wooden statue of Amon departed in his sacred bark from the darkness of his cell in his temple at Karnak to visit Hatshepsut's temple." Giedion, *op. cit.*, p. 426.

25. *Mortuary complex of Ramses III, Medinet Habu. 1198-1166 BC. Ground plan.*

26. *Mortuary complex of Ramses III, Medinet Habu. Great gateway.*

27. *Mortuary complex of Ramses III, Medinet Habu. External fortifications.*

(15) U. Hölscher, *Medinet Habu* (Tübingen, 1958).

(16) Baldwin Smith, *op. cit.*, p. 145.

role of the pyramid. The upward movement of the ramps also reproduces the vertical thrust of the pyramid. Vertical axiality has been unified with the theme of the longitudinal path in a new, expressive synthesis.

Articulation here is more varied and sensitive than in the megalithic structures of the Fourth Dynasty. While the outer face of the porticoes shows the rectangular shapes of pillars, their inside is subdivided by round columns, and the walls are decorated by beautiful reliefs. In the northwest corner of the second terrace there stands a chapel to Anubis preceded by a proto-Doric colonnade. Pillars forming the front of a hypostyle hall on the third terrace were faced by tall statues of Osiris bearing the face of the Queen. In general the Hatshepsut temple seems to have been designed at a happy moment in Egyptian history when security, represented in the organization of space, was sufficiently well-founded for the reintroduction of the human scale and the meaningful detailing attempted by Imhotep at Saqqara.

It follows from this that a process of spatial abstraction and systematization was needed to allow for a more varied use of characterizing detail. This process is also illustrated by the fact that the first fully grown obelisks were erected during the Middle Kingdom and thereafter became a standard symbol of the vertical dimension. The programmatic materialization of orthogonal space culminated with the great festival hall of Tuthmosis III (1504–1450 BC) at Karnak.

Medinet Habu

The development of the temple continued during the later phases of the Eighteenth Dynasty and reached its climax with the great constructions of the Ramsesides of the Nineteenth and Twentieth Dynasties. The best-preserved of these buildings is the mortuary temple of Ramses III (1198–1166 BC) at Medinet Habu in Thebes.[15] In current literature, the temple of Medinet Habu is often criticized as a degeneration in form and decoration.[16] It is certainly true that the classical purity and precision found in the works of the Eighteenth Dynasty are gone,

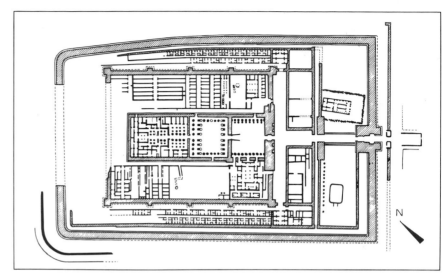

but rather than being discussed in terms of degeneration, Medinet Habu should be seen as a last, great baroque synthesis, where the basic intentions of Egyptian architecture are brought to their logical conclusion.

At Medinet Habu the temple proper is only the core of a complete holy city, which in many respects is analogous to the complex of Zoser at Saqqara. The approximately rectangular area measures about 200 by 300 metres (656 by 984 feet) and was surrounded by an immense brick wall, 10 metres thick and 18 metres high (33 by 59 feet) of which considerable remains are still standing. Within this great precinct there is a smaller rectangular area measuring about 130 by 160 metres (427 by 525 feet) which was surrounded by a 6-metre-thick (24 feet) wall incorporating the main pylon of the temple. Originally the complex consisted of the inner precinct only, but toward the end of his reign Ramses added the outer fortifications and used the area between the two walls for the dwellings of priests, soldiers, craftsmen and slaves. The inner area contains in addition the temple magazines along both sides and the royal palace at the southern corner.

The complex at Medinet Habu was approached from a canal and a quay which formed the continuation of the central, longitudinal axis. At the start of the dominant path, which constitutes the backbone of the composition, was a monumental gateway flanked by towers. After passing the great pylon, the path leads through two spacious courtyards and a hypostyle hall towards the innermost sanctuary. Between each of the main spaces a ramp is introduced to create an upward movement. The first court has pillars faced by statues of Ramses along the right side and round columns on the other. The latter form a portico which contains the Window of Appearances of the Pharaoh. The transverse axis so created represents a spatial accommodation to the royal palace behind the southern wall of the courtyard. The second court, in contrast, is symmetrically disposed and surrounded by a continuous cavetto cornice. The dominant longitudinal axis is emphasized by the introduction of a second pylon between the courtyards and a deeper portico in front of the hypostyle hall. Approaching the sanctuary the rooms be-

31. *Rock temple of Ramses III, Abu Simbel. 1301-1235 BC. Facade.*

32. *Temple of Horus, Edfu. After 332 BC. Pylon.*

come smaller and the floor rises. The path ends in a dark *sekos* which contained the sacred bark of Amon-Ra. This is the final and most convincing architectural interpretation of the Egyptian religious path.

The proportions and the decoration of the temple at Medinet Habu are characterized by an unusual plastic force. Reliefs are deep and create an expressive contrast to the general continuity of the surfaces. Everywhere a strong wish for spatial and formal integration can be felt, and in comparison the older temples appear as somewhat hesitant experiments. At Medinet Habu the original symbols are unified to create a truly great synthesis with a cosmic meaning. The imitative and additive forms encountered at Saqqara have grown into an integrated totality.

The baroque tendencies found at Medinet Habu were further developed during the Ptolemaic period, and the last Egyptian temples are distinguished by a florid richness of decoration and by a certain interpenetration of the architectural elements.

Space Conception and Development

These examples demonstrate the all-comprehensive and absolute character of the Egyptians' spatial organization, but they also indicate a certain development in Egyptian architecture. Most of the constituent formal ideas can be found as early as Saqqara, such as the defined enclosure, the axial hall, the courtyard, the megalithic mass, the orthogonal order and even the principal means of articulation such as columns, frames, mouldings and cornices. But they are still combined in a somewhat haphazard manner. A general axial disposition is lacking, and the layout may be characterized as a tentative geometrization of more primitive topological groupings. The great monuments at Giza bring us a step forward. Here the different

units of each pyramid complex form a linear sequence, and the stereometric precision is strongly emphasized. In these the pictographic approach of Saqqara has given way to a more general and abstract conception of architectural space. During the Middle Kingdom this intention led to the development of repetitive structures such as colonnades and continuous frames. This approach culminated with the temple of Queen Hatshepsut, which anticipates the comprehensive synthesis of the great trabeated structures of the New Kingdom.

In general the development of Egyptian architecture leads from a direct, imitative approach towards a concretization of more abstract relationships. The decisive step was the substitution of a symbolic grid of verticals and horizontals for the heavy amorphous mass.[17] In the Old Kingdom this grid was still applied to the mass, such as the pillar hall of Chephren's valley temple. Later the orthogonal grid assumed a constituent role and the buildings became true symbols of an absolute order, rather than direct expressions of some of its aspects. This process of abstraction obviously satisfied the Egyptians' desire for order and certainty, but in attendance to it was the danger of reducing the vital symbols of art and architecture to mere stereotyped formulae. The great temples of the New Kingdom, in fact, mark the end of development, and their plan became a formula which was repeated until the collapse of Egyptian culture.[18]

It is often maintained that Egyptian architecture shuns space, and that its formal language is primarily based on plastic relationships.[19] It is certainly true that Egyptian architecture does not possess embracing interior spaces, but this does not mean that the Egyptians suffered from spatiophobia. The basic wish for enclosure stems from the experience of a need for "being somewhere," that is, the need for an inside, but the Egyptians did not "dwell" in the space thereby created. Instead, the way they han-

dled interior structure expresses the idea that Egyptian man was always on his way. His space became the stage for an "eternal wandering."[20] This is not only symbolized by the longitudinal axis, but also by the intermediary spaces between the plastic members, for instance, between the columns of the hypostyle halls. These intermediary spaces are often smaller than the volume of the masses, whereby they become fragmented and do not invite calm. In this sense the masses are more important than the spaces, but the masses serve to define spatial relationships, which we have described as being all-comprehensive. However, within the general orthogonal system the spatial spaces (such as courtyards, halls and corridors) are still relatively independent and do not form a true continuity. Series of pylons or gates give emphasis to the staccato movement of the Egyptian wandering.

Meaning and Architecture

Some indications of the existential meanings implicit in Egyptian architecture have already been given, such as how the geography of the country favoured the conceptualization of basic natural elements and processes. These natural elements were central to Egyptian thought. Throughout Egyptian history the basic force was the sun. The sun god, Ra or Aton, had his principal sanctuary in Heliopolis ("sun city"). Ra later absorbed the gods of creation Atum and Amon. The children of the sun god were air (Shu), moisture (Tefnut), sky (Nut) and earth (Geb). The last begot the gods of fertility and resurrection (Osiris), of aridity and destruction (Seth), of motherhood (Isis) and of sisterhood (Nepthys). Atum first appeared as a rock which rose out of the primordial waters to receive the rays of the sun on its pointed top. This rock was represented in Heliopolis as a menhir, the so-called *benben* stone, which prefigured the later obelisks. The sun god was believed to reside in monolithic *pyrami-*

dions with gilt top. A large number of other gods completed the Egyptian pantheon. Their interactions were described in a complex mythology, which tells the tale of how the Egyptian world lived and functioned.

The primary gods represent *natural* elements which were embodied through analogy with human (and animal) properties.[21] In general these personifications enabled the Egyptians to achieve understanding of basic existential meanings, such as the interaction between elements of nature (fertility-aridity), and also more abstract relationships such as that of good and evil. We have seen that the Egyptians had a preference for highly ordered and formalized relationships, due partially to geography and partially to the rhythm of the seasons. Both determined this preference, for, as the country is entirely dependent upon the proper management of the Nile flood, continuous cooperative effort and strict discipline were required of its inhabitants. We may therefore talk about "environmental despotism, rather than social tyranny."[22]

In ancient Egypt man and nature were one. Man's intelligence was still engaged primarily with the problems of action, and although Egyptians developed the faculties of abstraction and concretization to a very high degree, they exercised these faculties in a direct rather than reflective way. The Pharaoh, therefore, was a symbol of the absolute and permanent character of the man-nature totality, rather than a personal tyrant. Any being, Pharaoh, common man or animal, was represented as part of the same general system. The basic task of Egyptian culture was to protect the experienced and desired totality against change. Change is a function of time, and hence the necessity of interpreting time as an eternal rhythm within a basically static order. This rhythm is made visible as orthogonally ordered spatial extension, neither infinite nor finite. It does not break all bonds as did Baroque extension later, nor does it lead to any final goal. Instead it leads symbolically to the world beyond death,

(17) "The laws of gravity, through even clearer crystallization of the abstract order derived from them, supersede the earlier physically felt weight of the solid blocks, and the mathematical-geometrical structure, thus derived from the gravitational effect, now becomes, as gravity itself was before, the symbol of eternity and indestructibility." Kaschnitz von Weinberg, op. cit., p. 162.

(18) See, for instance, the Horus temple at Edfu built 237-212 BC and completed as late as 57 BC. In the courtyards of the Egyptian mosques the old megalithic orthogonal character is still felt.

(19) Giedion, op. cit., p. 523, who refers to Riegel and Worringer, and Baldwin Smith, op. cit., p. 247.

(20) Giedion, op. cit., p. 352.

(21) I could, for instance, refer to Osiris and Seth as personifications of oasis (life) and desert (death).

(22) Baldwin Smith, op. cit., p. 248.

where life is reborn in Osiris.

The way the Egyptians organized space, therefore, was a realistic but highly imaginative interpretation in spatial terms of the basic existential facts of their world. Egyptian man was forever immobile and eternally on his way, represented by the great megalithic monuments which symbolize a whole society in an analogous situation. More than two thousand years have elapsed since the end of Egyptian culture, but we can still be deeply moved by its fundamental themes: the themes of place of belonging and path of life, of being and time.

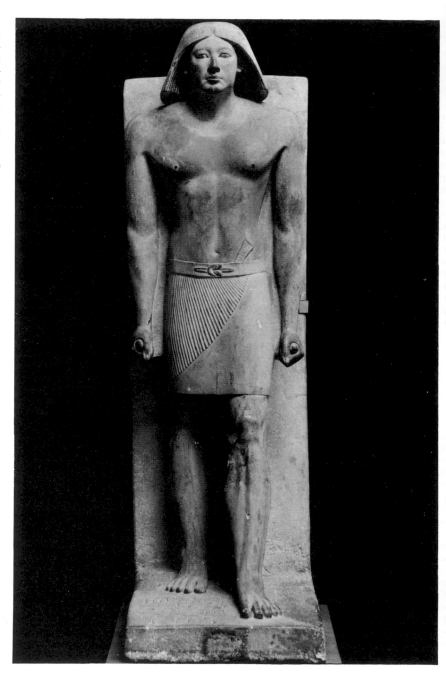

33. Ranofer. *Fifth Dynasty (2563-2423 BC).*
Cairo Museum.

2. Greek Architecture

34. Acropolis, Athens.

35. Temple of Apollo, Corinth. Mid-6th century BC.

Introduction

The course of Western architecture over two thousand five hundred years has been dominated by the achievement of the Greeks, a fact which invites us to approach Greek architecture with particular attention.

The architecture of ancient Greece is generally associated with temples, which in many places still impress with the power of their regular but articulate building. Their status makes them a richer source of fundamental meanings than other buildings which primarily offered physical protection. While the temples, appear as clearly organized individual bodies, their distribution seems irregular and haphazard, and the arrangement of space outside buildings, does not consist of easily recognizable relationships. As monumental interior spaces are also rare, some critics have been led to the conclusion that Greek buildings are "nonarchitectural" and have to be perceived as "large sculptures."[1] This unsatisfactory interpretation is probably due to the use of insufficient space concepts.

The beauty of the temples has closed our eyes to other less conspicuous aspects of Greek architecture, and thereby also has limited our understanding of the temple itself, which is often regarded as a mere aesthetic object. Variations in dimension, organization and detailing are interpreted in terms of stylistic development or as expressions of the wish for visual refinements. Whereas these factors are important, it is essential to understand the temple in relation to the total situation under which it was created. That is, it has to be related to its site and to the purpose it had to serve. An interpretation of this kind has been carried out with great skill by Vincent Scully, who, for the first time, has brought the Greek temples to life as individual concretizations of fundamental existential situations.[2] Not only has he confirmed the generally recognized fact that the regular buildings and the free distribution are complementary aspects of the same basic intentions, but he has also been able to explain this intention in terms of Greek religious and philosophical concepts.

What, then, are the fundamental phenom-

(1) B. Zevi, *Saper vedere l'architettura* (Turin, 1953), pp. 56-57.

(2) V. Scully, *The Earth, the Temple, and the Gods* (New Haven and London, 1962).

36. Doric temple, Segesta. Late 5th century BC.

37. Sanctuary, Olympia. Principally mid-5th century BC.

38. Miletus. Plan after Hippodamus, 466 BC (?), with later additions.

ena of Greek space? Basically, Greek sacred architecture is an architecture of plastic bodies. After the research of Scully, however,[1] we understand that their seemingly haphazard distribution has a meaningful spatial function in relation to the surrounding landscape. But it is evident that the spatial organization thereby implied cannot be described by means of the concepts of geometry and symmetry which determine the single Greek building, and which are usually employed to describe spatial relationships. In addition to these two spatial orders, we also find a third, more general orthogonal order, which was generally used in connection with the planning of Greek cities. Greek space is therefore characterized by its *heterogeneity*. It is not ruled by the same laws on all environmental levels, like Egyptian architecture, but is determined by a multiplicity of modes of organization. These modes interact in different ways according to the particular situation, producing totalities which have a pronounced individual value within a general system of related existential meanings.[3]

Landscape and Settlement

The Greek landscape is characterized by a great variety of natural sites. Rather than vast, monotonous expanses, it consists of defined spaces which seem predisposed for human settlement. The fertile valleys and plains, however, are small, and appear bounded by strong and barren mountains. Intense sunlight and clear air give the forms an unusual presence. Consequently the Greek landscape seems to embody a variety of natural forces, and does not easily accept human dominance. "Because of the ordered variety, clarity and scale in the landscape, the human being is neither engulfed nor adrift in Greece. He can come close to the earth to experience either its comfort or its threat."[4] One of the basic facts of the Greek environment, therefore, is the individual character of places—individual, however, not in the sense that the places were experienced as being entirely different. Rather they were manifestations of archetypal characters. In some places the surroundings appear to offer protection, in others they men-

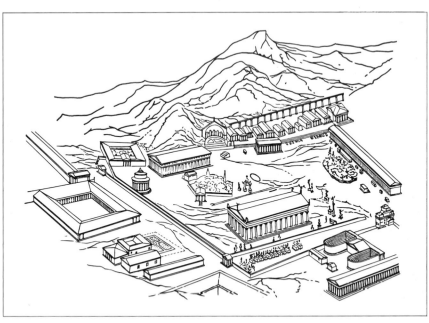

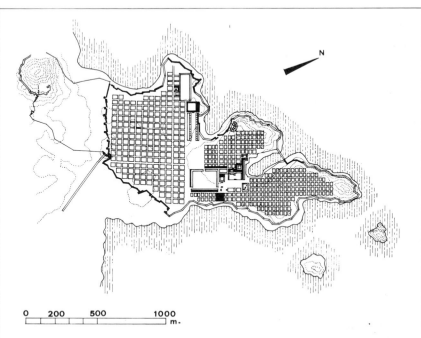

(3) Later, during the Hellenistic period, an abstract axial order became dominant, superseding thus the Classical Greek reconciliation of nature and man.

(4) Scully, *op. cit.*, p. 9.

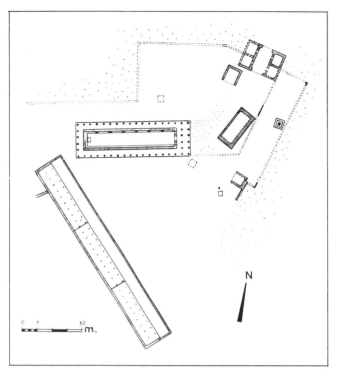

(5)   *Ibid.*, p. 45.

(6)   Doxiadis' attempt
to describe the grouping
of Greek buildings in
terms of mathematical
relationships is there-
fore meaningless, and
betrays a basic mis-
understanding of the
Greek intentions. See A.
Doxiadis, *Raumordnung
im griechischen Städte-
bau* (Heidelberg, 1937).

(7)   Scully, *op. cit.*, p.
147.

(8)   See A. von Gerkan,
*Griechische Städtean-
lagen* (Berlin and
Leipzig, 1924), pp. 28 ff.

(9)   In general the plan
is developed from the
ancient *megaron*, whose
symmetrical, longitu-
dinal plan with a porch
at one end, represents
one of the original types
of human dwelling.

ace. Some sites offer a dominant position for human settlement, while others make us feel at the centre of a well-defined *cosmos*. In some places there are natural elements of a very particular shape or function, such as horned rocks, caves or wells. All these properties are manifestations of a natural order, and induce a certain relationship between man and his environment. In interpreting these characteristics the Greeks personified them as gods, and any place with pronounced properties became a manifestation of a particular god. Thus places where nature is dominant are dedicated to the old chthonic deities Demeter and Hera, and places where man's intellect and discipline complement and oppose the chthonic forces are dedicated to Apollo. There are places where life is experienced as a harmonious whole, dedicated to Zeus, and places where men had come together to form a community, a *polis*, dedicated to Athena. Before any temple was built, open-air altars were erected "in the ideal position from which the whole sacred ['meaningful'] landscape could be grasped."[5] Siting, then, was anything but arbitrary; rather it is determined by the experience of the natural environment, as manifested by its particular forms, and interpreted by it.

The word "topology" can be used in its fullest sense in relation to Greek sanctuaries. They are determined by the character of the place, the *topos*, and do not admit any geometrical grouping of buildings which would symbolize a more abstract, general order.[6] Buildings are individual units representing archetypal human characters which participate in the situation symbolized by the site. Different topological groupings are established, according to the situation. In most cases a more or less well-defined *temenos* (a sacred enclosure) is formed, as any place may be understood as a "space within a space." At Olympia, for instance, this *temenos* is a true "centre of the world" within a larger, harmonious natural *megaron* The *temenos* is bordered by the sculpturally dense body of the temple of Zeus, the more open, ground-hugging building dedicated to Hera, and a series of treasure houses, symbols of all Hellas.[7]

Even though there was a certain regularity to Greek settlements, they were always in-

tended as an *individual place*, not allowed to grow beyond a certain size. During the fifth century BC an orthogonal grid became normal in Greek city planning,, usually connected with the name of Hippodamus from Miletus.[8] In contrast to the general symbolic importance of the orthogonal space in Egyptian architecture, it represented a practical tool which made the planning and building of new colonial cities easier, and as such it had no symbolic function beyond the definition of a neutral framework common to all the citizens of a democratic city-state. At the centre of the grid we find an enclosed space, the *agora*, which served as the communal meetingplace. Dominant axes are absent and the positions of the main buildings are still determined by the surrounding landscape.

Building

To a superficial eye Greek temples may look quite alike, but on closer scrutiny they reveal important differences in form and expression. The single temple may be characterized as an individual member of a "family," just as the gods formed a family which symbolized the various roles and interactions of men on earth.

Common to all temples is their appearance as clearly defined, plastic bodies. They are not simple masses, but articulate structures where an external colonnade or *pteron* is of primary importance. The general organization is orthogonal and the plan axial, but the axis is not emphasized and the stereometric grid does not possess the abstract, crystalline quality found in Egyptian architecture. Rather the temple resembles a sculpture in the round—like a statue with its face on one side—so it is actively related to its environment.[9] The orthogonal structure may be interpreted as a symbol of man's organizing intelligence, in relation to the experience of the horizontal surface of the earth and the force of gravity. Whereas the Egyptians stressed the latter aspect and abstracted an absolute order of verticals and horizontals, it was the human aspect that the Greeks took as their point of departure, making the trabeated structure an expression of the living forces of carrying and being carried. Accordingly, the Greek temple appears as a muscular body, as a truly organic form, which concretizes life as action in space and time. As an intelligible but variable building type, the temple also demonstrates that living action does not consist in casualness and arbitrary change, but manifests itself as interacting archetypal characters.

The only feature common to all temples is a longitudinal *cella* which housed the statue of the god.[10] This was quite spacious in the larger temples, but only obtained the status of a true "interior" towards the end of the fifth century BC. Size and particular function determined the plan of a temple, whose form then became a manifestation of symbolic content. As a plastic body the temple reacts and relates to other buildings and the surrounding landscape. When we say that the Greek temple is developed from within, we do not talk in spatial terms. Rather, this means that it expresses an individual immanent character which determines its articulation.

Among the other Greek building types, the dwelling, the *stoa* and the theatre have particular historical significance. The first of these, the city-dwelling, may be characterized as an introverted house, where the rooms are grouped around a courtyard. Originally a free standing *megaron*, it developed into a courthouse by the addition of wings and porches, a process which was determined by the need for a dense utilization of urban land. Its individuality is expressed by seclusion rather than by outer plastic appearance. The *stoa* is a long columnar portico used to screen off the *agora* and to offer shelter from sun and rain. As an extended, "one-sided" building it was treated as an element of secondary importance in Classical times, but became increasingly important during the Hellenistic period. The theatre, finally, represents, next to the temple, the most important Greek contribution to the history of architecture. Originally it was a ring in which the drama would be enacted by all those present. In Classical times the participants were separated into performers and spectators and the continuous ring was broken, but the Greek actor still appeared as a real plastic figure on the circular *orchestra,* which is embedded in the bowl con-

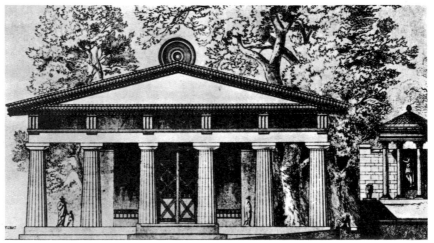

(10) Early Greek temples had a *cella* divided into two aisles by a central row of columns, as shown in the plan of the first Heraeum at Samos from about 800 BC. Kähler appropriately talks about "raumloser Raum." See H. Kähler, *Der griechische Tempel* (Berlin, 1964), p. 27.

(11) Scully, *op. cit.*, p. 206.

(12) Vitruvius, *De Architectura* I, ii, 5.

(13) *Ibid.*, IV, i, 6-8.

(14) The triglyphs actually represent the ends of transverse beams, and the whole structure is generally understood as a translation into stone of an original wooden construction. See A. von Gerkan, "Die Herkunft des dorischen Gebälks" in *Von Antiker Arcitektur und Topographie* (Stuttgart, 1959).

(15) In this context compare the Hera temples in Paestum to the temple of Apollo in Corinth with its straight columns. See Scully, *op. cit.*, p. 104.

(16) Le Corbusier, *Towards a New Architecture* (London, 1927), p. 191.

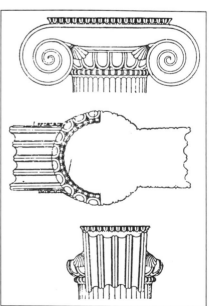

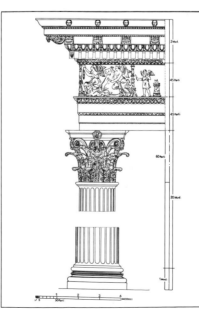

taining the audience. From their seats the spectators not only took part in the performance, but also experienced the surrounding landscape, "and the whole visible universe of men and nature came together in a single, quiet order."[11]

Articulation

We have seen how the Egyptians developed the basic means of architectural articulation, such as subdivision and framing, moulding and capital, so as to demonstrate the universality of their abstract order. The Greeks also needed abstraction and organization to gain security, but within the order thus established they also wanted to symbolize the individual characters and interactions which make experience vital. In general this was achieved by means of the so-called Classical Orders, usually understood through the oldest preserved theory of architecture, the "ten books" *De Architectura* by the Roman architect Vitruvius (first century BC). As early as the first book Vitruvius maintains that temples ought to be built in a different style according to their dedication,[12] and in the fourth book he proceeds by explaining the orders in terms of human characters. The orders represent different types of humanity. The Doric column, thus, "furnishes the proportion of a man's body, its strength and beauty." The Ionic, on the other hand, is characterized by "feminine slenderness," and its voluted capital resembles "graceful curling hair." The Corinthian, finally, "imitates the slight figure of a maiden . . . and admits of more graceful effects in ornament."[13]

The Doric order was particularly suited to concretize the plastic presence at the basis of the Greek temple. Doric columns rest heavily on the ground without a base, and their swelling, fluted shafts seem to embody masculine muscular strength. The capital is simple and consists of a compressed "cushion" (*echinus*) plus a square slab (*abacus*) on which rests the horizontal, smooth architrave. Over the architrave is the frieze, which consists of alternating decorative panels, *metopes,* and elements of a more structural appearance, the *triglyphs,* which correspond

to the columns.[14] The entablature is completed by a horizontal cornice, and by a triangular gable or pediment at the end elevations. The pediment may be interpreted as a synthesis of the horizontal and the vertical directions, like the pyramid, and was a distinguishing feature of sacred architecture. By means of slight variations in proportions and detailing, the character of the Doric order varies considerably. It may express a heavy ground-hugging weight appropriate to temples dedicated to the old goddesses of the earth, Demeter or Hera, or the geometrical purity and strength which is characteristically Apollonian.[15]

The Ionic order developed on the coast of Asia Minor, mainly in large temples, which somehow lack the plastic power of the Doric buildings. In contrast, they appear as holy groves, symbolized by a forest of columns, and it is no wonder that the largest Ionic temple built in antiquity was dedicated to Artemis (Diana). The Ionic column rests on an articulated base, and the slender shaft ends under a voluted capital, which like an elastic scroll carries the slight weight of a low entablature. The architrave is divided into three narrow fasciae, and the frieze is replaced by a plastic egg-and-tongue moulding (*cymation*) and a dentil course. Instead of muscular force, the Ionic order embodies feminine grace and beauty. Le Corbusier has said: "There was a breath of tenderness and Ionic was born."[16]

The articulation and refinements of Greek architecture cannot be understood in merely visual or aesthetic terms. Articulation meant making precise a particular character, and this character, simple or complex, determined every part of the building. So as to permit the concretization of more subtle nuances of human existence the two orders, Doric and Ionic, and their accompanying characteristics, were fused in different ways. Some Doric temples have Ionic proportions, and some Ionic temples have a Doric frieze, although as a continuous decorative band. Particularly interesting is the temple of Apollo at Bassae, built around 420 BC by Ictinos. Its exterior is Doric, but inside are tall, engaged Ionic columns, and at the end of the *cella* on the main axis was placed the earliest Corinthian column known in Greek architecture. For the first time the temple

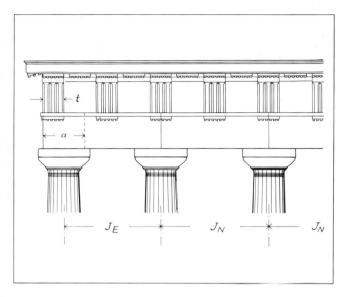

48. *Temple of Athena Nike, Acropolis, Athens. 427-424 BC.*

49. *Wall constructed in the technique of* opus quadratum, *Selinus.*

(17) Scully, *op. cit.*, p. 129.

(18) *Ibid.*, pp. 65, 170. The temples still maintained their normative orientation with the entrance towards the east.

(19) Scully. *op. cit.*, p. 171.

(20) For a thorough discussion of the temples see F. Krauss, *Paestum* (Berlin, 1941).

(21) H. Kähler, *Das griechische Metopenbild* (Munich, 1949). Quoted from Scully, *op. cit.*, p. 62.

expresses "a complex psychic structure in the god."[17]

Paestum

At the southern end of the gulf of Salerno in Italy stand the remains of the Greek colony of Poseidonia, later the Roman Paestum. The plan of the town was organized by means of an orthogonal grid, within which a large, centrally placed rectangle contained the *agora* and the sacred precincts. Three exceptionally well-preserved Doric temples are still standing. To the south, where the land is low, there are two buildings dedicated to Hera, placed close to each other with the same orientation. To the north, where the land rises, is a temple dedicated to Athena. The orientation of the temples is not parallel to the urban grid, and the slight deviation of the Hera temples is convincingly analysed by Scully as an accommodation to the strongly conical hill east of the coastal plain. He shows how the two temples "create a special perspective toward the sacred landscape. . . . But the temples of Hera thus sought to celebrate the city's unity with the earth and with its goddess."[18] The temple of Athena, on the other hand, rises above the landscape, and "seen from ships approaching the town, the temple of Athena, on the highest ground, and with the most pronounced of upward thrusts, would have stood out more than the other temples against the mountains and stated the fact of the city . . . the polis which helped to liberate men from their terror of the natural world with its dark powers and limiting laws."[19]

Each temple has a different symbolic function which determines its plastic form and articulation.[20] The first Hera temple shows how important a role the column played in Greek architecture. Usually known as the Basilica, it was built around 550 BC, on a plan with a row of supports along the central axis. Its exterior columns are low, relative to the width and the length of the building, and their large number (nine by eighteen) creates an atmosphere like that of a sheltering grove rather than a unified plastic body. Yet the temple still possesses a singular plastic force. This is due to the pronounced swelling

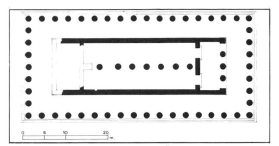

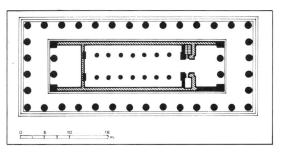

or *entasis* of the columnar shaft, as well as the unusual size and shape of the capital. Where the shaft meets the *echinus*, a circular groove expresses the upholding of a tremendous compressive weight. As a symbol the column embodies the basic earth-hugging character which ought to be concretized by the building.

The second Hera temple no longer symbolizes the tremendous chthonic forces encountered in the first temple. Although it conserves a strong megalithic power, its articulation seems to represent the victory of the Olympian gods, that is, the human will.[21] Previously known as the temple of Poseidon, it dates from about 450 BC. Here the Ionic extension into space has completely disappeared. The temple is fully Doric, and possesses the power of a unified sculptural body. Although it is bigger than the first temple, the number of columns has been reduced to six by fourteen, and the plan has got the balanced classical layout where an *ophistodomos* at the rear corresponds to the entrance porch, each with two columns *in antis*. The overall proportions also express a wish for integration and unity, which represents an important step beyond the "security through repetition" found in Egyptian and archaic Greek architecture. Again the general character is clearly expressed by the single column. Where in the first temple there was a struggle between the vertical and the horizontal, here there is a continuous rising movement where the shaft only slightly swells and contracts again under the upward-thrusting *echinus*. The shaft and the capital are defined as *one* element by means of an ambiguous zone of transition.

The temple to Athena, dating from about 510 BC, illustrates a third variation on the Doric theme. Here proportions and detailing collaborate to create an unusual vertical effect which culminates in a high pediment not separated from the trabeation by the usual cornice. The verticality is enhanced by the considerable inward slant of the columns. As shown above, this trait becomes of special significance when understood in relation to the town as a whole. As a temple of Athena, it moreover shows a fusion of characters. Thus Ionic prostyle columns were

53. *Second temple of Hera, Paestum. Interior.*   54. *First temple of Hera, Paestum.*

55. *First temple of Hera, Paestum. Capital.*

introduced in front of the *cella;* the earliest known example of a direct combination of the two basic orders.

Delphi

At Paestum the basic determining situation was man's settlement on a fertile plain between the sea and the hills, and its character was symbolized by the peaceful togetherness of the goddesses of the earth and of the city. In Delphi, too, the old and the new, nature and man, are brought together, but here as a great contest between opposed forces. Here, at the place which the Greeks honoured as the centre of the world, the drama of human existence on earth is enacted in symbolic, architectural terms. Since immemorial times Delphi has been particularly important as a sanctuary of Gaia, the original goddess of the earth and of fertility. She was worshipped at a ravine in the depths of which her child, the serpent Python, dwelled. From the cavern prophetic vapours emanated. A priestess, or Pythia, who sat on the edge of the cavern, fell into trance and uttered oracular words. In a parable about the victory of man over the original forces of nature, legend tells how Apollo, four days after his birth, killed the serpent and took possession of the sanctuary, where he resided ever since. But the victory was not clear cut, as shown in Aeschylus' *Eumenides;* it was more of a reconciliation.

Hardly any other landscape in Greece has such an imposing grandeur. Over the deep valley of the Pleistos the steep rocks of Mount Parnassos rise into the sky. From above, the visitor looks over the plain of Cirrha (Itea) towards the gulf of Corinth. The sacred place is located in a shadowed cleft in the southern slope of the Parnassos, surrounded by terrible cliffs. The rocks reflect and intensify the sunlight, a spring gushes forth and earthquakes shake the ground. Inspired and awestruck, men beheld the majesty of the earth and tried to understand its message. Within the grand natural space a steep *temenos* rises stepwise up the mountainside towards the shining, Doric temple of Apollo. The present remains stem from a late construction (*c.* 350 BC), but a wooden

(22) A Doric Apollo temple from the sixth century was destroyed by an earthquake in 373 BC.

(23) Scully, *op. cit.*, p. 112.

(24) H. V. Herrmann, *Omphalos* (Münster, 1959), pp. 98 ff.

(25) Scully, *op. cit.*, p. 115.

temple was probably erected on the site as early as the eighth century. Most of the other structures, as well as the *temenos* wall, were erected during the sixth century BC.[22]

The different elements of the sanctuary are distributed in an apparently haphazard way, and well illustrate the topological planning of Greek sacred architecture. Scully's analysis has, however, revealed a deep inner meaning. From afar the sanctuary seems small, but at the entrance to the *temenos* the scale changes and the man-made forms begin to act. From the entrance a sacred way runs up through the *temenos*. Directly west of the entrance, the temple is lost to sight and the path leads past the treasuries and memorials of the different city states. As representatives of Greek democratic society, none of them were allowed to dominate the others. "The movement is like that of free persons in a crowd,"[23] and the buildings are conceived as individual plastic units. After the turn of the path, the cliffs appear again, and under them the smooth, polygonal wall of the temple terrace. As a symbol of tamed and transformed nature, this terrace prepares for the experience of the abstract but anthropomorphic order of the temple. Only when the pilgrim turned the corner of the altar of Chios in front of its western façade, could he perceive the building as a whole in its natural setting and contemplate the pure form of its straight columns. A cavelike *adyton* contained the stone *omphalos* or "navel of the world." This conical stone of primary symbolic importance probably covered the original *bothros* or offering cave of the Great Goddess.[24] In enclosing the symbols of the earth in Apollo's temple, they have been taken over by the god and made a part of a new total vision of nature and man. This reconciliation becomes manifest when the site is seen from the theatre above the temple: "It is a throne, from which 'excess,' both natural and human, has been exorcised and where a grand gentleness reigns."[25]

As the god of poetry and wisdom Apollo assumed the role of mediator of existential meanings, and inspired human creation replaced revealed truth.

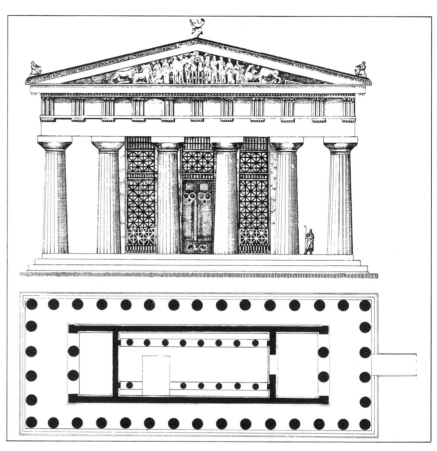

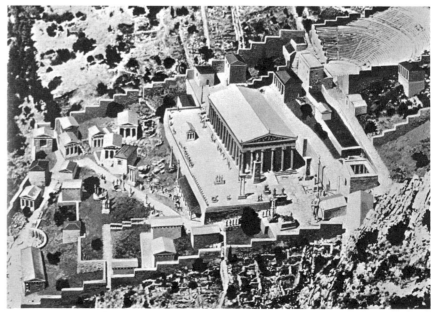

58. *Sanctuary of Apollo, Delphi.*

59. *Tholos, Delphi. c. 390 BC.*

The Acropolis of Athens

(26) *Ibid.*, p. 169.

Aeschylus' *Eumenides* ends with the Panathenaic procession after the reconciliation of Apollo and the ancient powers represented by the Furies giving a blessing to Athena's city. This ending portrays the Greek *polis* as the symbolic result of a new way of life. And ever since its great epoch during the fifth century BC, the name of Athens has been a token of the social and cultural achievement of Greek civilization. As Athena Polias, the goddess has already much before resided over the settlements of men. In the Homeric myths her image protected the town of Troy, which could not fall until that image had been stolen from the town.[26] But it is in Athens that we find the greatest manifestation of the Athena concept, and the buildings of the Periclean Acropolis fully realize in architectural terms the great human synthesis of classical Greece.

The Acropolis rises steeply out of the Attic plain, and forms the luminous centre of a grand space bounded by mountains and islands. By means of a great substructure the hill was transformed into a large platform which carries the splendid buildings of Athena's citadel. The entrance is at the western end where the slope was less precipitous, and here can still be found the impressive remains of Mnesicles' Propylaea (437 BC, left unfinished in 431). Traditionally the gateway to a Greek *temenos* was an unassuming structure in the shape of a small gabled temple. The Propylaea represents a revolutionary break with this tradition. Here flanking wings on either side create an open forecourt which receives the visitor, and embraces the landscape axis from Salamis to Hymettos. A great Doric portico in the middle shows a significant widening of the central intercolumnium which corresponds to a passage flanked by rows of Ionic columns. This, the first conscious creation of a continuous spatial transition, radically diverges from the Greek idea of the building as a plastic body. The combination of Doric and Ionic also indicates the synthesis of characters which was an aim in Attic architecture. The gravity of the mainland is here combined with Ionic grace. The Ionic interior of the Propylaea is echoed in the small

60. Acropolis, Athens. Reconstruction, c. 400 BC.

61. Acropolis, Athens. Ground plan.

62. Ictinos and Callicrates: the Parthenon, Acropolis, Athens. 447-432 BC. View from the Propylaea, 437-431 BC.

(27) ibid., p. 183.

temple of Athena Nike, or the "victorious Athena," which hovers on the bastion to the right of the forecourt. Here Athena is truly represented as a charming maiden with graceful curling hair. Other aspects of her complex personality meet us when from the Propylaea we enter the grand *temenos*. Straight ahead Phidias' 7-metre-tall (23 feet) statue of Athena Promachos ("the champion") used to stand out against the sky, and on both sides the temples of Erechteion (420–406 BC) and Parthenon (by Ictinos, 447–432 BC) flank the significantly free central space.

The Erechteion has a complex form, which results from the need for enclosing a number of traditionally holy places, and forms an ideal contrast to the simple purity of the Parthenon. "In the asymmetrical, gently scaled Erechteion the old traditional earth cults are humanized and made extraordinarily articulate, lucid and civil, while in the Parthenon what might be called the human view of Athena becomes unexpectedly splendid, dominant and divine."[27] Both buildings combine Doric and Ionic properties. In the Erechteion the Ionic dominates, and is moreover naturalistically interpreted in the Caryatid porch with its six *Korai*. But its other porches have a tall entablature of almost Doric weight. The Parthenon, on the other hand, is mainly Doric, but possesses little of true Doric gravity. Its large number of relatively slender columns already give an Ionic feeling which is heightened by the introduction of prostyle colonnades behind the main *pteron*, with its famous continuous frieze of the Panathenaic procession. The *cella* and the approximately square west room have the quality of true interior spaces. The *cella* with its nave and two aisles contained a colossal gold-and-ivory statue of Athena by Phidias, whereas the west room, which was the treasure house of the goddess, had a coffered ceiling supported by four Ionic columns. Interior space and plastic body combine in this building, which represents an ideal synthesis of female grace and male strength.

The timeless value of the Athenian Acropolis consists in its symbolization of human society as a reconciliation of nature and man. Here man knows himself without losing

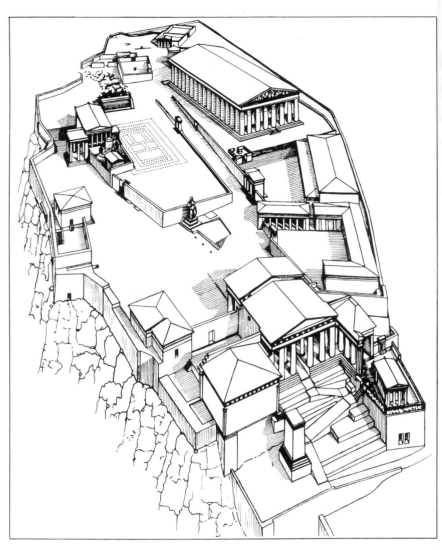

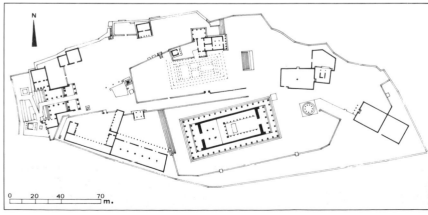

64. *Ictinos and Callicrates: the Parthenon, Acropolis, Athens. Cella.*

65. *Erechteion, Acropolis, Athens. 420-406 BC. North portico.*

66. *Erechteion, Acropolis, Athens. South side with the caryatid porch.*

his reverence for the earth on which he lives; he has come to know himself because of a deep understanding of his position in the natural surroundings.

Priene

The city of Priene is situated near the Ionian coast of Asia Minor between Miletus and Ephesos. Its urban structure is particularly well known, thanks to successful archaeological excavations,[28] and offers a good illustration to the city planning of antiquity. Priene was founded anew around 350 BC under the influence of Athens, which was regarded as its mother city. Its population is believed to have been about four thousand.

The town was built on the southern slope of the mountain Mycale, just under a precipitous rock, a part of which was incorporated in the urban enclosure as a citadel or acropolis. Whereas the city wall follows the natural topography of the site, the urban layout is orthogonal. The main streets run east-west and are connected with three city gates, two on the east side and one on the west. Steep streets run north-south with narrow flights of steps. The directions of the urban grid allowed for a southern orientation of the main public meeting places, such as *stoa,* stadium and theatre. A standard block of houses measured *c.* 47 by 35 metres (154 by 115 feet), and the main street between the western gate and the *agora* is 7.36 metres wide (24 feet). The *agora* is situated approximately at the centre of the urban area. On a terrace above to the northwest is the *temenos* of Athena Polias and to the east, at about the same height, the theatre. Under the steep cliff there is a sanctuary of Demeter, while a temple to Zeus stands adjacent to the *agora.* The gymnasium and stadium are at the lowest end of the city.

Priene thus contains all the main buildings of a Greek *polis,* and their planning and location offer a complete illustration to its structure. The *agora* was the public place *par excellence.* Here men came together for social life, business and politics. As an institution, it represented the new democratic way of life, and its fundamental importance as the living heart of the city was expressed by its being a spatial enclosure at the centre

(28)   For a general presentation see M. Schede, *Die Ruinen von Priene* (Berlin, 1964).

67. *Priene. Reconstruction, c. 350 BC. Pergamon Museum, Berlin.*

68. *Agora, Priene, c. 350 BC. Ground plan.*

of the urban area. In Priene this enclosure is defined by continuous porticoes. Along the northern side runs the principal colonnaded *stoa* where the history of the community was engraved on the walls. The *stoa* was rebuilt about 130 BC and extended beyond the *agora* to a length of 116 metres (381 feet). Behind its extension is the Bouleuterion, or hall of the city council, with 640 seats, and on the other side of the main street, which runs along the *stoa*, a temple to Zeus dating from the third century BC. The *agora* itself was populated by statues and monuments, freely distributed but maintaining the general orthogonal organization of the space. In contrast to the public character of the *agora*, with its open colonnades, the houses of Priene are turned inwards. Of various size, they form a tightly knit, orthogonal pattern of courtyards around which the rooms are located. The exterior walls are continuous and practically without windows, expressing thereby the private character of the dwelling.

A third kind of spatial quality is represented in the sacred *temenos* of Athena Polias. Within the precinct the temple is still conceived as a freestanding plastic body, acting as a symbolic force, and from its terrace it dominates the bustling main street and *agora* below. Built by the famous architect Pytheos shortly after the foundation of the polis in 350 BC, its order is a pure and elegant Ionic, but its plan and general plastic compactness is Doric in character. Again, the temple expresses the synthesis of human properties symbolized by Athena Polias. From the theatre nearby we may, as in Delphi, contemplate a meaningful whole. Finally, near the tall and menacing cliff to the north, it is possible to experience again the ancient forces of nature, which found their manifestation in the sanctuary of Demeter. Her *temenos* does not contain any proud, plastic

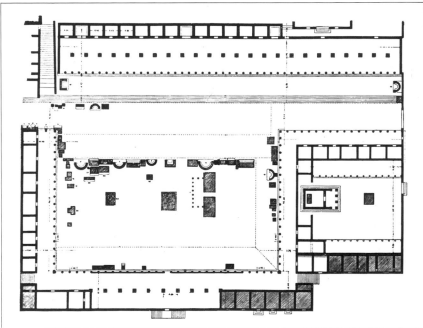

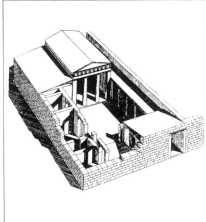

building, but a low Doric pavilion with widely spaced columns and no pediment. Like a holy grove of stone it is immersed in nature.

Priene illustrates how the Greek city consisted of qualitatively different spatial domains, each of which corresponded to a particular function and meaning. It illustrates that it is not possible to understand Greek architecture in terms of building types and Classical orders alone, and that it is hardly satisfactory to exclude the concept of space from a meaningful interpretation.

Space Conception and Development

Our examples have shown the general characterization of Greek space to be heterogeneous. We have seen that the places of Greek sacred architecture do not represent one all-comprehensive spatial image, but symbolize individual meanings. We have also demonstrated that the form of the single building and the grouping of several buildings are based on different organizing principles. Moreover we have pointed out that Greek settlements consist of several, qualitatively different domains. The Greeks, thus, did not only want to define individual places, but also recognized that different functions demand a different kind of space. The Greek concept of space, hence, is pluralistic. For the Greeks space was not *one* thing, but *many,* and the Greek language does not have a single word for "space."[29] This pluralism was a highly important solution to the problem of giving a meaningful structure to man's environment, as it liberated man from the fetters of an all-comprehensive system, and allowed him to transcend the world of casual improvisation.

The harmonious interaction of different modes of spatial organization in Classical Greek architecture was the product of an historical development. In archaic times the modes of organization were less clearly defined, or not yet present. Builders needed the experience of several generations to give their temples the articulate, integrated form which enabled them to act as strong, individual forces in the environment. Development was also needed to make the urban pattern a true expression of a unified *polis* where each dwelling maintained a certain freedom. Taking the simple *megaron* as their common point of departure, the temple and the dwelling moved in opposite directions. The temple became ever more a manifestation of a well-defined character, whereas the house developed towards functional differentiation. The self-knowledge represented by sacred architecture obviously made man free in the actions of his daily life. Classical Greek architecture is the ideal result of this general development, as an illuminated instant when every participant in the existential process knows itself.[30]

A brief summary can be given of the modes of organization referred to above. The simple enclosure plays an important role as a concretization of a particular place or domain and the spatial relation outside-inside is thus recognized as a primary means of environmental differentiation. Topological clusters are fundamental in sacred architecture, as they conserve the individuality of each element. Domestic architecture combines topological and orthogonal properties to allow for functional freedom within the regular orthogonal system of the city. We must, however, repeat that this orthogonal system is functionally and spatially confined, and does not constitute any general idea as in Egyptian architecture. The Greek path is usually the topologically defined way (Del-

phi), but strict axial organization is also used, mainly to make the temple an independent, symmetrical organism.[31] But the axis is neither employed to let one building dominate, nor to represent a general superior order.

The pluralistic approach to space also includes interior spaces. It is significant to notice that they are usually connected with the old chthonic forces and female deities. The sanctuary of Demeter at Eleusis with its large Telesterion furnishes an important example. But interior space is also potentially present in the sacred groves of Ionic architecture,[32] and the development of the Corinthian column implies a memory of the sacred grove, and was obviously developed to symbolize the reconciliation of nature and man, which is the fundamental meaning behind Greek spatial pluralism. The growing interest in interior space during the period of the greatest perfection of plastic form stems from the same basic intention.

Meaning and Architecture

The fact that they chose different spatial organizations according to each individual situation implies that the Greeks wanted to concretize a multitude of existential meanings, rather than a few general relationships. But the choice was never casual; it happened within the limits of an integrated language of building types and means of articulation ("orders"). In classical Greek thought the individual phenomena of daily life were seen as manifestations of interacting archetypes or "ideas." Plato presented the ideas as absolute, and argued that man ought to consider them the ideal of perfection, that is, the goal of his aspiration. Self-knowledge implies the recognition of this true reality.[33]

(29) The Greeks only talked about space as the "in-between," which is a rather neutral concept allowing for many concrete interpretations, at the same time as it recognizes the fact that the character of any space is highly dependent upon the articulation of the space-defining elements ("the wall").

(30) During the later, Hellenistic period this harmonious union of interacting character was weakened. For instance, the sanctuary of Asklepios at Kos (third to first centuries BC) still conserves some of the Classical Greek freedom of the parts, but there are the beginnings of a dominant, superior axis.

(31) On the urban level, the axis may be introduced in connection with entrances, the most famous example being Mnesicles' Propylaea.

(32) The interiors of the circular *tholoi* at Delphi and Epidauros are surrounded by Corinthian columns, as in the *cella* of the interesting temple of Athena at Tegea. All buildings date from shortly before or after 400 BC.

(33) The theory furthermore maintains that knowledge of the perfect archetypes is at all times present in the soul itself. The knowledge is there, but latent and unconscious. What is called "learning," or the discovery of truth, is the recollection of this latent knowledge, raised to the level of consciousness.

71. *Telesterion, sanctuary of Demeter, Eleusis, 5th century BC. Reconstruction.*

72. *Telesterion, sanctuary of Demeter, Eleusis. Reconstruction of the interior.*

Similarly Platonism seeks the key to natural phenomena in perfect final causes, and in Greek *cosmos* means beauty as well as order.

The Classical image of the world slowly emerged from a complex multitude of interacting natural and human forces, which were concretized in the wonderful tales of Greek mythology. Like the Egyptians, the Greeks symbolized the recognized meanings as gods. Whereas the Egyptians gave the natural elements and processes primary importance and accommodated human phenomena to a natural order, the Greeks concentrated their attention on the human aspect. Thus the Greek projected elements of his own personality into external objects, and symbolized the results as the personalities of anthropomorphic gods. "In the beginning," Hesiod says, "there was chaos, vast and dark. Then appeared Gaia, the deep-breasted earth." Uranus, son and husband of Gaia, was the starlit sky. Their children, the Titans and Cyclopes, symbolized the tumultuous forces of nature, but they were soon beaten and put in chains by the new generation of Olympian gods. Primarily the Olympian gods represent archetypal human properties and characters, but also analogous natural phenomena. The goddess Hera, for example, was understood as a (jealous!) wife and mother, and often took over the role of the old fertility goddess Demeter. Other goddesses, such as Artemis and Aphrodite, symbolized the feminine qualities of capriciousness and beauty respectively, among other related properties. Athena maintained the fundamental feminine qualities but combined them with a sense for peaceful work and applied intelligence. Therefore she became a (rather militant!) protectress of towns, and the patron of architects and sculptors. Among the male gods, Hephaistos represented man as the master of the forces of nature, and hence was the god of fire and handicraft. Apollo, the most truly Greek among the gods, represented man's capacity to acquire knowledge and to express himself, and accordingly he also was the god of light. Zeus, to conclude our few examples, was the omnipotent ruler of good and evil, of right and wrong, who punished or showed mercy. "Finally," Hesiod says, "Eros appeared, the love which softens

hearts, whose fructifying influence would
thenceforth preside over the formation of
beings and things." In telling the story of
how man obtained knowledge of himself and
the world, Greek mythology naturally prepared him for a systematic development of
philosophy and science. Thus, while Thales
of Miletus could still say that "all things are
full of gods," he also made the decisive step
of freeing intelligence from the immediate
interests of action. In this way man became
free to organize his knowledge of himself
and the world.

Polycleitos' *Doryphoros* may serve to represent the Greek image of man: an organic,
acting human being, but idealized as a perfect archetype. The play of his muscles resembles the articulation of the members of
a Greek temple, which also symbolizes the
ideal truth of a particular situation fully
understood, so that each part is reconciled
with the others. No wonder that Greek medi-
cine was governed by the principle that heal-
ing is the restoration of a balance or proportion dislocated by disease. In modern eco-
logical thinking we have rediscovered the
Greek ideal of a harmonious unity of interacting forces.

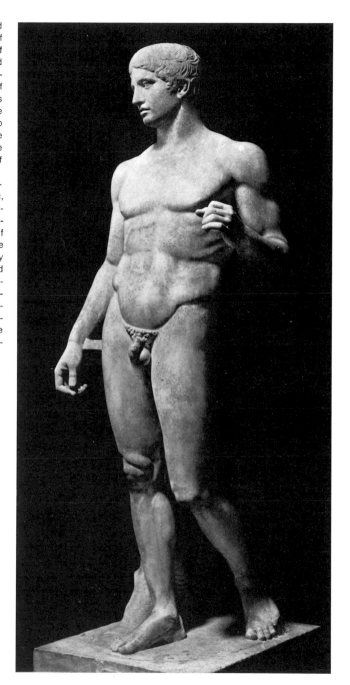

73. *Polycleitos: Doryphoros. c. 450 BC.
(Roman copy). Museo Nazionale, Naples.*

3. Roman Architecture

(1) It is due to the pioneering works of such scholars as Wickhoff, Riegl, von Gerkan, L'Orange, Boëthius, Kaschnitz von Weinberg, Lugli and Kähler.

(2) See G. Kaschnitz von Weinberg, *Mittelmeerische Kunst* (Berlin, 1965), ch. VII, pp. 479 ff.

(3) K. Kähler, *Wesenszüge der römischen Kunst* (Saarbrücken, 1958), p. 9.

(4) W. Müller, *Die heilige Stadt* (Stuttgart, 1961), pp. 36 ff.

(5) *Ibid.*, p. 16.

Introduction

Roman architecture has been admired for its splendour for centuries, but for a long time Roman and Greek art were confused. After Winckelmann (1717–68), and the researches that followed him, Roman architecture generally came to be considered a degeneration of Classical Greek architecture. A true understanding of the original value of the Roman achievement is therefore of fairly recent date.[1] Although much research remains to be done, we are today in a position to carry out a structural analysis of Roman architecture and the meanings it represents.

Roman architecture cannot be associated with one particular leading building type, such as the temple. Instead there are a *multitude* of building types, which in part were unknown prior to Roman times, for example the grandiose structures of the *termae*, basilicas, amphitheatres, and circuses. This multiplicity indicates more complex social functions and structures, and thereby also a widened range of existential meanings. Yet in spite of the functional differentiation, Roman buildings and layouts have fundamental traits in common. Above all, they are usually organized on a rather strict axial basis, making the *axis* the distinguishing property of Roman architecture.[2] We have already met the axis in Egyptian architecture, but there it was secondary to a more general, orthogonal space. In Rome, orthogonal and rotational elements are combined to form complex, axially organized totalities. We should also point out that the Roman axis is generally related to a *centre*, which is often defined as a crossing of axes. The meaning of the Roman axis correspondingly differs from the symbolism of the Egyptian path.

A second distinguishing property of Roman architecture is its extensive and varied use of interior space, as well as "active" exterior space. Roman architecture is, in fact, generally characterized as being spatial, in contrast to the plastic architecture of classical Greece. In Roman architecture for the first time there are grand interior spaces and complex groups of spaces. These spaces show a large variety of forms, and are covered by vaults and domes which so far had only played a sec-

ondary role in building. In general the Romans treated space as a substance to be shaped and articulated, making it active and no longer an "in-between," secondary to the surrounding plastic bodies. It becomes the primary concern of architecture, and is defined by walls which are intended as continuous surfaces, rather than by masses. To make such walls possible, the Romans developed a new building technique: Instead of the trabeated systems of the Egyptians and Greeks, they employed a kind of concrete, which was cast to form continuous walls, vaults and domes *(opus caementicium)*.

How, then, was it possible to confuse Greek and Roman architecture, or to consider the Roman a degeneration of the Greek? The reason is that the Romans took over the Classical orders, but used them in a fundamentally new way. What had been constituent elements before were "reduced" to surface decoration. But it would be unfair to judge Roman architecture with Greek standards. The Classical members certainly lose much of their plastic force and independence in Roman architecture, but instead they give character to a new kind of spatially integrated environment. The character, however, is no longer the character of individual places. Space and articulation become functions of highly codified types, which may be used without fundamental changes in any place. Roman architecture, therefore, may be characterized as an "international style," which is independent of the particular geographical situation.

Landscape and Settlement

It is not possible to talk about the "Roman landscape" as it was about the Egyptian or Greek landscape. Whereas the Greek world consisted of a multitude of individual places, the Roman was always centred on the capital. Rome was *caput mundi*, and the roads of the *Imperium* led from the *Miliarium Aureum* column at the foot of its Capitol. In fact, if we were to make a symbolic map of the Roman world, its most conspicuous feature would be a centralized network of

roads.[3] The Romans mastered nature, technically and spatially, and their dominant system of roads and aqueducts manifests this achievement. It is highly significant in this connection to mention the Roman god Janus, who appears in no other mythology. Janus was the god of all doorways and of public gates through which roads passed. His two faces allowed him to observe simultaneously the exterior and interior of a building. Being the god of gates he also was the god of departure and return. We recognize here a new existential fact: man's wish to conquer the world, parting from a known, meaningful centre. The network of roads thus represents the most basic property of Roman existential space. In such a network the nodes are particularly important, and the Romans gave them due attention by means of gateways and triumphal arches.

This does not mean that the Romans had no feeling for nature. In the Roman world places were chosen or considered sacred because of their particular character. *Genius loci* is, in fact, a Latin concept. But instead of interpreting the natural character, the Romans as a rule introduced a different, dominant order. When a Roman place was consecrated, the *augur* seated himself in the middle and with his stick, or *lituus*, he defined two main axes through the centre, dividing space into four domains: left and right, before and behind. This division was not arbitrary, but represented the cardinal points and was also accommodated to the forms of the surrounding landscape. The space which was thus defined within the boundary of the horizon was called the *templum*.[4] The Romans, then, took a general spatial image as the point of departure for their layouts, rather than a particular character embodied in plastic forms. Any Roman place is a manifestation of this basically cosmic order.

The Roman *castra* and city—and Rome itself—are based on the same model: The square or rectangular area is divided into four parts by two main streets intersecting at right angles; the primary *cardo* and the secondary *decumanus*. The *cardo*, running from north to south, represented the axis of the world, and the *decumanus* the course of the sun from east to west.[5] The main streets lead to four gates in the city wall.

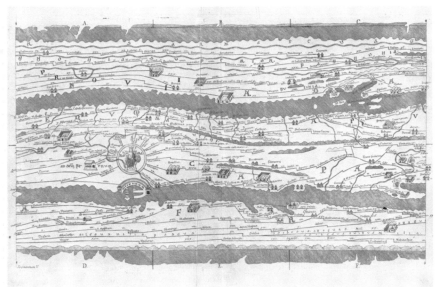

The first settlement on the Palatine was called *Roma quadrata,* a name which refers not to a square shape but to a division into four parts. The centre was represented by a pit which was called *mundus,* that is, the world. The *mundus* obviously symbolized a contact with the chthonic forces man had to come to terms with, like the cavern under the omphalos stone in Delphi. Later, when Rome became a large town, the division into four parts was maintained and a new *mundus* was made at the Forum Romanum, close to which the Miliarium Aureum was later erected by Augustus. In other Roman towns the forum usually became an axially organized rectangular space, close to the symbolic centre.

This general organization, common to both landscape and settlement, concretized a cosmological image, and the town was intended as a microcosm, a fact which is furthermore indicated by the close affinity of the words *orbis* (world) and *urbs* (city). The relationship to Egypt is evident, but by making a centre the origin of orthogonal and axial order, the Romans transformed the eternal static image of the Egyptians into a dynamic world where the possibility of departure and return, that is, of conquering the environment, became a primary existential meaning. But this conquest happened as the manifestation of a preestablished cosmic order, "in agreement with the gods."[6]

Building

Through their concern to use space as an active means of architectural expression the Romans lent primary importance to the interior, and to the integration of the building in the urban setting. This is evident even in the most conservative of Roman building types, the temple.[7] Right from the outset, the Roman temple was conceived in a fundamentally different way from its Greek counterpart. For example, the temple of Jupiter Capitolinus (509 BC) cannot be understood as a plastic body "in the round," rather it is frontally *directed.* It had widely spaced and relatively slender columns. Its central intercolumnium is larger, to accentuate the longitudinal axis which is intro-

(6) Thus Vergil said, "When you comply with the gods, you are Master."

(7) For a concise discussion of the Roman temple see H. Kähler, *Der römische Tempel* (Berlin, 1970).

76. Diagram representing the subdivision of space made by the Roman augur when consecrating a place.

77. Timgad. Plan, c. AD 100.

78. Arch of Constantine, Rome. AD 315.

79. Via Biberatica in Trajan's market, Rome. c. AD 110-12.

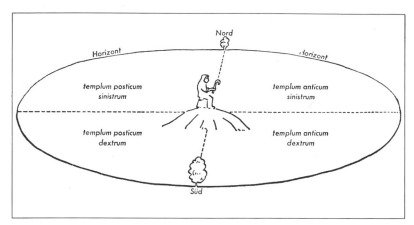

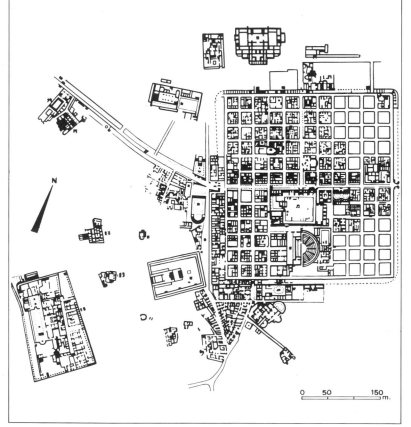

80. Hadrian's villa, Tivoli, c. AD 118-33. Reconstruction.

81. Temple of Fortuna Virilis, Rome. 2d century BC.

duced by a frontal flight of stairs leading up to a mighty podium. The *cella,* dedicated to the Capitoline triad Jupiter, Juno and Minerva, had a blank wall in the back extending to embrace the lateral rows of columns.

As it developed further, the Roman temple assimilated elements from Greek architecture, but conserved its original traits and even emphasized them. The forest of columns of the Capitoline temple thus developed into a deep porch, and the *cella* became a unified space occupying the full width of the podium. Generally, the Roman temple is not freestanding, but connects at the back with the boundary walls of an axially organized space which it dominates. The primacy of space, thus, is evident, and as a logical consequence the *cella* of late temples such as the temple of Venus and Rome (AD 135) was covered with a vault, which completes the cosmic symbolism of the spatial image.

In other less conservative types of building, the Roman interest in space is perhaps still more evident. A good example is the basilica, which in several respects had a function analogous to that of the Greek *stoa,* usually forming one of the sides of the forum, opposite the temple. The axis of the temple may thereby join the transverse axis of the basilica.[8] This axis is crossed at a right angle by another longitudinal axis. The biaxial layout of the basilica hence repeats the basic scheme of Roman space. Its section, with a higher nave accompanied by aisles, not only allows for sufficient daylight in the central part of the space, but also contributes essentially to the grandeur of the interior. In the Basilica of Maxentius in Rome (AD 307–312) this effect is emphasized by the introduction of three large groinvaults over the nave. The thrusts of these vaults are neutralized by three barrel-vaults on either side.

The Roman house, with its main room, the *atrium,* is usually considered a major manifestation of the Roman concept of space. It is a centralized space, lit from above, penetrated by a longitudinal axis which runs from the entrance to the peristyle garden at the opposite end. In certain respects the *atrium* house has an affinity to the Greek courtyard house, but whereas the Greek house was characterized by its seclusion, its axial dis-

(8) See, for instance, Augusta Raurica, Lugdunum Convenarum, Lutetia Parisiorum, Leptis Magna, and, above all, the Forum of Trajan in Rome itself.

82. *Basilica Ulpia, Rome. AD 110-13. Reconstruction of the interior.*

83. *House of the Silver Wedding, Pompeii. 2d century BC. Atrium.*

84. *Theatre of Marcellus, Rome. Dedicated 13 or 11 BC. Reconstruction. Museo della Civiltà Romana, Rome.*

85. *Apartment houses, Ostia. Mid-2d century AD. Reconstruction.*

(9) Originally, in smaller houses without peristyle, the *tablinum* which faced the entrance on the other side of the *atrium*, had analogous function, or the functions of the two rooms might be interchangeable. See A. Boëthius and J. B. Ward-Perkins, *Etruscan and Roman Architecture* (Harmondsworth and Baltimore, 1970), p. 153.

(10) Robert Venturi says: "Architecture occurs at the meeting of interior and exterior forces of use and space. These interior and environmental forces are both general and particular, generic and circumstantial. Architecture as the wall between the inside and the outside becomes the spatial record of this resolution and its drama." Robert Venturi, *Complexity and Contradiction in Architecture* (New York, 1966), pp. 88-89.

position makes the Roman house part of a comprehensive spatial system. As a result the *atrium* house is a synthesis of private and public functions, simultaneously enclosed and connected. The axis may also be interpreted as a symbol of authority, like the dominant axis of the Roman temple, for it ended in an *exedra* which was the reception room of the *pater familias.*[9]

Finally, the theatre well illustrates the basic Roman intentions. Whereas the Greek theatre may be characterized as a relatively passive space which served as a background to the active, plastic figures of the performers, the Roman theatre is an active space in its own right. Its steeply sloping rows of seats and the high *scaenae frons* create a strong feeling of interior space. Within this space the performers did not act freely, but were confined to a narrow *proscaenium* opposite the spectators; they appeared like a relief. Together with the spectators; they have become dependent parts of a dominant space which at a closer scrutiny reveals itself as axial: In the centre of the *scaenae frons* over the main door was placed the statue of an "authority," and facing it, above the spectators, there is often a small temple. Thus the action of the performers was integrated into a comprehensive existential system, and the building illustrates the general Roman wish for functional differentiation as an expression of the multitude of actions which constitute this system.

Articulation

New problems of formal articulation naturally grew from the increased importance of active interior and exterior space. Whereas the Classical orders were developed to characterize relatively independent and small architectural units, the extended, continuous surfaces of the larger Roman buildings demanded a new kind of subdivision and textural treatment. Although the Egyptians had already developed some of the most important means of architectural articulation, we may say that the modern problem of the wall as "the meeting of exterior and interior forces of use and space" was first encountered by the Romans.[10]

86. *Sanctuary of Bacchus, Baalbek. Mid-2d century AD. Interior.*

87. *Basilica, Trier. Early 4th century AD.*

88. *Basilica, Trier. Early 4th century AD. Aula of Constantine (Aula Palatina).*

It is generally recognized that Roman wall articulation does not correspond to the technical structure of the building. Although technical elements appear, such as the arch, the formal treatment of the wall hides rather than explains the construction. Roman concrete buildings consist of a continuous system of vaults, arches, walls and pillars, which incorporates hardly any horizontal elements. The appearance of the walls, however, is usually conditioned by the application of the horizontal and vertical members of the Classical orders. Only in utilitarian buildings of secondary importance is the construction exposed, a fact which indicates why the orders were introduced in connection with more important public tasks. But the Roman use of the orders differs fundamentally from the Greek. The Romans wished to create a symbolic form of a new kind, and did not simply imitate Greek architecture. Rather than making a particular ideal character manifest, the Classical members here form a complex dynamic totality of interacting parts.

The best-known example of the Roman use of the orders is the so-called "superimposition," where Doric, Ionic, and Corinthian columns, engaged columns or pilasters are placed above each other. The masculine and stout Doric thus carry the more graceful Ionic which in turn carry the slender Corinthian. A relatively simple play of forces is expressed this way, which represents a new kind of relationship between the parts of a building. They act together, not as individuals but as parts of a system, each part being subordinate to the superior idea of system. In contrast to Greek architecture, where every part contained the immanent character of the whole, the single part in isolation does not tell us anything about the building as a whole.

A more complex example of such systems is offered by walls where the Classical orders are combined with rustication—even in the sixteenth century this device was interpreted as an expression of an interaction between man's organizing power and the forces of nature.[11] If the Romans, then, wanted to characterize the building as a dynamic system, why did they not use the system of construction directly for this purpose? The

(11) S. Serlio, *Tutte l'Opere d'Architettura IV.*

(12) "Man is surrounded not only by the dimension of space, but also that of time." K. Schefold, *Pompejanische Malerei* (Basle, 1952), p. 83.

(13) H. Kähler, "Das Fortunaheiligtum von Palestrina Praeneste," *Annales Universitatis Saraviensis,* vol. VII, no. 3/4, (Saarbrücken, 1958), pp. 189 ff.

answer is that the play of forces in a continuous construction would be too complex and out of tune with the strict, spatial order of Roman layouts and buildings. The large baldachins of the groin-vaults, however, represent an important step towards employing the real technical structure as a means of spatial organization.

In general, Roman articulation represents an answer to the problem of how to give space continuity and rhythm, that is, dynamic order. Its basic intention is to characterize space as the stage of god-inspired human action. Space becomes the varied and dynamic, but ordered stage where history takes place. The Pompeian wall paintings support this interpretation. By means of perspective illusion they make the walls dissolve, whereby the room becomes part of a comprehensive spatial totality, and the actions which take place in the room are related to the divine, historical plan which is symbolized by the pictorial motifs. Thus Roman space concretized the dimension of time, not as eternal, static order such as the orthogonal space of the Egyptians, but as the dimension of action.[12]

Palestrina

One of the most important sanctuaries of Roman antiquity was situated near Rome at Praeneste, now called Palestrina. It was dedicated to Fortuna Primigenia, the firstborn of Jupiter (who at the same time is reported to have been the nurse of Jupiter and Juno!)— a very different dedication from those we have encountered in Greece. An anthropomorphic god is replaced by the vague concept of fate, that is, the principle which makes things come to be and events to happen. The sanctuary of Fortuna which we will discuss here stems from the Republican period (*c.* 80 BC), but the cult of Fortuna in this place is certainly much older.[13] From the outset of the Roman development destiny was seen as a dimension of human existence.

Two old sacred places in the steep hillside were taken as the point of departure for the great Sullan layout: the circular temple of Fortuna Primigenia from the third century BC, and, about 100 metres (328 feet) below,

91. *Temple of Fortuna Primigenia, Palestrina.*
c. *80 BC. Perspective reconstruction.*

92. *Temple of Fortuna Primigenia, Palestrina.*

a statue of Fortuna with Jupiter and Juno in her lap. These two elements were incorporated in a grand scheme of axially disposed terraces. A semicircular portico was attached to the old temple. It embraced a "theatre" which offers a commanding view of the campagna. Hardly anywhere else in Roman building is the use of landscape so evident. To both sides the space is defined by hills, but a north-south *cardo* leads the eye towards the distant sea. A valley running east-west crosses this axis below the sanctuary, like a *decumanus*. The sanctuary dominates this ordered domain, and the "theatre" is the place from which its cosmic implications may be perceived and understood. (The altar of Fortuna probably was placed within the "theatre" as its "stage.") A series of terraces below prepares the visitor for this concluding, meaningful experience. To "prepare" here implies a continuous movement through an organized space. The sanctuary is entered from both sides, where symmetrically disposed stairs lead up to a kind of *propylaea* with columnar porticoes and fountains. Here long access ramps start, running at a right angle to the main axis of the layout. The ramps were closed-in between walls, and did not allow for any contact with the landscape before the visitor reached their common landing at the centre. Here a breathtaking view of the plain below makes manifest the significance and power of the main axis. The ramps give access to a long terrace which is accompanied by a Doric colonnade. At the centre of each half of the terrace, Ionic *exedras* are inserted; the western one to accommodate an altar, the other for the statue of Fortuna with Jupiter and Juno in her lap. A central staircase leads on to another terrace whose back wall is articulated by engaged Ionic columns. Continuing along the main axis, one reaches a large platform accompanied by Corinthian columns on three sides. The temple of Fortuna now becomes visible above the theatre and its columnar, semicircular portico.[14]

Continuity is a basic formal property of the sanctuary at Palestrina. It is not composed of individual plastic bodies, such as its Greek counterpart in Delphi, but consists of terraces, colonnades, ramps and stairs, which are unified to form an integrated whole. The general spatial and plastic con-

(14) According to Kähler's reconstruction: *op. cit.*, pp. 204, 206.

93. *Temple of Fortuna Primigenia, Palestrina. First terrace.*

94. *Pantheon, Rome. AD 118-28.*

(15) Ward-Perkins says, "With the building of the Pantheon . . . architectural thinking had been turned inside out; and henceforth the concept of interior space as a dominating factor in architectural design was to be an.accepted part of the artistic establishment of the capital." A. Boëthius and J. B. Ward-Perkins, *op. cit.*, p. 256. Perhaps we should rather say: Architectural thinking had been turned "outside in!"

(16) See H. P. L'Orange, *Romersk idyll* (Oslo, 1952), p. 69.

tinuity is combined with a dominant axial disposition. A series of significant characters rises up towards the final goal: great polygonal wall under the first terrace, and Doric, Ionic and Corinthian orders of the main levels. Each element becomes a dependent part of a dynamic whole, which seems to concretize a meaningful action. From the moment the visitor enters the sanctuary he experiences the layout as a spatial force which leads him towards the goal. The temple of Fortuna thus extends its influence beyond its immediate surroundings, and becomes the agent of a cosmic order which embraces the whole landscape. The sanctuary has to be "read" starting from the temple, and the Roman path *extends* from a centre. Egyptian "return" has been replaced by Roman departure and conquest.

Pantheon

Whereas the sanctuary in Palestrina was the first major treatment of active exterior space, the Roman Pantheon introduces interior space as an expression of a new existential dimension.[15] The building standing today was erected by Hadrian (AD 118–128), and its dedication to all the gods again indicates a general principle rather than a particular, individual force. The Pantheon, in fact, has always impressed visitors by its cosmic character. "It resembles heaven," Dio Cassius said, and recent studies subscribe to this simile.[16]

The Pantheon consists of two major elements, a huge domed rotunda and a large columnar porch. The general effect of the exterior did not differ from that of other Roman temples: The porch resembles the portico of a normal Roman temple, and was originally preceded by a flight of stairs, as the ground level was considerably lower in antiquity than now. It was flanked by lower columnar porticoes extending forward on both sides. The rotunda was not conceived as a plastic body, but as a shell containing the great *cella,* which seems to manifest a new image of man's universe. These two major parts of the Pantheon apparently do not form an integrated whole. The traditional porch and the revolutionary rotunda seem added together without inner necessity. A

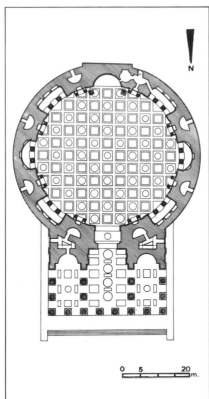

N

0 5   20
m.

95. *Pantheon, Rome. Detail of the construction.*

96. *Pantheon, Rome. Ground plan.*

97. *Pantheon, Rome. AD 118-28. Isometric drawing and section.*

closer scrutiny, however, reveals formal traits which contradict this (rather common) interpretation. A rectangular volume has been introduced between the porch and the rotunda, which serves as a natural transition. The entablatures of the two main volumes do not correspond, but both continue across the transitional element, producing an interpenetration of forms, which can only be due to a *total* conception of the building. Furthermore, a longitudinal axis runs from the porch through the transitional volume and across the rotunda to end in an apse. This apse is flanked by columns which through breaks in the entablature are connected visually with an arch penetrating the upper zone of the drum. When inside, however, the axis is less evident than the centralizing effect of the circular space and the hemispherical dome. It has often been pointed out that a sphere, with a diameter of 43.20 metres (142 feet), could be described within the space. But it is important to note that the coffers of the dome are not related to the centre of this sphere, but to the centre of the floor and to the spectator who would stand there.[17] A vertical axis thereby defined, which rises freely towards heaven through the large opening in zenith, means that the Pantheon integrates the sacred dimension of the vertical in the organization of interior space.

The Pantheon unifies a celestial dome and a longitudinal, extended axis into a meaningful whole. It unifies cosmic order and living history, and makes man experience himself as a god-inspired explorer and conqueror, as a maker of history according to divine plan. This is also evident in the horizontal division of the space. The drum consists of two zones, and both are articulated by means of the classical members: large Corinthian pilasters and columns below and small pilasters above.[18] These members, their entablatures, and the coffers of the dome hide the complex, arched construction behind, and give the interior the intended calm, cosmic order. The lowest zone has a rich and plastic articulation with deep niches and freestanding columns, representing, so to speak, action in space. The upper zone presents a simple order of anthromorphic members, and the dome the heaven-

(17) Kähler, *Der römische Tempel*, figs. 11, 12.

(18) Only a small fragment of the original upper wall is visible today.

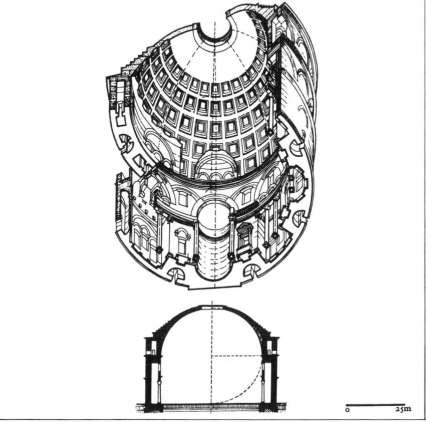

0   25m

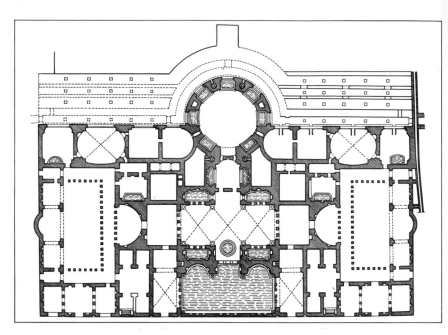

98. Baths of Caracalla, Rome. AD 212-16. Reconstructed ground plan of the thermal building.

(19) Heidegger says, "But 'on earth' really means 'under heaven.' . . . The four belong to an *original* unity: Earth and Heaven, Mortal and Divine . . . . The Mortals are Men . . . . Only Man dies and keeps on dying while remaining on earth, under heaven, in the presence of the Divine," M. Heidegger, "Bauen Wohnen Denken," *Vorträge und Aufsätze* 11 (Pfullingen, 1967).

ly harmony of geometric perfection. Architectural space is used to symbolize man's existence in space.[19]

The Baths of Caracalla

The Roman *termae* certainly represent the grandest manifestation of the Roman interest in concrete interior space. In the great imperial baths not only is there a rich variety of vaulted and domed interiors, but also a new wish for joining such spaces together to form complex groups. This is naturally related to a differentiated functional programme, but cannot be explained in terms of functional pattern only. Whereas the baths in Pompeii still show an irregular distribution of spaces, the Baths of Titus (AD 80) had a strictly symmetrical layout relative to a north-south axis. In the Baths of Trajan (AD 109) we also find a fully developed east-west axis. This scheme, with its affinity to the *cardo* and *decumanus* of the Roman settlement, was repeated in the Baths of Caracalla (AD 212–16) and Diocletian (AD 298–306).

The Baths of Caracalla exploited all the possibilities of concrete construction, and the ruins still give testimony to an impressive layout. The bathhouse forms a rectangle measuring 214 by 110 metres (702 by 361 feet), freely placed within an enclosed area of 450 by 450 metres (1476 feet), with which it has the main north-south axis in common. The outer enclosure consists of constructions of considerable bulk. The northern wing contained offices and dwellings, and in the middle the main entrance. To the south were water cisterns and along them rows of seats for watching the games in front of the bathhouse. The axis of the sports ground is indicated by large *exedrae* to the east and the west. The bathhouse itself has a complex, but strictly ordered distribution of spaces. The intersection of its main axes defines the place which must be considered the core of the building: a lofty hall covered by three groin-vaults. In the corners four smaller bays are joined to the hall, which contained cold plunges, indicating that the hall was the *frigidarium,* or cold bath of the *termae.* Along the main axis to the north is

99.	Baths of Caracalla, Rome. Aerial view.

100.	Giovanni Battista Piranesi: View of the
Baths of Caracalla. 18th century print.

the swimming pool or *natatio,* and to the south the *tepidarium* and the circular *caldarium,* or hot bath. The latter is flanked on both sides by identical rows of smaller heated rooms. The rest of the rectangle is taken up by two *palaestrae* (possibly covered) surrounded by suites of changing rooms *(apodyteria).* After changing, the visitors probably entered the heated rooms, from which they passed into the *caldarium.* From there they followed the main axis through the *tepidarium* and the *frigidarium* to the *natatio.* We see, thus, that the intersecting main axes only partly correspond to the functional pattern.

As the layout of the Roman *termae* cannot be fully explained in functional terms, we may infer that it has symbolic implications. Or rather, the use comprised functions which go beyond the physical acts of bathing and gymnastics. The *termae* had to possess a spatial organization and an articulation which made them transcend the purely utilitarian structures. They gave the visitor occasion to cultivate his mind by conversation, reading and other intellectual activities, and during the imperial epoch they served as true civic centres, where important political decisions were made. As one of the important stages where Roman life took place, and hence an expression of existential meanings, the *termae* naturally had to possess the spatial structure we have encountered when talking about the Roman landscape, settlement and principal building types. It is therefore no mere coincidence that the organization of the *termae* resembles that of the city. But it would be too superficial to explain this affinity as a result of similar functions. Rather, both manifest the same basic order; a fact which proves that the Romans applied the same spatial model on all levels.

Spalato

When he retired in AD 305 Diocletian built an impressive retreat on the Dalmatian coast. It is difficult to decide whether the ruins are of a palace or a small ideal city. In fact, the plan closely resembles that of the Roman *castra* with its intersecting main streets and

the *praetorium* located at the end of the north-south axis, and the palace of Diocletian did actually house a garrison, and was fortified like a permanent military fort. But it also incorporated elements from villa and palace architecture, such as a continuous loggia along the southern façade.[20]

The plan of the imperial palace in Spalato is inscribed within a rectangle measuring 216 by 180 metres (709 by 591 feet). It is surrounded by high walls with projecting square towers, and monumental gateways flanked by octagonal towers in the middle of the north, east and west walls. The gates are connected by colonnaded streets which intersect at the geometrical centre of the plan, defining thus the basic Roman pattern of *cardo* and *decumanus.* The streets divide the urban area into four equal parts, two of which were reserved for the garrison, and the other two, towards the south, for the palace proper and two spacious precincts. The eastern precinct contains the emperor's mausoleum, the western one a temple to Jupiter and two small rotundas. The main north-south axis led up to a circular vestibule and a large rectangular audience hall which was directly connected with the southern loggia overlooking the sea. The axis, then, did not stop, but indicated the integration of the palace in a larger, natural space. Of particular interest is the spatial sequence formed by the Golden Gate in the northern wall, the *cardo,* the peristyle beyond the main intersection, the domical vestibule, the *aula* and the central opening in the loggia.[21] The gate was crowned with an arcade which had statues of the emperor and the gods in its niches. Inside the gate there was a square vestibule covered with a "celestial cupola." The processional way led from the gate through the arcaded peristyle to the main domical vestibule which served as the *salutatorium* of the emperor. Between the peristyle and the vestibule is a "glorification pediment" where the horizontal entablature is interrupted by an arch in the middle. Instead of just being a building the place was intended as a meaningful succession of spaces, related to the "divinity" of the emperor.

Within this integrated, dynamic whole, the mausoleum and the temple form a comple-

mentary, symbolic composition. Whereas the temple faces the rising sun, the mausoleum is oriented towards the west. Together, thus, they represent beginning and end, and their common axis has a truly metaphysical character. Anybody who approaches the imperial vestibule has to cross this reminder of the mystery and limits of human existence. Appropriately, the two buildings are screened off behind the lateral arcades of the main way.

In general, the palace in Spalato is characterized by strict order and regularity. But this order represents something much more profound than the military organization of contemporary society. By repeating the order of the Roman *templum,* the palace became a true *palatium sacrum.* Thus Diocletian built himself a palace in the form of a *castra* not so much for physical protection, but because the plan symbolized a divine world order. As *Cosmocrator,* the emperor was the supreme power controlling this world, and the palace was a manifestation of his role. "The *palatium,* therefore, was a concept rather than a specific building, which implied a universal and divine power that came from the gods and was made manifest in the person of the ruler."[22]

Space Conception and Development

Our examples have shown that, regardless of building task and environmental level, the Romans employed the same fundamental spatial image. We have seen that this image represented a world order abstracted from certain natural phenomena, such as the cardinal points, and from ancient symbolizations, such as the "spiritual" vertical, the "profane" horizontal and the concepts of centre and path. In contrast with the pluralism of Greek architecture, Roman architecture therefore is characterized by uniformity. This is not only due to the employment of the same basic image, but also to the wish to make this image a dominant principle which determines the choice and articulation of detail. Roman architecture is truly systematic; but, at the same time, it is functional. The Romans were practical, well-

(20)	An analogous loggia is found in the Flavian Palace on the Palatine, overlooking the Circus Maximus.

(21)	See E. Baldwin Smith, *Architectural Symbolism of Imperial Rome and the Middle Ages* (Princeton, N.J.: 1956), pp. 141 ff.

(22)	Baldwin Smith, *op. cit.,* p. 98.

101. Palace of Diocletian, Spalato (Split). AD 300-306. Ground plan.

102. Palace of Diocletian, Spalato (Split). Peristyle court.

103. Palace of Diocletian, Spalato (Split). Reconstruction. Museo della Civiltà Romana, Rome.

(23) See Kaschnitz von Weinberg, *op. cit.*, ch. VI.

(24) The term "Dominate" is introduced in H. P. L'Orange, *Art Forms and Civic Life in the Late Roman Empire* (Princeton, N.J.: 1965).

organized people, and demanded from their buildings that they should work, so they have a rich variety of spatial forms and dimensions, and ingenious technical solutions such as hypocaust heating.

As in Egyptian architecture, the basic Roman intentions were present from the very outset, and to a certain extent they stem from more ancient Italic sources.[23] But Roman architecture also has an historical development, which consists both in the gradual working out of basic intentions and in their interaction with temporary circumstances. In general three main periods can be distinguished: the Republican period, the Principate and the Dominate.[24] In Republican architecture active exterior space is developed as an expression of the general role of the Romans in the world. At the same time its articulation illustrates the integration of the Greek anthropomorphic characters in a new systematic totality. The architecture of the first emperors is still characterized by variety and by the organic life of members and details. After the peaceful classicism of Augustus follow the mannerist experiments of the Claudian period. A decisive turning point is represented by the rebuilding of Rome under Nero after the great fire in AD 64, when extensive use of concrete and new spatial forms supported each other, and the first great manifestation of interior space is found in Nero's Golden House. Here a domed, octagonal hall, lit from above, gave a new divine interpretation to the role of the emperor. During the reigns of Trajan and Hadrian the mastery of space reached its climax with such creations as Trajan's Forum and Hadrian's villa. The island villa (*teatro marittimo*) of the latter has a centralized plan of unsurpassed richness and complexity, interpenetrated by the fundamental intersecting axes. It represents, so to speak, the baroque phase of the Roman development. The later Imperial period, the Dominate, is characterized by increasing systematization and rigidity, as well as an almost ascetic lack of traditional articulation and detail.

In Roman architecture the basic notions of centre, path and domain are unified to form a hierarchical system. On the most comprehensive level, Rome itself was the centre, the *caput mundi,* of a system of ways

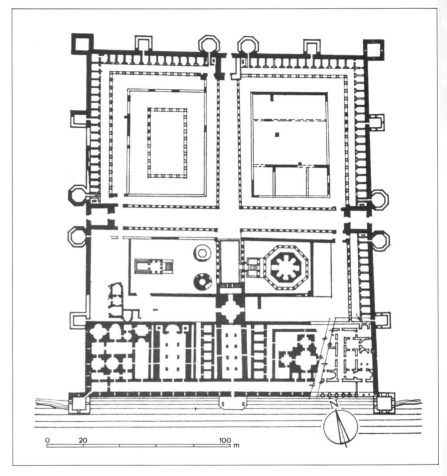

104. *Palace of Diocletian, Spalato (Split). Reconstruction of the peristyle court.*

105. *Imperial forums, Rome. Ground plan.*

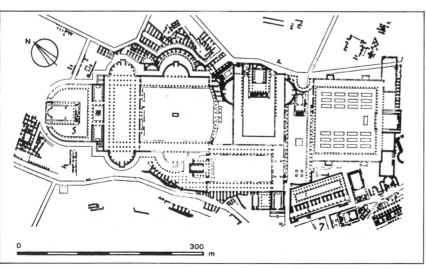

0   300
m

and domains. Cities were intended as microcosms having an analogous structure, and the single building repeated the same model. Every building thus represented the totality, and every place reminded the Roman citizen of the world order to which he belonged. This does not mean, however, that Roman space was continuous and open; it consisted of clearly defined and structured units which were added together. This is, for instance, evident when we look at the composition of the imperial forums or the general layout of Hadrian's villa. Roman space offered maximum security without confining man physically and psychologically to one particular place.

Meaning and Architecture

Although the Romans took over the orders of Classical Greek architecture, their intention was not primarily to symbolize a multitude of ideal archetypes. The new concept of system rather implies that the parts are conditioned by a general, comprehensive image. The individual elements of the Greeks thus were replaced by the concept of systematic interaction. The Stoic philosophers stressed the common essential nature of all men, and as a result maintained that there was only one Law and one country. Poseidonias (185–51 BC) regarded nature as one great system and every detail as being arranged by divine providence. This attitude is still present in the philosophy of Marcus Aurelius (emperor AD 161–180) who said: "O world, I am in tune with every note of thy great harmony."[25] Rather than pursue ideal perfection, the Romans, then, felt they should live in accordance with divine plan, that is, to participate actively in *history*. For the Romans life on earth was not a mere imperfect reproduction of the ideal archetypes, it was a direct and meaningful manifestation of divine will. Thus we understand that the contradiction between cosmic order and practical action is only apparent; in reality order and action were understood as aspects of the same historical process.

The recognition of history as a basic dimension of human existence naturally implied a new interpretation of the gods. The Roman gods are not primarily abstracted

(25) Marcus Aurelius, *Meditations* 4, 23.

106. *Hadrian's villa, Tivoli. AD 118-25. "Teatro Marittimo." Ground plan.*

107. *Hadrian's villa, Tivoli. "Teatro Marittimo."*

(26) "Ask in vain where the Roman gods really are. They are always there, constantly at work. In their activity they embody the forces which correspond to that peculiar quality which we consider Roman: the relationship to history as the temporal dimension, as the here-and-now." His gods are the forces behind these events. Their myth is to a certain extent history." Kähler, *Der römische Tempel*, p. 11. See also F. Altheim, *Romische Religionsgeschichte* 1 (Berlin. 1956), pp. 52, 62, 68.

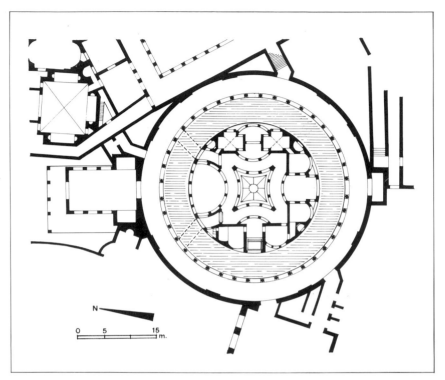

from the experience of natural forces and anthropomorphic characters, but were envisaged as the agents of the historical process and as symbolizations of its different aspects. We have already mentioned Janus who in general was the god of all beginnings. We may also mention another typically Roman god, Mars, the god of battle and war. Of supreme importance, however, was Jupiter, who was the great protector of the city and the state. All the Roman gods have in common that they are conceived as forces rather than personalities. They do not belong to particular places and do not form part of an original mythology.[26] During the Imperial epoch, the Emperor ever more took over the functions of the gods. Divine authority was invested in his person, and a pseudo-cosmos was established around him. His actions were manifestations of divine will, and hence were marked by monuments such as columns, arches and buildings. Whereas we do not know the foundation date of any major Greek building, all Roman monuments represent important historical occasions. The built environment thus became a concretization of the cosmic Roman state and its history. The Emperor and his *palatium sacrum* acted as its meaningful centre. Herodian wrote, "Where the Emperor is, there is Rome."

We understand that it is a misunderstanding to consider the Romans only as practical engineers with a strong talent for organization. Roman organization was founded on a comprehensive religious attitude, and Roman *praxis* was the historical manifestation of the divine order. The Romans did not stress the pursuit of knowledge of the timeless. Rather they recognized *time* as a basic existential dimension. They did not enquire after the "what," but the "how." Stoic philosophy teaches about the "how" of human conduct, and that ethical behaviour means

o live in accordance with divine plan, to be
the instrument of the course of history. Roman art is correspondingly characterized by
a new realism, that is, the wish to present
the historical moment, or the succession of
such. This is particularly evident in histor-
cal representations such as the reliefs of
the columns of Trajan and Marcus Aurelius,
but also in the portraits of the Roman emperors, up until later imperial art when living
history was replaced by the abstract system
as such.[27] The architecture of Diocletian is
characterized by an almost Egyptian wish
for eternal form. It is as if the freedom of
action which resulted from the Roman image
of the world was lost. Man no longer found
security in action and conquest, and had to
return to the origins. Thus Roman history
repeats the course of a natural process.

108. Caesar Augustus (Augustus of Pri-
maporta). c. 20 BC. Vatican Museums, Rome.

(27) See L'Orange, op.
cit.

57

4. Early Christian Architecture

(1) R. Krautheimer, *Early Christian and Byzantine Architecture* (Harmondsworth and Baltimore, 1965), pp. 21, 41.

(2) P. Sherrard, *Constantinople. Image of a Holy City* (London, New York, and Toronto, 1965).

Introduction

For centuries the church has been the leading building task of European architecture. Even today most European towns are dominated by a centrally located church which gives visible structure and meaning to the townscape. Whereas Greek and Roman settlements had a more complex appearance, the Christian town was characterized by its churches, and only the castle sometimes formed another focus. In spite of an extremely rich historical development, the basic themes of ecclesiastical architecture can be traced back to the Early Christian epoch. From the very outset a few profoundly symbolic spatial relationships were taken as the point of departure for the building of churches; that is, the concepts of "centre" and "path." Fundamental existential meanings, thus, were given a new Christian interpretation. In addition to these properties, a more general interiority is a distinguishing characteristic of Early Christian architecture, a characteristic which has always kept its basic importance.

Central and longitudinal spaces have already been found among the most significant manifestations of Roman architecture. The centralized space of the Pantheon was simultaneously a cosmic symbol and an expression of man's new experience of being an "actor" in space. The longitudinal spaces of Roman basilicas or the Aula Palatina at Trier had an analogous double meaning with the addition of the path motif to symbolize the directed character of human action. Both forms were taken over by Early Christian architecture, and the plan of most early churches tends toward a combination or synthesis of longitudinality and centralization; the former being dominant in the West and the latter in the East. At the outset the church proper was based on the longitudinal basilica, whereas a centralized space was used when the building task was a baptistry, mausoleum or *martyrium*.[1] Centralizing tendencies can be seen in the early churches as well, and in sixth-century Byzantine architecture the central plan was adopted for major ecclesiastical buildings, churches generally incorporating a secondary longitudinal axis. We will return later to an interpretation of these basic phenomena.

A pronounced interiority is common to all early churches. By late Roman architecture there was a tendency to interpret the exterior as a shell around a richly articulate interior. A wish for transcendence was thereby made manifest, which prepared for the meaning of Christian space. The early churches are conceived as interior worlds, as places which represent the eternal *Civitas Dei*. Summary treatment of the exterior and the articulation of the interior served to emphasize this character. Continuous decorative treatment deprived the walls of their material, tectonic character, so that the visitor does not enter another earthly space, where physical laws reign, but feels transported to a qualitatively different world.

Early Christian man did not obtain security by means of abstractions from natural, human or historical phenomena. Only by negating these phenomena could he receive that grace which made his existence meaningful. Christian existential space, therefore, is not derived from man's concrete environment, but symbolizes a promise and a process of redemption, which are concretized as a centre and a path. By building the centre and the path as a church, the new meaning of existence was made visible.

Landscape and Settlement

When Constantine moved the capital of the Roman Empire to Constantinople in 330, his intention was to mark the beginning of a new era.[2] With the dedication of a new city the old order was absorbed by a new one based on the Christian faith. The location of the new capital is very significant. As it was to represent a synthesis of the old Empire and "the new pact," that is, of Rome and Jerusalem, it was set where Asia and Europe meet. But it is not only the continents of the East and the West that meet here, the Black Sea and the Mediterranean are also connected to form a north-south axis. Constantinople, thus, is located at the intersection of the great *cardo* and *decumanus* of the new Empire. At this intersection the city seems to hover between heaven and earth.

Although it was built on seven hills like the old Rome, the character of Constanti-

109. Anthemius of Tralles, Isidorus of Miletus: Hagia Sophia, Constantinople (Istanbul). 532-37. Interior.

110. *Rossikon monastery, Mount Athos, Greece. Reconstruction.*

111. *Wall of Theodosius II, Constantinople (Istanbul). 412.*

112. *Abbey of Montecassino, Italy. Reconstruction, 1075 (after Conant).*

(3) W. Braunfels, *Abendländische Klosterbaukunst* (Cologne, 1969).

(4) K. J. Conant, *Carolingian and Romanesque Architecture* (Harmondsworth and Baltimore, 1959), p. 4.

nople is entirely different. Rome's architectural forms have always been characterized by a certain gravity and plastic power, but Constantinople is the city of silhouettes, of dematerialized contours and surfaces. Legend tells that Byzas, who founded the first town there, was the son of Poseidon, and over and over again it has been repeated that Constantinople/Istanbul ought to be approached from the sea. Then its character as a promised land comes alive; like a mirage, like an unreal, heavenly city it floats over the shining surface of the Sea of Marmora. A new, transcendent dimension is thus added to urban space; and Constantinople represented a worthy start to the new concept of the city as a manifestation of the *Civitas Dei*.

The buildings erected under Constantine before and after the dedication in 330 were still based on Roman models, but with the passing of time it must have become evident that the place demanded another kind of architecture. During the first half of the sixth century under Emperor Justinian development was initiated which gave the city its characteristic skyline dominated by the innumerable domes of churches. Over them all rose Hagia Sophia, which according to a contemporary chronicler "far surpasses the power of description."

However the image of a Christian environment found an expression which was more radical than the creation of a new capital. With the introduction of monasticism and monastic buildings, a truly Christian way of life was concretized.[3] During the fourth century the cenobitical system developed in which the congregation lives together in a monastery consisting of cells, refectory, church, and secondary functions such as kitchen and guest house. Usually the different elements formed an enclosure around a centrally placed church. Within the enclosure, silence, humility and asceticism reigned. Monasticism was introduced in the West during the second half of the fourth century, and received its main impulse from St. Benedict of Nursia (*c.* 480–553) who founded the Benedictine order. The monasteries were "orderly and peaceful islands within a society which was struggling out of deep confusion,"[4] and made a vital contribution to the economic and cultural basis of medieval civilization.

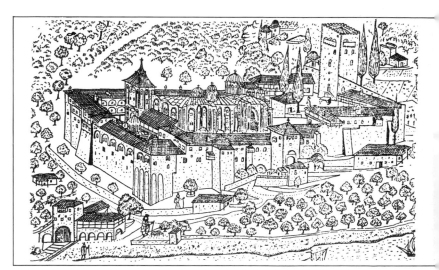

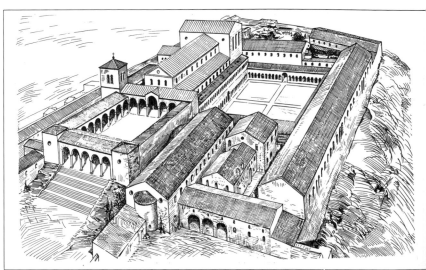

113. Monastery of Christ Pantocrator, Constantinople (Istanbul). c. 1150.

114. S. Sebastiano, Rome. 312-13. Reconstruction.

115. S. Giovanni in Laterano, Rome. 313-20. Ground plan.

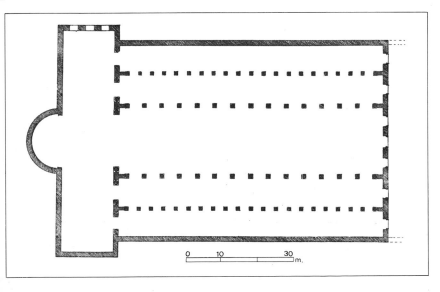

Although Constantine repeated many of the structural properties of the old Rome in his new capital,[5] the city of Constantinople as well as the monasteries of the Early Christian period was characterized by topological enclosure rather than by the strict geometrical organization of Roman settlements. The aim of this was to express the otherness of the sacred enclosure, and it was defined as such by means of symbolic motifs like towered gateways and "heavenly" domes. The Early Christian enclosure did not represent a particular place, like the Greek *temenos,* or a general order like the Roman *templum,* but concretized a way of life.

Building

It is significant that the basic theme of Western ecclesiastical architecture was introduced as early as the first major church built after the decree in favour of Christianity of 313. The church, which today is known as S. Giovanni in Laterano, was originally dedicated to Christus Salvator, and was attached to the residence of the Bishop of Rome. We know the original plan in spite of later rebuildings. A vast columnar basilica with double aisles ran from the east to the west and terminated in a tall apse which held seats for the bishop and the clergy. The transept is a medieval addition; originally the inner aisles were continuous, while the outer were stopped by relatively low sacristies.[6] The plan may be compared with the colonnaded street or peristyle leading up to the imperial throne in the Roman *palatium sacrum.* Like the emperor, Christ was revealed at the end of a symbolic, axial succession of spaces. From the beginning, churches consisted of two major parts: the congregational nave and the chancel. What was fundamentally new, however, was the idea of bringing these two elements together within the same interior space, for in Greek and Roman temples the *cella* was always reserved for the priests alone. The Christian church thus expresses a new conception of the function of giving and receiving.

During the Constantinian epoch other types also developed. There is a very interesting group of basilicas in Rome where the

(5) Thus the roads of the new Empire started from the "Million" in the central square of the Augustaeum, as they formerly did from the Miliarium Aureum in the Roman Forum.

(6) H. Kähler, *Die trühe Kirche* (Berlin, 1972), pp. 61, 62.

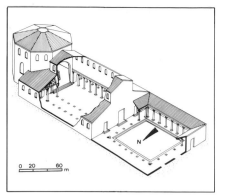

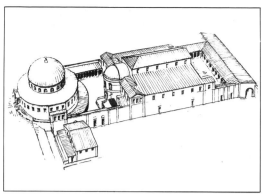

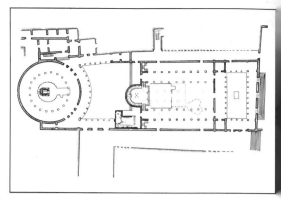

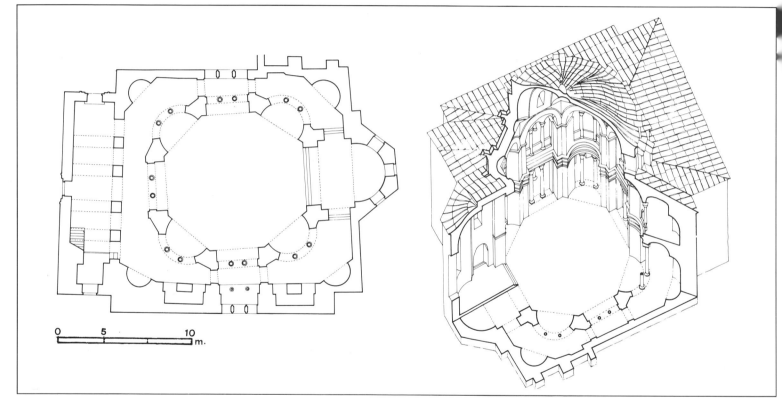

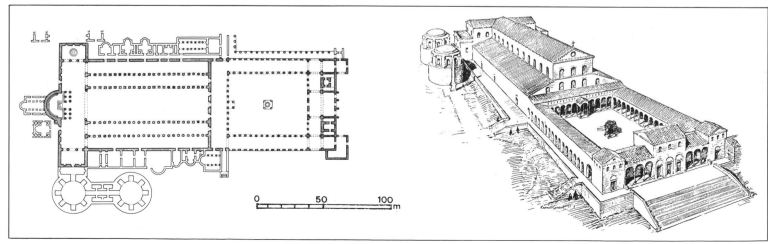

aisles are carried around the apse to form an ambulatory,[7] expressive of a wish for centralization. This relates the buildings to the centralized mausolea of Roman and Early Christian architecture, and, in fact, these basilicas were funerary halls connected with a martyr's grave.[8] However, this style was soon abandoned. Instead we encounter a type of *martyrium* which is more closely related to the "normal" basilica, as developed in the Laterano church. The huge basilica of St. Peter's (after 324) thus repeats the basic scheme, but a tall transept offers additional space for the functions of a funerary hall. The great building was preceded by an *atrium* with a central fountain for purification. Although the apse, and the *ciborium* or baldachin in front of it, forms a symbolic and architectural centre in the Early Christian basilica, the plan is basically a longitudinal path. Constantine only erected two structures, in the Holy Land, which were true combinations of longitudinal and centralized spaces. In the church of the Nativity in Bethlehem an octagon was added to a basilica, the latter located near the Grotto of the Nativity (c. 330). In Jerusalem the church of the Holy Sepulchre was planned along similar lines. In addition, it contained a large open apse around the Tomb of Christ. The plan, thus, is obviously related to the Roman funeral halls mentioned before. Somewhat later a large rotunda, the *Anastasis,* was erected over the tomb.

In the Eastern Empire, on the other hand, the centralized plan was adopted for the major churches. From the time of Emperor Justinian centralization became the distinguishing property of Byzantine ecclesiastical architecture. The first example is the domed, octagonal H. Sergios and Bakchos (begun before 527)[9] which was attached to Justinian's residence as heir to the throne. After the great experiment of Hagia Sophia, however, to which we will return later, Justinian church architecture fell back upon a simple cross-domed plan, where a dome surmounts the crossing of nave and transept. In larger structures, such as the church of the Holy Apostles in Constantinople (536–50), five domed units were arranged to form a Greek cross. In later Byzantine architecture the cross-domed church developed into the

standard cross-in-square church (quincunx), where the corners are surmounted by smaller domes, and the chancel is accompanied by smaller apses on either side. These lateral spaces, the *diaconicon* and the *prothesis,* served as depositories for the gospel book and the Eucharist respectively. During mass they were brought into the central nave, where they were exhibited to the congregation which assembled in the aisles, the narthex and the galleries, and from there to the chancel. Christ revealed himself to the faithful under the central heavenly dome, in a unity of liturgical function and architectural form.

Articulation

The interiority of the Early Christian church has already been mentioned. The exterior of basilicas and Byzantine domed structures is usually intended as a neutral envelope of continuous masonry walls. To avoid any general tectonic effect, columns only appear as isolated elements, and bricks are used rather than ashlar, achieving in this way a deliberate contrast to the rich, "heavenly" interior. The articulation of the interior is fundamentally different from the anthropomorphic organisms encountered in antiquity. Colonnades accompany the nave without any tectonic function. In most cases the columns are spoils, and their height, diameter and capitals vary considerably. Therefore they do not represent any particular anthropomorphic character, but must be simply understood as an emblematic motif and a means to emphasize the longitudinal movement.[10]

It is today generally assumed that the colonnades of the Laterano church originally had a straight entablature and that the same solution was used in old St. Peter's. The horizontal lines of the entablature do "visualize" the movement in depth, but at the same time the nave is divided into two distinct zones: a tall upper wall resting on a row of columns. This solution echoes the classical play of forces and moreover contradicts the idea of the wall as a continuous surface. Hence it is not surprising that the wall system of the first Constantinian basilicas was abandoned.[11] In the great church of S. Paolo

fuori le mura (385), the straight entablature has been replaced by an arcade, a solution which previously was only used in the secondary divisions between the aisles. The arcade makes the wall appear as one continuous (although perforated) surface, without the traditional conflict between vertical and horizontal members. The wall hence is "dematerialized," an effect which was emphasized by its treatment as a flat surface. Arched windows lit the nave and the transept, whereas the aisles remained dark. With the introduction of glass mosaic the walls were transformed into a shimmering skin: Thousands of minute tesserae were pressed into the plaster at slightly different angles to make the mass of the wall dissolve in a play of coloured lights. Space in the interior of the Early Christian church was intended to make the visitor forget the properties of everyday things: plastic form, weight, size, scale, material texture, and shape-defining shadows.

In Byzantine architecture we encounter the same basic intention, but also, due to the different building types, new structural principles of fundamental importance. In the Early Christian basilica the space-defining wall is the primary element. The space is covered by a secondary wooden roof which creates a certain vertical openness.[12] The centralized space of the Byzantine church, on the other hand, is covered by a dome. A dome, as such, does not represent any innovation, but the domes of Justinian architecture are more than domes in the traditional sense: They are conceived as complete baldachins. Thus the dome proper is superimposed on a polygonal volume, and the transition is taken care of by squinches or pendentives. Between the vertical supports of the baldachins, secondary membranelike walls are filled in. As these walls have no structural function they may be perforated by numerous openings, replaced by columnar screens, given a curved form, or simply eliminated. It is also possible to add several baldachin-shaped elements together. The Justinian architectural system therefore offers a new fundamental freedom of planning, and was of basic importance for the development of Romanesque and Gothic.[13] In Byzantine architecture several

(7) The first S. Agnese on the Via Nomentana, the first S. Lorenzo on the Via Tiburtina, S. Sebastiano and SS. Marcellino e Pietro.

(8) Krautheimer, *op. cit.*, p. 32.

(9) We ought also to mention the singular, centralized structure of S. Lorenzo in Milan (c. 370), which was probably also an imperial court church.

(10) Traditionally the columns are understood as representations of the Prophets and Apostles which carry the Church, and the colonnade as an abbreviation of the city.

(11) See H. Sedlmayr, "Spätantike Wandsysteme" in *Epochen und Werke I* (Vienna and Munich, 1959), pp. 31 ff.

(12) It is not clear whether the wooden construction was originally visible, or hidden by a "plat-fond." In any event, the ceiling was gilded, or blue with painted stars.

(13) See H. Sedlmayr, "Das erste mittelalterliche Architektursystem" in *Epochen und Werke* I, pp. 80 ff.

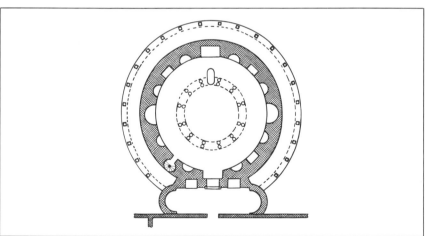

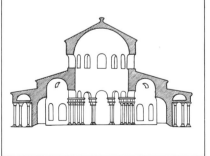

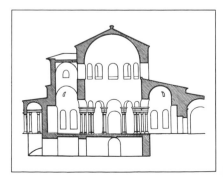

of the possible variations were utilized, but the structural properties of the system were not explored; the logical and systematic definition of primary and secondary elements was not visualized. In the Byzantine churches the baldachins were still immersed in the continuous shimmering boundary of Early Christian space.

The iconographic scheme of the Byzantine church shows that the building was intended as an image of the cosmos. The dome represents heaven while the lower parts form an earthly zone. The higher a picture is placed in the architectural framework, the more sacred it is held to be.[14] Divine light emanated from the heavenly dome and spread to the centralized space below.

Santa Costanza

On the Via Nomentana outside the city wall of Rome stands a particularly interesting group of buildings from Early Christian times. The main structure is today the basilica of S. Agnese fuori !e mura, built in 625–38 over the tomb of the virgin martyr, a church which concludes the history of Early Christian architecture in Rome. Previously the tomb was housed in a separate catacomb next to a funeral basilica of the type mentioned above. Impressive fragments of this building are still standing. It was erected by Constantine's daughter Constantina, in about 345. Better preserved is the mausoleum of Constantina herself, which was attached to the southern façade of the basilica. It was later used as a baptistry and in 1254 became a church, dedicated to a saint who never existed, S. Costanza.

S. Costanza is the best preserved building in Rome from the Constantinian epoch. Whereas the great basilicas have been destroyed or rebuilt, the mausoleum of Constantina is completely intact, except for the interior decoration. It testifies to the high quality of planning and execution still possible in Early Christian Rome, and is a singular architectural masterpiece. The exterior of the circular building shows the plain treatment of late antiquity. It was originally encircled by an open colonnade which carried a barrel vault. This ambulatory probably

(14) O. Demus, *Byzantine Mosaic Decoration* (London, 1953), p: 15. In the Early Christian basilica the apse was the most sacred place.

(15) See F. W. Deich-mann, *Frühchristliche Kirchen in Rom* (Basel, 1948), p. 50. In this connection we ought to mention the Piazza d'Oro in Hadrian's villa, where the dome rests on an undulating colonnade. However, this solution did not have any following; in later Roman buildings with a central plan the vault rests on massive walls or on engaged columns.

(16) Deichmann, *op. cit.*, pp. 25 ff.

(17) Only in S. Paolo fuori le mura were fluted columns introduced. After the fire in 1823 they were unfortunately replaced with smooth columns which give the interior a rather schematic character.

gave access to a subterranean space. A similar colonnade surrounded Diocletian's mausoleum in Spalato, but in contrast to late Roman mausolea S. Costanza has a "basilica" section. The drum rises above a lower, circular volume which contains the inner ambulatory. The revolutionary idea of adopting the spatial disposition of the basilica in a centralized building gives S. Costanza particular importance in the history of Christian architecture, being the origin of the concept of "double-shell" domed structures.[15] The adoption indicates that the basilican section meant something more than a mere practical solution to the creators of Early Christian architecture.

The interior of S. Costanza is preceded by a narthex which has lost its barrel vaulting. We therefore enter the main room today somewhat unprepared. As in the longitudinal basilicas, the centre is flooded by light, whereas the ambulatory remains in semi-darkness. A tall drum is inserted under the dome proper, perforated by large, arched windows. The drum rests on a continuous arcade with twelve pairs of composite columns. Between capital and drum entablature fragments are inserted, which may be considered the point of departure for the impost blocks of Byzantine architecture. S. Costanza, thus, was not only a revolutionary building in its general disposition, but also in its articulation. A cross of intersecting axes is superimposed on the circular twelve-part plan. The axes are defined by slightly wider arches and by larger niches in the outer wall. The longitudinal axis is further emphasized by giving the outer pair of columns a different colour, and by interrupting the ambulatory with a tall light-chamber which illuminates the place where the princess's sarcophagus once stood. A decorative scheme was organized in accordance with the architectural disposition.[16] The vault of this inserted baldachin was originally decorated with a mosaic representing the Heavenly Jerusalem, and the mosaic decoration of the ambulatory which is fairly well preserved, formed part of an integrated scheme which combined pagan and Christian symbols of death and eternal life.

Formally and symbolically S. Costanza forms a link between the central buildings of antiquity and the central churches of Western architecture. It combines the ancient cosmic symbolism of centre in relation to the problems of life and death, with the Christian concept of redemption and eternal life. When its mosaic decoration was complete, the shimmering interior must have been experienced as a singular manifestation of the new existential image.

Santa Sabina

"The best preserved Early Christian basilica in Rome is S. Sabina on the Aventine hill, built between 422 and 432. Here the experimentation of the Constantinian period is over, and the basilica has found its classical form." The plan is very simple: a nave accompanied by one aisle on either side, and a deep, spacious apse. The nave is relatively tall, and the slender proportions give the interior a new lightness and elegance. Elegance also characterizes the splendid rows of fluted Corinthian columns. Being less closely spaced than in S. Paolo fuori le mura the arcades create a particularly easy movement in depth. The nave is flooded by light from very large arched clerestory windows, thirteen on either side. As a contrast the aisles were windowless and dark. (During the Middle Ages small openings were made in the outer walls of the aisles, but they do not seriously disturb the original effect.) The clerestory windows are fitted with modern copies of the original grating, and the light quality is probably fairly correct. Recently, however, the roof construction has been covered by a flat ceiling, which contradicts the general lightness and hidden verticality of the interior.

Only fragments of the original decoration are preserved, but it is still possible to see that the wall was completely dematerialized. The aisles probably had simple plaster walls, while the nave carried a marble revetment and mosaic panels. The spandrels still show the original revetment, which consists of an abstract linear pattern of chalices and patens. Mouldings are entirely absent; the decoration defines a smooth surface which seems to extend infinitely. Fluted columns below seem to continue the linear pattern of the marble revetment. During the Constan-tinian age, columns were very smooth and kept a certain plasticity.[17] Here the plastic roundness dissolves in a bundle of vertical lines which foreshadows the shafts of Gothic architecture. Appropriately Corinthian capitals are used rather than the more tectonic Ionian.

Architectural form, illumination and decoration form a convincing artistic totality in the interior of S. Sabina. The space is conceived as a luminous hall, an idea which appeared for the first time in the imperial Aula of Constantine in Trier (c. 310) where smooth walls are perforated by numerous and large arched windows. Even the apse has openings, like in S. Sabina. Here the Emperor appeared as the sun, and represented the majesty of the Imperium Romanum. In S. Sabina it is Christ who is the light of the world; and the light which floods the interior through the large clerestory windows is of decisive importance for the character of the space. The semidark aisles below give the luminous upper part of the church a heavenly appearance. We see, thus, how the basilica section which originally was a practical device, invented to give light to the central part of an interior, had become a symbolic form which expresses the transcendence and grace of God. From the exterior only the row of large clerestory windows indicates the role of the building as a receptacle of divine light.

The basic intention of Early Christian architecture is the concretization of spiritualized space. This is achieved through dematerialization, that is, by means of a particular treatment of the surface and a particular illumination. The idea may become manifest in central as well as longitudinal buildings, but in Early Christian architecture the directed basilica was of primary importance, as it combines spiritualized space with the great theme of the path of life as a road to salvation. Both themes found a most convincing interpretation in the infinitely sensitive and delicate interior of S. Sabina.

Hagia Sophia

During the Nike Riot in 532 the old Constantinian basilica of the Holy Wisdom in

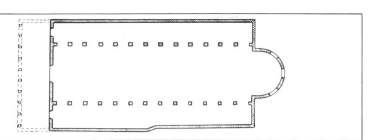

130. S. Sabina, Rome. 422-32. Ground plan.

131. S. Sabina, Rome.

132. S. Sabina, Rome. Interior.

Constantinople burned down. Justinian immediately decided to build a new and much more splendid church. He must have had in mind for some time a new kind of sacred architecture, as he had erected H. Sergios and Bakchos about 525, and even exported the solution to Ravenna, where the related S. Vitale was begun shortly afterwards. In 536, before the new Hagia Sophia was dedicated (on December 27, 537), Justinian also had the construction of a new church of the Holy Apostles begun to replace Constantine's Apostoleion. It is probable that the mathematician Anthemius of Tralles was the architect of all the three buildings in Constantinople, assisted by another theorist, Isidorus of Miletus. The first dome of the Hagia Sophia collapsed in 558, and was replaced by a steeper one, which was completed in 562. The finished building has been considered one of the greatest masterpieces in the history of architecture right from its completion. It even convinced the Islamic conquerors, whose great domed mosques, built after the fall of Constantine in 1453, are unthinkable without the Christian model.

The Hagia Sophia is a genial combination of central and longitudinal structures.[18] Its main element is a central baldachin. A longitudinal direction is introduced by the addition of half-domes to the east and the west, while the lateral "arms" are closed off by screen walls. Smaller, diagonally placed conches are added to the half-dome spaces, and the longitudinal movement is completed by an apse. The plan displays a logical use of the possibilities inherent in the baldachin system, but the particular solution is most original, and represents a convincing synthesis which has hardly been equalled since. The main nave with its great baldachin, half-domes and conches is placed within a larger rectangle, measuring about 71 by 77 metres (233 by 253 feet). A double-shell structure is thereby obtained, where the main rooms seem surrounded by an illuminated spatial stratum. The aisles and galleries thereby formed were used by the people during service, while the nave and the chancel were reserved to the clergy and the emperor. The secondary spaces were also formed by numerous small baldachins. The main dome,

(18) For a complete analysis see H. Kähler, Hagia Sophia (New York and London, 1967).

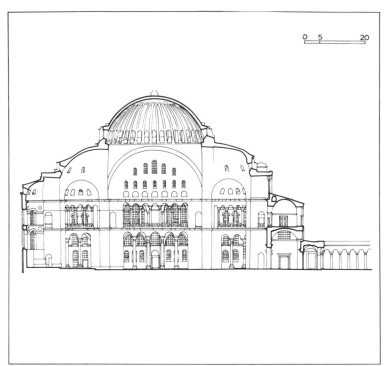

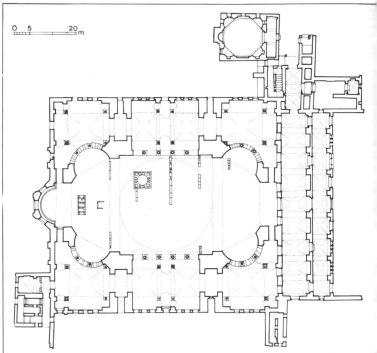

133. *Anthemius of Tralles, Isidorus of Miletus: Hagia Sophia, Constantinople (Istanbul). 532-37. Section.*

134. *Anthemius of Tralles, Isidorus of Miletus: Hagia Sophia, Constantinople (Istanbul). Ground plan.*

135. *Anthemius of Tralles, Isidorus of Miletus: Hagia Sophia, Constantinople (Istanbul). View from the south.*

136. *Anthemius of Tralles, Isidorus of Miletus: Hagia Sophia, Constantinople (Istanbul). Vaulting.*

137. *Anthemius of Tralles, Isidorus of Miletus: Hagia Sophia, Constantinople (Istanbul). View of the interior toward the southeast.*

which has a diameter of over 30 meters (98 feet), is perforated by a row of windows at its foot. It rests on pendentives which are carried by huge piers. Inserted between the piers is a screen wall of superimposed columns and clerestory windows, which echoes the nave of the Early Christian basilicas. The piers and the walls are not, however, characterized as structurally different elements; like the whole interior, they are covered with a continuous skin of marble revetment and mosaics. Together with the double-shell space and the general "transparency," this decoration creates a spiritualized interior of unsurpassed beauty. The complex, but unified space was "permeated by the light of the Divinity which emanated from the centre of heaven and spread to the angels, patriarch, clergy and emperor. Thus the spatial shapes, the light and the colours all emanate from the central dome."[19] The somewhat inarticulate exterior is of secondary importance to the interior, but anyhow the majestic domed volume dominated the city and gave it its characteristic silhouette.

The meaningful synthesis achieved in the Hagia Sophia was clearly recognized at the time. Thus it is reported that Justinian said on the day of consecration: "Solomon, I have vanquished thee!" And the court poet, Paul the Silentiary, added: "When the first gleam of light rosy-armed driving away the dark shadows, leapt from arch to arch, then all the princes and people with one voice hymned their songs of prayer and praise; it seemed to them as if the mighty arches were set in heaven. And above all rises into the immeasurable air the great helmet, which, bending over like the radiant heavens, embraces the church. . . . The golden stream of glittery rays pours down and strikes the eyes

(19) Krautheimer, *op. cit.*, p. 160

138. S. Marco, Venice. 830; rebuilt 1063-94.
Ground plan.

139. S. Marco, Venice. Aerial view.

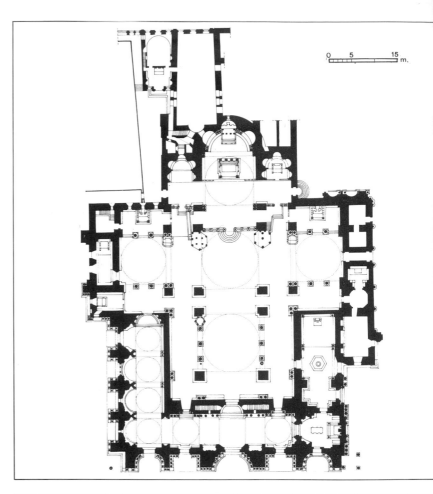

138. S. Marco, Venice. 830; rebuilt 1063-94.
Ground plan.

139. S. Marco, Venice. Aerial view.

(20) Another building
on a similar plan is St.
Front in Perigueux (after
1120).

(21) Krautheimer, *op.
cit.*, pp. 46 ff.

of men, so they can scarcely bear to look.
. . . Thus through the spaces of the great
church come rays of light, expelling clouds
of care, filling the mind with promise, showing the way to the living God. . . . Whoever
sets foot within this sacred place, would
live there forever, and his eyes well with
tears of joy.''

S. Marco

The first church of St. Mark's in Venice was
built in 830 to house the relics of the Evangelist. It was laid out as a copy of Justinian's
church of the Holy Apostles in Constantinople, with a cross-shaped plan and five
domes: one over each arm and one over
the crossing. In 1063 a new church was
erected on the foundations of the original
structure. As the Apostoleion in Constantinople was torn down after the conquest in
1453 to make room for the mosque of
Mehmed the Conqueror (el Fatih), St. Mark's
today remains the most important record of
the fundamental ideas embodied in the Justinian church.[20] The basic concept, however,
predates that era. Constantine had built a
church of the Holy Apostles in Constantinople on a cross-shaped plan, about which
a contemporary description tells us that the
crossing was surmounted by a drum under
which the emperor's sarcophagus was
placed. The building, thus, was intended as
a mausoleum, with arms added to shelter
the faithful.[21] A similar church was erected
over the tomb of St. John the Evangelist in
Ephesos after 400. This was also replaced
with a larger structure by Justinian (548–56)
where again we find the layout of the second
Apostoleion in Constantinople. From the
fourth to the ninth century, then, a continuous tradition of cross-shaped churches dedicated to the Holy Apostles can be traced. We
may in this connection also recall the introduction of a transept in the great basilicas of
St. Peter's and St. Paul's in Rome. The symbolism is clear. The Apostles were the first
to take up the Cross of Christ, and the simple
longitudinal path of the congregational
basilica did not suffice to symbolize their
role. Moreover, the centralized form of the
martyrium was integrated in the symbolic
plan.

In the imperial architecture of Justinian,

centralization becomes a dominant theme. As God is the centre of the cosmic order, so the King—the *basileus*—is the centre of the terrestrial order. The latter is nothing but a manifestation of the former, and the *basileus* is the symbol of the Deity, a living image of the incarnation. In Hagia Sophia, the church of Divine Wisdom, this image is concretized as a great centralized space, which contains the longitudinal path as a secondary element. In the church of the Holy Apostles the path and the cross become the primary motifs as symbols of the following of Christ, but Byzantine centralization is also present in the Greek-cross plan. As we have pointed out before, both buildings were based on the same baldachin element; in the Hagià Sophia as a complex study in integration, in the Apostoleion as simple addition, but this does not mean that the Apostoleion was more commonplace.[22] The additive movement of the great baldachins along the cardinal axes is a meaningful and most convincing expression of the diffusion of the Christian creed to the whole world.

The church of St. Mark's repeats the layout of the Apostoleion. Five hemispherical domes are carried on broad piers, forming a succession of clearly defined baldachins. The main spaces are accompanied by aisles which penetrate the piers, creating a complete double-shell structure. In contrast with the Justinian churches the aisles rose to the full height of the arches which carry the dome. A certain wish for spatial unification is thereby made manifest, which is emphasized by the reduction of the screen walls between nave and aisles to mere galleries.[23] The interior surfaces are covered with marble revetment and mosaics, and are treated as a continuous skin. The upper zones are well lit, whereas the lower remain dim. This was the last great manifestation of the Early Christian interpretation of spiritualized space. The exterior of the church shows a complex combination of forms and styles. Whereas the group of domes belong to Byzantine architecture, the richly ornate façade and the deep portal niches are late medieval additions. In general, the church is permeated by oriental mysticism, and it did not have any influence on the further development of ecclesiastical architecture in the West.

(22) As suggested by Krautheimer, *op. cit.*, p. 171.

(23) The solution foreshadows the "wall-pillar" halls of late Gothic churches in Central Europe.

141. *Jacob of Kokkinobaphos: 12th-century
miniature representing the church of the Holy
Apostles in Constantinople. Bibliothèque
Nationale, Paris.*

(24) When Michelan-
gelo wanted to express
the tragic situation of
man, he introduced the
heavy mass as a symbol
of earthly imprisonment,
and he shut out the
divine light from above
(project for St. Peter's).
Thus the basic mean-
ings of mass and light
were still alive.

Space Conception and Development

Our examples have shown that Early Christian architecture is characterized by certain
fundamental properties regardless of functional differences and local circumstances.
In any Early Christian church we find the
same wish for dematerialization and interiority, that is, for "spiritualized space." The
believer who entered the building was really
meant to experience entering heaven, "and
his eyes well with tears of joy." Spiritualization is achieved by contradicting the inheri-
tance from Greek and Roman architecture,
which is transformed rather than negated.
Anthropomorphic elements, such as columns, are still present, but they have lost
their bodily weight and plastic force. This
is mainly due to two factors: the treatment
of the surface, and the use of light. The surface is conceived as a shimmering skin, and
the basilican section adds to the effect by
making the spatial boundary dissolve. In the
basilica the boundary of the lower zone is
hidden in darkness, while the upper wall
seems to emit divine light. The double-shell
structures of Justinian architecture represent
a most convincing solution to these intentions, which remained basic to Christian
architecture throughout the Middle Ages.24

We have also seen that the idea of spiritualized space does not demand one particular type of building. Central, longitudinal and
synthetic plans have all been encountered,
and the spatial organization of the Christian
church has been shown to consist in a transformation of inherited forms. The ancient
symbols of centre and path are present in
any church, but their relationship differs.
Although the spiritual centre is the altar, it
is rarely placed centrally in an architectural
sense, and even in the centralized Byzantine
church, it is found at the end of a longitudinal path. The architectural centre, instead, is the vertical axis defined by the
heavenly dome. In Byzantine architecture
this axis is of primary importance, while
the longitudinal path is less emphasized.
The opposite is the case in the Early Christian basilica, where a vertical axis is hardly
indicated. In the Constantinian buildings we
only find a general vertical openness, whereas the introduction of a transept implied

crossing which formed the point of departure for integrating a true centre in the longitudinal plan. However, centralized structures in Early Christian architecture are found in connection with baptistries, mausolea and funeral chapels. All these attempts at meaningful spatial organization happen inside the building. Early Christian architecture literally starts from within in contrast to Roman architecture where an absolute order was applied on all environmental levels.

The development of Early Christian architecture does not consist of great experiments and changes. The basic intentions are present from the outset and are partly related to the wish for transcendence in late Roman architecture. We have seen, however, that spiritualization was enhanced by the introduction of the arcade, and by changes in proportion and longitudinal rhythm. Whereas Early Christian dematerialization is achieved by optical means, the Justinian baldachin system made a true dissolution of the wall possible; hence its constitutive importance for medieval architecture. But although later development in the West adopted the baldachin, it could not accept Justinian's particular interpretation of the themes of centre and path. In the West the longitudinal basilica became the great symbolic form, until the heavenly dome was reintroduced in the fifteenth century.

From the beginning Christian architecture was international. The house of God does not belong to any particular place. God is where his plan of salvation is made visible. The same spatial themes are therefore found everywhere, the themes which concretize the Christian image of the world. The only diversity of basic importance was the different interpretation of the image in the East and the West, which, in fact, led to the schism of 1054.

Meaning and Architecture

The Christian image of the world cannot be understood as an abstraction from natural, human or historical phenomena. Christian man realized that existential security cannot be achieved by mastering nature, understanding oneself or by purposeful action. This does not mean that he negated those

(25) R. Schwarz, *Vom Bau der Kirche* (Heidelberg, 1947), p. 24.

(26) The theme was taken up by Charlemagne in his palace chapel in Aachen, dedicated in 805.

(27) The concept of time as limited by a beginning and an end was brought to our understanding by St. Augustine, but as an existential image it is of Jewish origin.

existential dimensions, but that he considered them subordinate to a new spiritual dimension. Only by developing his own *inner* self can man find true existential meaning, and that development meant to follow Christ. The centre of the Christian world, therefore, is something more than a concrete natural or man-made place. It is the abstract point where the meaning of life is revealed. The idea of participation introduced in Christian liturgy also gives the centre a new power of bringing men together. "In this point men are unified . . . [they know] that the real road inwards, to the hearts of others, goes through the centre. The meeting now becomes a meeting in the common centre of meaning."[25] But the following of Christ does not imply that the centre is reached at once. The way is long, and in architectural terms it was concretized as a longitudinal axis, as a path of salvation leading to the altar, the symbol of the communion with Christ. The eternal wandering of the Egyptians, thus, is contradicted; the path of life has been given a meaning. When man returns from the communion with Christ to the world, he is ready to contribute to its transformation into a true *Civitas Dei.*

As the place where God reveals himself, the church had to contain a centre and a path. From Early Christian times other symbolic forms were combined with these basic elements. As a manifestation of the *Civitas Dei,* the church represented the "Heavenly Jerusalem," and naturally assimilated the forms of the Roman town, such as the colonnaded street. The apse is also taken from Roman architecture, where it contained the seat of the *pater familias* or the throne of the emperor. In the Early Christian church the apse was used for the bishop's throne. The apse, thus, represents a centre almost as important as the altar and the two elements were coordinated spatially to form a sanctuary or chancel. The cross is also integrated in the plan of most churches. As it is the major Christian symbol, that is not surprising. We may, however, also ask why the Romans used crucifixion for the execution of traitors. Obviously the cross represented the cosmic order they had acted against, the *cardo* and *decumanus* of the Roman world. The reappearance of the cross in the spatial layout of the church therefore sym-

bolizes Christ's conquest of this order. The dome, finally, is also a cosmic symbol, a representation of heaven. We have already pointed out that its vertical *axis mundi* does not usually correspond to the spiritual centre of the church, the altar. Evidently, Christian truth is distinguished from the general cosmic order concretized by the dome. Its use in baptistries and mausolea is natural, as its static form is eternally resting in itself and its vertical axis unifies the depths of the earth with the zenith of heaven. The use of the dome in imperial chapels may be understood in connection with the cult of the Emperor as *Cosmocrator.*[26]

The different choice and combination of symbolic forms in Western and Byzantine architecture stems from different interpretations of the dimension of time in relation to the idea of salvation. In the West *beginning* and *end* are of basic importance, as expressed by the very first and very last words of the Bible.[27] Between these two stations is the time given to man to decide for or against God. Western man therefore is always on his way, and his spatial form is the path. In the East however, salvation is understood as a total, cosmic event. The world is conceived as a harmonious, static whole which rests in itself "from eternity to eternity." As a consequence the centre, the circle, and the dome became the primary spatial forms. The East here took over ancient oriental concepts of cosmic order and eternal return and slowly stagnated culturally and socially. The Early Christian West in contrast initiated the great historical development which has given us our civilization, and which is closely connected with the Judaeo-Christian concept of time as directed movement.

5. Romanesque Architecture

143. *Abbey of Cluny, France, in 1043 (after Conant).*

144. *Medieval pilgrimage routes to Santiago de Compostela.*

Introduction

Innumerable Romanesque churches, monasteries and castles still give a characteristic note to the European landscape. From southern Italy to Scandinavia, from Spain to Poland, we find these records of an age which possessed a strong cultural unity for all its political division and unrest.

The most conspicuous property of Carolingian and Romanesque buildings is their combination of massive enclosure and manifest verticality. The tower became a formal element of primary importance for the first time in architectural history. And the tower came to stay: It was taken over by later periods for its importance as a concretization of fundamental existential meanings.

In Roman architecture, round, square and octagonal towers were used to reinforce the city walls, and city gates were usually flanked by towers which together with the gate proper formed a characteristic tripartite unit. As the entrance to a qualitatively different domain, these gateways acquired symbolic significance. Thus "the gateway became a kind of architectural ideogram denoting a *Sacrum palatium* as the seat of government and the place from which emanated the divine wisdom of the State."[1] The towered façades of medieval churches should be related to this symbolism, which combines the existential significance of protection and transcendental aspiration. The *sacrum palatium*, however, was also denoted by another architectural form: the *pentyrigion,* a five-towered structure with a major central element, and smaller towers at the four corners. Evidently the symbolism of centre and cardinal points is present here, in direct descent from the Roman *castra.* The basic properties of pre-Romanesque and Romanesque churches appeared when the towered façade and the *pentyrigion* (complete or in reduced form) were combined with the longitudinal basilica.[2]

To achieve this combination architects had to solve difficult problems of formal coordination. In early examples the towers are superficially attached to a conventional columnar basilica, whereas in the mature Romanesque church the different elements are fully integrated. This was achieved by a

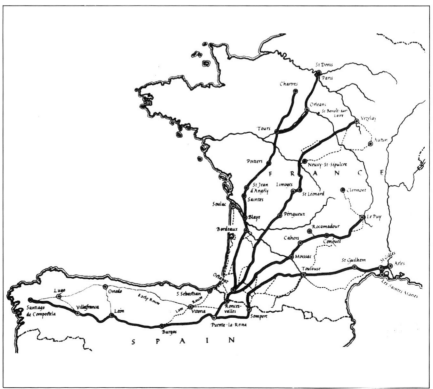

(1) E. Baldwin Smith, *Architectural Symbolism of Imperial Rome and the Middle Ages* (Princeton, N.J., 1956). pp. 10 ff.

(2) In Byzantine architecture the *pentyrigion* developed into the static, self-sufficient quincunx.

145. Monastery of St. Gall. Switzerland. 820. Plan.

(1) church: (a) scriptorium on ground floor, library on upper level; (b) sacristy on ground floor, wardrobe for liturgical vestments on upper level; (c) lodging for brothers of the order in transit; (d) residence of the rector of the day school; (e) residence of the guardian; (f) entrance for guests and for the day school; (g) reception hall for all visitors to the monastery; (h) entrance to the pilgrim house, shelter and administrative building; (i) residence of the administrator of the pilgrim house and shelter; (j) monks' parlor; (k) tower of St. Michael; (l) tower of St. Gabriel (2) sacristy (3) monks' dormi-tory on upper level, auxiliary boiler on ground floor (4) monks' latrine (5) monks' baths (6) monks' refectory on ground floor, wardrobe on upper level (7) monks' cellar for wine and beer on ground floor, pantry on upper level (8) monks' kitchen (9) monks' bakery and brewery (10) kitchen, bakery and brewery for guests (11) house for guests (12) day school (13) abbot's house (14) abbot's kitchen, pantry and bath (15) house for blood-letting (16) doctors' quarters (17) novitiate and hospital (18) kitchen and bath of the hospital (19) kitchen and bath of the novi-tiate (20) gardener's house (21) poultry yard (22) coop for chickens and geese (23) enclosure for geese (24) barn (25) workrooms for craftsmen (26) annex to the craftsmen's workrooms (27) mills (28) mortars (29) lime kiln (30) coopery, joinery and ale granary (31) pilgrim house and hospital (32) kitchen, bakery and brewery for pil-grims (33) stable for horses and cattle, lodging for stableman (34) lodging for retinue of the emperor (identification not certain) (35) sheep pen and lodging for shepherd (36) pen for goats and lodging for goatherd (37) stable for cows and lodging for cowherd (38) lodging for workers on the estates and for workers attached to the emperor's retinue (39) pigsty and lodging for keeper (40) stable for mares in foal and unbroken colts, and lodging for stable-man (W) cloister (X) monk's garden (Y) cemetery and orchard (Z) garden of medicinal herbs.

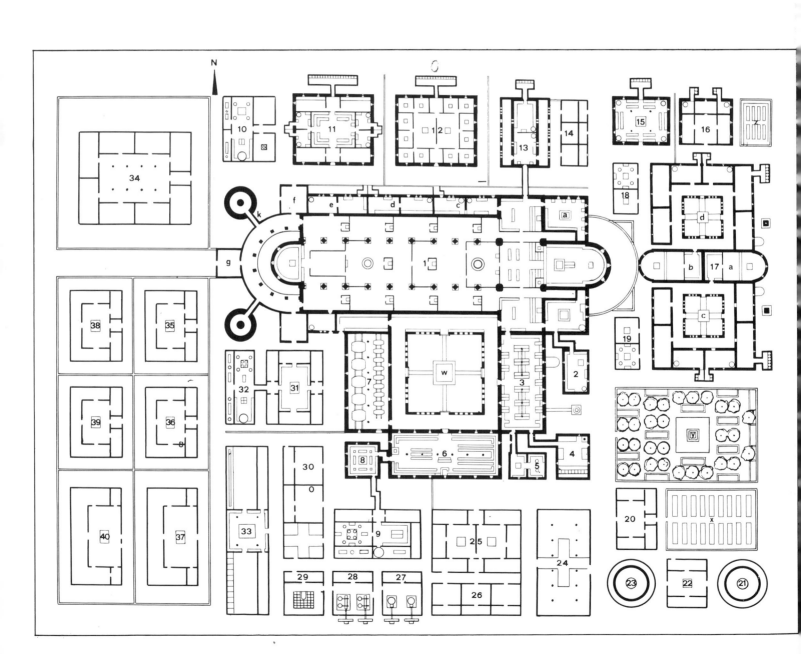

process of subdivision of the main volumes, whereby all of them seem composed of the same constitutent elements. A basic property of Romanesque architecture is a resulting rhythmic articulation of space which relates the original interiority of the Early Christian church more closely to the dimensions and movements of man.[3] The introduction of towers, of excessively long and narrow naves, and of rhythmic articulation can be interpreted as expressions of the same desire for a more active human participation. In general, the Romanesque church is characterized by a certain redundancy which gives emphasis to the meanings concretized by the single elements.

The spatially active forms of Romanesque buildings are apparently at odds with the pronounced wish for massiveness and enclosure. These latter properties can, however, be seen as an expression of the need for assurance and protection, that is, for a basis which makes divinely inspired human action possible. So the Romanesque church is simultaneously stronghold and gate to heaven, and the two main building types of the period, the church and the castle, are profoundly related. Both stem from the Roman *palatium,* and their conjunction deserves Martial's praise of Domitian's palace, which he compares to a temple and describes as "so high in the air that it approaches the stars."[4]

Landscape and Settlement

After the fall of the Roman Empire, and especially after the expansion of Islam during the seventh century, urban civilization degenerated. Down to the eleventh century the monasteries served as cultural and economical centres and, like the feudal castles, they gave rise to the formation of new settlements. For instance, a large village grew up around the monastery of St. Riquier (790), inhabited mostly by craftsmen and their families. Geographically the monasteries were relatively isolated from each other, but as they were based on the same basic values and the same way of life, they formed a well-distributed set of related places. Individual character was relatively less important than

fundamental similarity, and as a result there was a unity to European culture, in spite of political division and poor systems of communication. With the growing importance of the veneration of relics and the appearance of local saints, certain places gained particular importance and were visited by large numbers of pilgrims. Wherever he went, the pilgrim had the experience of simultaneously reaching a goal with a particular meaning and finding himself "at home."

The major goal of pilgrimage was Santiago de Compostela, shrine of the relics of St. James, the patron saint of Spain. During the eleventh century the roads to Santiago from France became grand routes of communication used by myriads of people. The pilgrimage roads connected several important ecclesiastical centres, and their cultural importance can hardly be overestimated. In general they were the expression of an epoch of faith, an epoch when the Church was on its way to giving Europe a common cultural basis. In terms of existential space the system of sacred places made the manifestations and the history of Christianity visible, and granted new psychological security in a difficult and frightening world.

Monasteries were concentrated settlements which unified sacred and temporal functions. A good illustration is offered by the ideal plan from *c.* 820 which is conserved in the monastic library of St. Gall. Early monasteries have a simple interiority which is here replaced by a differentiated organism with the monks' *claustrum* at its centre. Around a cloister are church, dormitory, refectory and storehouse. The church is a longitudinal basilica, whose main axis represents an ideal contact with the world. The axis is emphasized by two cylindrical towers flanking the entrance to the church and perhaps by a square tower over the crossing. As a place of more exploit interiority, the centralized space of the cloister is introduced, which significantly forms the innermost core of the monastic complex. A place for meditation, it concretizes that cultivation of the spirit on which the medieval world was based. From this core emanates an order, which is reflected in the buildings and in the cultivated fields surrounding the monastery. When visitors entered the *claustrum,* their feet were washed while the

monks chanted: *"Mandatum novum do vobis: ut diligatis invicem."*[5] Medieval monasteries had an ordered programme of Benedictine invention, which expresses how the Christian values had become the basis of a meaningful, common life in this world.

During the Middle Ages this "sacred landscape" concretized the operation of Christianity in space and time. The new image did not stem from an abstraction of natural properties and characters, as had been the case in Egypt, Greece and Rome, but expressed the diffusion of meanings of new spiritual kind. However, it should not be forgotten that the new system of meanings absorbed many of the ancient symbols.

Building

It has been suggested above that the basic properties of Romanesque architecture stem from a combination of the Early Christian basilica with the protective and aspiring motif of the tower. This process was begun as early as the first church of St. Martin at Tours (470). "The composition of St. Martin was not horizontal, self-contained, and inward-looking, as classical compositions are; rather it was made up of aspiring and intersecting forms. In St. Martin, with its two axial towers, the new dynamic mode is unmistakable."[6] Still earlier, the *pentyrigion* had been combined with the basilica in the cathedral of Trier, probably to symbolize the role of Trier as an imperial residence. Also the contemporary palatine church of S. Lorenzo in Milan (*c.* 370) had a centralized, double-shell space flanked by four towers. In the imperial buildings of the Carolingian epoch the basic themes are further developed. The church of the important monastery of St. Riquier (after 790) was a columnar basilica with the transept and an elaborate "westwork" preceding the nave. The crossing and the westwork were crowned by tall towers surmounted by pointed spires. These towers were flanked by smaller, circular stair turrets, and furthermore the three entrances to the *atrium* were crowned by square towers. Thus the longitudinal organism was interpenetrated by nine vertical elements! The structure is repeated and varied in the great

(3) The problem of rhythmic articulation in Romanesque architecture was introduced by Wilhelm Pinder in his pioneer work *Rhythmik romanischer Innenräume in der Normandie* (Strasbourg, 1904-5), but the theme has so far not been developed much further.

(4) Baldwin Smith, *op. cit.*, p. 53.

(5) W. Braunfels, *Abendländische Klosterbaukunst* (Cologne, 1969), p. 58.

(6) K. J. Conant, *Carolin-gian and Romanesque Architecture* (Harmondsworth and Baltimore: Penguin, 1959), p. 10.

(7) It may, however, also be interpreted as an incorporation of the emperor in the Church.

(8) Conant, *op. cit.*, p. 117.

(9) Baldwin Smith, *op. cit.*, pp. 181 ff.

German churches of the following centuries: St. Michael at Hildesheim (1001) and the cathedrals of Mainz, Speyer and Worms. A particularly impressive *pentyrigion* group of towers is preserved in Tournai (1110 and later).

A differentiation and integration of the plan went together with the introduction of towers. A characteristic addition to the traditional basilica is the "westwork" mentioned above, consisting of an elevated, tall space preceding the church proper. Serving as a *capella imperialis* from which the emperor could participate in the service, the westwork may be understood as a manifestation of the ruler's claim to authority over the church.[7] (It was also known as a *solarium*, and in some buildings the emperor sat in front of a circular "sun window.") Similar in function, a western apse was introduced into some churches at the same time, and the resulting double-enders concretize *regnum* and *sacerdotium,* between which the path of redemption is spanned. Their biaxial plan is relatively static and self-sufficient, and related to the centralized composition traditionally used in imperial buildings. The westwork and the western apse later disappeared, but the flanking towers came to stay, as did the choir gallery which originally surrounded the main westwork space on three sides.

Another characteristic type of plan is found in the great shrines on the pilgrimage roads, St. Martin at Tours again showing the way. In 918 a new church was dedicated on the site with the revolutionary feature of an ambulatory around the apsidal sanctuary. Radiating apsidioles were attached to its outer wall. Forming a continuation of the aisles, the ambulatory represented a decisive step towards spatial integration of the building. This general intention is enhanced by the addition of aisles to the transepts as well, whereby the whole plan seems made up of similar spatial units.

The development of the Romanesque plan culminated with the third church of the great monastery of Cluny in southern Burgundy (1088). In Cluny the basic motifs of path and goal are strongly emphasized: The eastern part was augmented by a second transept, and was surmounted by four towers. "These aspiring forms were clustered in the part of

the building which was devoted to prayer. The nave, with the narthex beyond, used for processions, gave a tremendous contrasting horizontal to the composition."[8] The whole layout was based on a strict modular system.

In general the mature Romanesque churches manifest a growing wish for true formal integration, and in particular for an integration of centralization and longitudinality, as becomes apparent when they are compared with the simple addition still used in St. Bénigne at Dijon (1001). The development reflects a gradual change in the concept of the Divinity. God comes closer, and hence the symbolic division of nave and sanctuary is weakened.

Articulation

With the incorporation of towers and the differentiation of the plan, the uniform Early Christian basilica developed into an articulate, modular organism. The process becomes manifest as a progressive subdivision and plastic articulation of the interior and exterior walls, and may be followed step by step. During the Carolingian epoch the continuity of the interior colonnades is already interrupted by the introduction of piers, a device usually denoted by the German term "*Stützenwechsel*" (St. Salvator, Werden 809). The rhythmic articulation thereby achieved marks a first step towards the medieval bay system. About the same time we find the first attempts at exterior articulation by means of pilaster strips and arched corbel tables (S. Vincenzo in Prato, Milan 833). The latter motif was probably derived from the crowning arcade of the Roman *palatium,* which served as a celestial symbol.[9] In the Early Christian basilica the arcade belonged to the interior. By applying it to the exterior, the missionary function of the medieval church becomes evident, and the order it represents generally visible. It is therefore natural that the growing importance of the church is accompanied by a weakening of its original massive and enclosed character. This process was to culminate in the skeletal structures of Gothic architecture.

The development was slow and gradual. Massive, continuous exterior walls are still evident in the original design for Mainz ca-

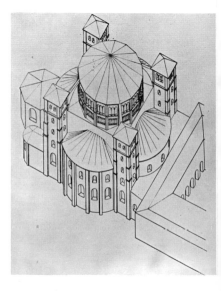

149. *St. Michael, Hildesheim. 1001. Reconstruction.*

150. *Second church of St. Martin, Tours. 918. Drawing of the apse under excavation.*

151. *St. Bénigne, Dijon. 1001. Reconstruction (after Conant).*

thedral (978), and the interior of St. Michael in Hildesheim (1001) is still based on the simple *Stützenwechsel*. In the second church at Cluny, however, an important step was taken by subdividing the upper walls of the nave by pilaster strips, probably in connection with the introduction of tunnel-vaulting (about 1000). The pilaster strips rested on corbels, and carried transverse arches. The next step consisted in bringing the pilaster strips down to the floor. To make this possible, the traditional columns were replaced by square piers, and the pilaster strips transformed into round shafts. This solution is found at Speyer (1031), and was adopted in the great pilgrimage churches of the eleventh century. With the introduction of groin-vaulting, a double-bay system was developed, where every other pier is strengthened to carry the weight of the vault, while the intermediary ones become part of a secondary in-filling wall (Speyer after 1080). The result bears some resemblance to the baldachin system of Byzantine architecture, and marked the decisive step towards a true dematerialization of the wall.

The bay system transformed the structure into a skeleton, and was naturally accompanied by a progressive articulation of the intermediary wall surface. In churches with basilican section a third storey was introduced between the main arcade and the clerestory, called the triforium (Jumièges 1037). This new feature relates to the corbel table and arcade motifs of the exterior, and also serves to emphasize the horizontal rhythm of the building. Sometimes it is developed into a full gallery (Caen, St. Etienne 1067).[10] In the great pilgrimage churches a two-story partition was employed, with a spacious gallery over the main arcade and no clerestory—a design which stresses the continuous encircling movement of aisles and ambulatory.

In general, the articulation of the wall brought about a differentiation of the architectural members. Thus the lateral and transverse arches of the interior are carried on independent shafts, and as a consequence the square pier tended to become a composite bundle of vertical elements. The basic intention of transforming the building into a skeleton is thereby confirmed. Local structures in wood have been indicated as a pos-

(10) In a few cases there is a gallery as well as a trifotrium; Tournai 1110 and several early Gothic churches.

152. *S. Vincenzo in Prato, Milan. 833.*

153. *S. Maria in Cosmedin, Rome. c. 1100. Interior.*

154. *St. Michael, Hildesheim. 1001. Interior.*

155. *Parish church, Maursmünster. Mid-12th century. Westwork.*

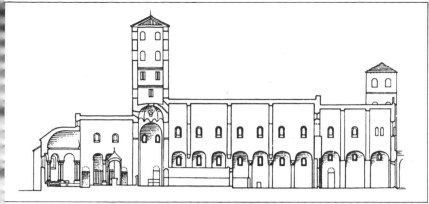

156. St. Etienne, Caen. Begun 1067. Wall of the nave.

157. Second church (Cluny II), Abbey of Cluny, France. 955-81. Longitudinal section, in part of hypothetical.

158. Cathedral, Modena. Begun 1099. Apse.

sible source of inspiration,[11] but the meaning of medieval articulation transcends the technical aspect. Insofar as it represents a further development of the wall articulation and rhythmic articulation of Roman architecture, the term "Romanesque" is quite appropriate. A basic difference of character, however, results from the elimination of the anthropomorphic, classical members. In Romanesque architecture Roman action has become an act of faith.

(11) W. Horn, "On the origins of the Medieval Bay Stream," *Journal of the Society of Architectural Historians*, vol. XVII, no. 2, 1958.

Speyer

The cathedral at Speyer has preserved much of its original character, and is a good example of the architecture of the German *Kaiserdome*. Started in 1029 by Conrad II, the Salian, it was consecrated in 1061. Between 1080 and 1106 the nave was vaulted. In 1689 the church was severely damaged by French troops, and in 1772–78 was partially reconstructed. Again damaged during the Napoleonic wars, the church was reconsecrated in 1822, and between 1854 and 1861 the shape of the original westwork was restored by the architect Heinrich Hübsch.

Its architects were in no doubt about the importance of this building, as is shown by its extraordinary dimensions; with a length of 132 metres (433 feet) it surpassed old St. Peter's in Rome. The plan is based on the biaxial scheme developed during the Carolingian epoch, but shows considerable modification on the layout of St. Riquier and St. Michael in Hildesheim. An exceptionally massive westwork is surmounted by a great octagonal tower flanked by two tall, square towers containing the stairways. The eastern part shows a similar disposition, but is augmented by the introduction of a wide transept and a spacious apse. The longitudinal axis is also emphasized by the placing of the flanking towers *behind* the transverse axes of westwork and transept. Hardly anywhere else are the basic intentions of Romanesque architecture so clearly manifest. The grouped, vertical masses at the east and the west end contrast most emphatically with the long stretch of the nave. The regular volumes and the restrained articulation contribute to the overwhelming effect of stout

159, 160. Cathedral, Speyer. 1029-61; 1080-1106. Ground plan and view from the north-east.

161. Landscape with Speyer cathedral. Engraving.

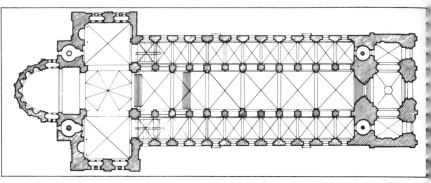

(12) The crowning arcades and the differentiation of the transept walls stem from the rebuilding after 1080.

(13) Speyer has the highest Romanesque vaults ever built: 32.61 metres (107 feet) in the nave and almost 50 metres (164 feet) over the crossing.

simplicity, emphasizing the dominance of the function of *sacerdotium*.

Unlike earlier churches exterior articulation is highly significant. Before the over-elaborate nineteenth-century reconstruction, the westwork appeared as the most massive part of the building. It rose higher than the nave and must have resembled a tower. A sophisticated use of continuous horizontals joined it to the rest of the building, making the lower cornice of its crowning arcade the upper cornice of the corresponding arcade of the nave, which also embraces the transept. Whereas the high wall of the nave is continuous with cutout windows, the transept is treated as a kind of skeleton with stout pillars and richly decorated windows between them. The apse, finally, is articulated by means of slender, round shafts and unusually tall windows.[12] From the entrance to the apse the structure becomes gradually lighter and more open. A similar progressive dematerialization characterizes the vertical development of the building.

Inside the church is distinguished by serene simplicity. Before the introduction of groin-vaults after 1080, the nave was separated from the aisles by a regular succession of square piers with engaged shafts, which rise up to support a blank arcade incorporating the clerestory windows. This monumental approach has been related to the wall articulation of the Constantinian *aula* in Trier. Later every other pier was strengthened to sustain the groin-vaulting. The immense double bays which result gave the nave a very solemn rhythm which well prepares for the lofty and luminous vault of the crossing.[13] The space finds a worthy conclusion in the apse, which is articulated by a blank arcade incorporating alternating windows and niches.

With Speyer the imperial architecture initiated by Charlemagne reached its conclusion. Whereas the octagonal palatine chapel in Aachen (792–805) may be characterized as a self-sufficient westwork expressing the divine majesty of the ruler, Speyer symbolically reduces the emperor to a protector of the existential meanings concretized by its long nave and luminous crossing. The simple, powerful massing of Speyer is truly German. The building does not possess

162. Cathedral, Speyer. View of the interior toward the apse.

163. Cathedral, Santiago de Compostela. After 1075, Isometric drawing.

much charm, but its articulation is logical and significant.

Santiago de Compostela

Unfortunately the great churches of the pilgrimage roads have suffered considerable damage during the course of the centuries. St. Martin at Tours and St. Martial at Limoges have been destroyed, whereas St. Sernin at Toulouse and Santiago de Compostela have been considerably altered, and only the relatively small church of Ste. Foi at Conques is still fairly intact. But at Santiago, built between 1075 and 1125, the interior is preserved and transports us back to the great age when it was conceived. Unfortunately the exterior was dressed up during the eighteenth century in the rather dubious Baroque known as Churrigueresque, and only the south porch, or Puerta de las Platerias, remains of the original exterior. The much more splendid main entrance, the Portico de la Gloria, is today hidden behind the Baroque façade.

The plan is based on a Latin cross, a disposition stemming from Early Christian and Byzantine apostle churches, and which is common to all the shrines on the pilgrimage roads. The large transept, 70 metres (230 feet) long, makes the exterior of the chancel very impressive. Its general effect of simultaneous expansion and concentration is enhanced by the addition of numerous apsidioles, a plan also found in St. Sernin in Toulouse. In general we may say that the pilgrimage plan symbolizes a horizontal extension which is not found in previous medieval churches. It is tempting to relate this property to the function of the church as a goal for pilgrims coming from "all corners of the world," and this interpretation is supported by the cathedral's monumental entrances in the transept as well as the nave. However symbolic verticality is present everywhere, in the wall arcades, in the apsidioles and in the numerous turrets. The main façade illustrated the transformation of the traditional westwork into a "transparent" screen between powerful, flanking towers, and gave an inviting effect enhanced by the deep Portico de la Gloria.

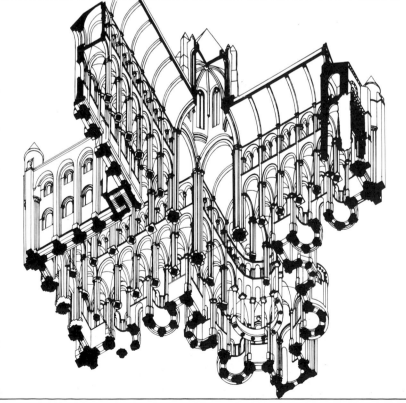

164. *Cathedral, Santiago de Compostela. Ground plan.*

165. *Cathedral, Santiago de Compostela. Reconstruction of the original plan (after Conant).*

166. *Cathedral, Santiago de Compostela. Reconstruction of the facade, 1168-1211.*

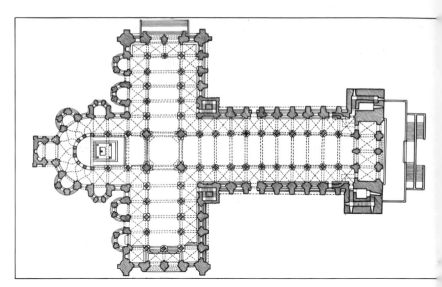

Its well-preserved interior is undoubtedly one of the most beautiful Romanesque spaces in existence. Gone are the heavy masses and continuous walls of early medieval churches, and in their place is a fully developed, logical skeletal system. Yet simple volumetric shapes and substantial proportions of the members conserve the fundamental sense of protection characteristic of Romanesque. In Santiago this protection has lost all frightening implications, and manifests itself as something warm and assuring.

The spatial character is simultaneously open and enclosed. It is determined by continuous aisles and galleries which encircle the interior, a system based on St. Martin at Tours. This extraordinary achievement offers a truly convincing answer to the problems posed by the architects of the Early Christian churches. The effect would have been weakened by conventional clerestory walls; at Santiago the tunnel-vault starts immediately above the galleries, and only in the apse is the height of the gallery reduced to allow for clerestory windows. The luminous centre of the space, however, is the crossing which is lit from an octagonal lantern on squinches.

The fully integrated, double-shell space of Santiago de Compostela represents one of the decisive moments in the development of Western architecture. It fulfills the promises of the past and points towards the transparent skeletons of Gothic churches as well as the geometrically simple structures of the Renaissance. At the same time it testifies to the fundamental importance of the pilgrimage in making the Christian values penetrate the Western world. In Santiago path and goal are unified in a synthesis which endows human existence with an immediate and profound meaning.

Cluny

During the eleventh century Cluny in southern Burgundy developed into the most important monastic centre of Western Christendom. Although the Benedictine rule called for independent houses, there was a process of centralization which led to the creation of a network of monasteries under

167. *Cathedral, Santiago de Compostela. Interior.*

168. *Landscape with the Abbey of Cluny, France, Drawing by Lallemand.*

Cluny's rule.[14] Three monastery churches in all were built: the second (Cluny II), finished after 955, soon proved too small, and the construction of a new church was started in 1088. When finished about 1220, it had a total length of 187 metres (614 feet). Unfortunately it was destroyed during the French Revolution, and only a fragment of the south transept remains today.[15]

Cluny II still had the fortresslike character of Early Romanesque churches, but the tunnel-vaulting, transverse arches and pilaster strips of its interior formed a point of departure for further development.[16] Cluny III, in fact, took over basic traits from the former building but it also incorporated the ambulatory, radiating chapels and modular design of the pilgrimage churches. As a monastic building, Cluny III did not have the spatial integration of, for example, Santiago de Compostela. The transepts had no aisles, and as a consequence the church did not possess an encircling double-shell structure. As has been mentioned above, Cluny III gives instead maximum emphasis to the two basic themes: the longitudinal path of the nave and the aspiring, vertically directed chevet. Path and goal, thus, are not unified in one synthetic form, but are treated as two distinct meanings. From the outside the many vertical elements of the chancel dominate, echoing contemporary representations of the Heavenly Jerusalem. Inside, however, the long path of the nave tells us that the true goal cannot be reached once and forever, but has to be conquered over and over again. Monastic life was the systematic attempt at such a perpetual conquest of a meaningful existence.

Cluny III is a most interesting combination of basilica with transept, cruciform plan and centralized sanctuary. The grand nave had double aisles on either side. A section shows a stepped basilica with light coming in at three levels, and an unusually high arcade. Pointed arches were introduced, and above them the wall was treated as a skeletal screen between engaged shafts which rose up to carry the transverse arches of the tunnel-vaulting. The clerestory consisted of a uniform series of windows, three in each bay, and the triforium was subdivided to correspond with the windows, creating a

(14) Conant, *op. cit.*, p. 108.

(15) See K. J. Conant, *Cluny: Les églises et la maison du chef d'ordre*, (Cambridge, Mass: Medieval Academy of America, 1968).

(16) See K. J. Conant, *Early Medieval Church Architecture* (Baltimore, 1942), plate XXXVIII. The character of Cluny II may be illustrated by the related church in Payerne (1040).

169. Abbey of Cluny. Ground plan in 1157.

170. Third church (Cluny III), Abbey of Cluny.
Begun 1088. Transverse section (after Conant).

unified zone which visually balanced the tall arcade below. The main shafts were divided in three superimposed elements, a rather unusual classical trait, which may be interpreted as an attempt at a kind of explanation of the different parts of the structure.

Light flooded into the great transept from numerous windows, and with its three domed vaults it must have been a breathtaking preparation to the complex and elaborate sanctuary. By the introduction of a second transept the chancel was augmented to form a centralized structure in its own right. This structure is prefigured in St. Bénigne at Dijon, where a rotunda was added to a cruciform basilica, and prepares for the deep chancels of the Gothic cathedrals. The west front of Cluny (1109–15) had a great, deeply embrasured portal at the centre, the first grand specimen of a kind which was to become a standard element in the Gothic cathedrals. During the twelfth century a large narthex (or "Galilee") was added to the nave, serving as a waiting place before the processions entered the church, and preceded by two stout fortresslike towers.

With the destruction of Cluny III Romanesque architecture lost its major monument. To get an idea of what it looked like, we must today visit the smaller churches influenced by Cluny, such as Autun cathedral (1120–32), the small Paray-le-Monial (c. 1100), and Ste. Madeleine in Vézelay (after 1096).

Pisa

Italy has scarcely figured in the discussion of the development of Romanesque architecture and has appeared only in relation to a ninth-century Lombard building and its exterior articulation by means of pilaster strips and blind arcades. The Italian contribution was only essential in the absorption of traditional forms from Roman times. In fact, the Romanesque architecture of Italy remains outside the main lines of development and has its own particular character. This is due to several factors: first, the church did not have to show the same missionary zeal in Italy as in the transalpine countries; secondly, the classical tradition was of a more

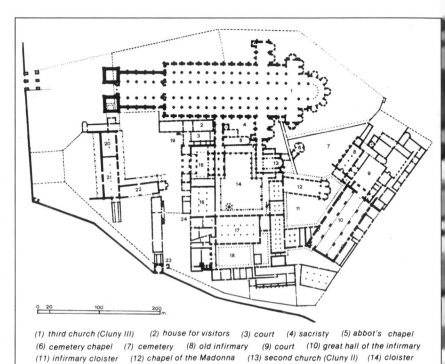

(1) third church (Cluny III)   (2) house for visitors   (3) court   (4) sacristy   (5) abbot's chapel   (6) cemetery chapel   (7) cemetery   (8) old infirmary   (9) court   (10) great hall of the infirmary   (11) infirmary cloister   (12) chapel of the Madonna   (13) second church (Cluny II)   (14) cloister   (15) atrium   (16) storerooms   (17) second refectory   (18) novitiates' cloister   (19) palace   (20) shelter   (21) stables   (22) shelter   (23) southern gate   (24) kitchen

direct importance; and finally, Byzantine influences were more strongly felt. As a result, in Italy we hardly find a true integration of basilica and tower.[17] The tower is there, but is placed next to the church as an independent *campanile.* Neither do we find the complex wall treatment of the mature Romanesque churches described above. Italian exteriors are usually articulated by means of uniform series of arcades, often superimposed, with members of obvious classical derivation. The interiors are either columnar or based on the simple, large units of the double-bay system. In general Italian Romanesque aims at formal separation and addition rather than integration, and is Romanesque mainly in so far as it makes use of Roman elements. As these elements lose their traditional anthropomorphic implications, a general medieval character becomes manifest.

The cathedral group in Pisa is one of the most representative monuments of medieval Italian architecture. Its extraordinary beauty is first of all due to the interaction of four, formally related buildings: cathedral (1063–1118), baptistry (1153), belfry (1174) and *campo santo* (1278). The large baptistry is placed in front of the cathedral on its main axis, and the famous leaning belfry forms a counterweight at the other end. The *campo santo* has a long wall which serves as a kind of background; this enhances the plastic independence of the three main elements. Unity is assured by a uniform treatment of walls: All the buildings are faced with white marble panelling and articulated by superimposed arcades. Rather than expressing a real structure, the walls appear as a precious gown which is wrapped around the volumes. The optical approach of the Early Christian interior has, so to speak, been extended to the exterior. The effect is splendid and must have had a particular fascination in the past, when the Ligurian Sea came to the outer limit of the cathedral area.

The cathedral is a large columnar basilica with double aisles and deep transepts which are formed like semiindependent single-aisled basilicas. Galleries screen off the transepts to emphasize the continuity of the nave. The crossing is marked by an oval

(17) There are exceptions in the north, such as S. Abbondio in Como (1063), and in the Norman south, such as the twin-towered façade of Cefalù cathedral (1131). The cathedral of Modena (1099) has a particularly beautiful exterior wall articulation which combines nordic complexity and Italian clarity.

172. *Campo Santo, Pisa. Aerial view.*

173. *Cathedral, Pisa. 1063-1118. Ground plan.*

(18) R. Krautheimer, *Early Christian and Byzantine Architecture,* (Harmondsworth and Baltimore, 1965), plate 11A.

(19) In this connection we may recall the typically Italian decorative work of the *cosmati.*

dome, and there is a circular baptistry, derived from the Anastasis rotunda in Jerusalem and whose conical roof it repeats.[18] Overall, the effect of the interior is conservative and no attempt has been made at a formal integration of arcade, gallery and clerestory. The upper part of the exterior was remodelled in Gothic style after 1250, but the belfry conserves the Romanesque articulation, although it was finished as late as 1350.

The Italians rejected the complex symbolism and formal integration of mature Romanesque architecture, maintaining the Early Christian idea of optical dematerialization of the wall.[19] By extending this concept to the exterior, however, the church became an active environmental factor, its elaborate exterior forming a meaningful contrast to the enclosed masses of other buildings. In Italy the Romanesque church was not conceived as an independent stronghold, but as the core of a differentiated urban environment, and in this sense it anticipates the role of the Gothic cathedral.

Space Conception and Development

The examples discussed above have demonstrated how the spiritualized space of Early Christian architecture developed into more articulate spatial images. Within this process three general aspects can be distinguished: introduction of vertical elements, spatial rhythmic articulation and integration, and a new relationship between inside and outside. We have understood that the vertical elements served the double purpose of protection and aspiration, as the tower is simultaneously stronghold and *axis mundi.* Rhythmic articulation served to relate the longitudinal axis more directly to man's movements, whereby it could be experienced as a real path rather than an abstract symbol. In both cases the intention was to integrate the existential meanings of Christianity into everyday life. This is also reflected in the third aspect: the symbolic opening up of the building. What had been a refuge started to become an active environmental force. As a work of art the Romanesque church unifies

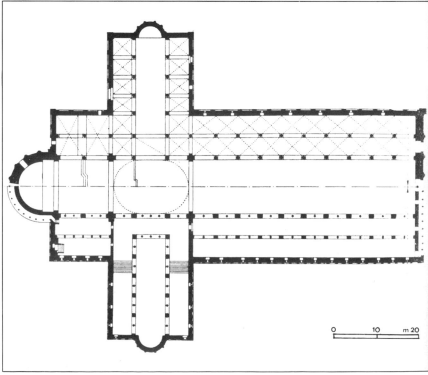

74. Cathedral and belfry ("Leaning Tower"), Pisa. 1063-1118; 1174.

75. Palatine chapel, Aachen. 792-805. Interior of the dome.

74. Cathedral and belfry ("Leaning Tower"), Pisa. 1063-1118; 1174.

75. Palatine chapel, Aachen. 792-805. Interior of the dome.

contradicting factors: Dematerialization and solidity are simultaneously expressed. To achieve this end, Early Christian optical dematerialization was replaced by a differentiated structure consisting of primary and secondary parts.

The Romanesque style was capable of concretizing significant differences in function and content. For all its basic cultural unity it incorporates several significant building types, as well as regional variants. The plan of the pilgrimage churches, for instance, is based on the symbolic forms of cross and ambulatory, whereas the monastic churches give primary importance to the longitudinal path. A typological differentiation of this kind was suggested already during the Constantinian epoch. and a more particular variant is represented by the bipolar plans of the German *Kaiserdome*. In addition to functional types we also encounter manifest regional characters. The German buildings generally aim at powerful and fantastic effects, whereas the French are distinguished by logical organization and structural clarity. Italian Romanesque emphasized the ordered, but rich and somewhat flashy façade. In England we encounter a stout, masculine character distinguished by extraordinarily thick walls and huge, cylindrical piers.

The development of Romanesque architecture is usually interpreted as a Western phenomenon. However some authors relate it to the Early Christian architecture of Syria and Asia Minor, where similar forms, such as integrated towers and subdivided nave, are found.[20] But their most quoted example, the church of S. Sergios in Rusafa from the sixth century, really represents only a provincial variation on late Classical motifs. Although Syrians played an important role in the commercial life of the early Middle Ages, it is farfetched to derive the Romanesque style from Syrian prototypes.

It is possible to follow the development of medieval Western architecture step by step from the deliberate *Rinovatio Romanorum* of Charlemagne. Charlemagne adopted the centralized palatine chapel (Aachen) as well as the basilica (St. Denis), and he combined the basic forms in a new way (St. Riquier). The further development of Romanesque

(20) S. Guyer, *Grundlagen mittelalterlicher abendländischer Baukunst* (Einsidln, Zürich, Cologne, 1950), *passim*.

176. Mission of the Apostles, *tympanum of the central portal of the narthex, Ste. Madeleine, Vézelay.* c. 1120

architecture reflects the problems of relating the Christian existential image to everyday reality. Thus the organized monastery was created, the monastic church, the pilgrimage church, the parish church, and the cathedral, which is the urban church containing the chair of a bishop. Through the opening-up of the originally enclosed church due to a growing interpenetration of Christian values and everyday life Romanesque architecture manifests Christendom on its way to the great synthesis of the Gothic epoch.

Meaning and Architecture

"Christendom on its way" implies the wish to realize the *Civitas Dei* in this world. Whereas Early Christian architecture represented man who turned inwards to find God, Romanesque architecture was the creation of a man who wanted to bring God to the world. To do this he had to instil civil society with the divine principles of conduct in accordance with Augustine's conception of the Christian church and her mission. This was essentially a dynamic and social conception, decreeing that the Church must permeate the state with her principles.[21] Romanesque architecture hence proves Heidegger's words that " 'auf der Erde' heisst schon 'unter dem Himmel'."[22] The integration of the ancient symbols of the vertical and horizontal directions in the Romanesque churches is therefore profoundly meaningful. For the first time in history God is with man on his wandering: He is no longer a distant goal, but continuously present in the vertical direction which permeates the building. Beyond their function the vertical members of the Romanesque wall are not anthropomorphic elements but the manifestation of a symbolic direction.

The operation of the Church in the world did not only manifest itself through hierophanies, such as the appearance of local saints, but first of all through the establishment of an order founded on Christian values, deriving from the order created by St. Benedict of Nursia. During the Middle Ages, Europe was educated from forty thousand Benedictine monasteries, where the monks lived a life based on obedience and self-discipline, prayer and practical work. The monasteries were not a refuge from the world, but a vital part of it, and the world was experienced from the inside out. The monasteries and their churches made the *Civitas Dei* visible, they preserved the manifestations of God and made them part of history, thereby establishing *stabilitas loci* as the basis of medieval civilization. As to settle down first of all means to define limits, to gain a foothold Romanesque architecture combines spiritualized space with its apparent contradiction: massive solidity. Romanesque buildings have a powerful effect which is due to a return to a preanthropomorphic concept of mass and proportion, and Romanesque articulation never aims at the creation of a skeletal wall as such. The skeleton is always secondary to the primary mass. The environmental image of Romanesque man may be defined as a system of *protected places;* protected from within by the experience of the existence of God, and from without by symbolic enclosure and solidity.

How, then, can medieval architecture be related to the concept of history as the growth of existential possibilities? When discussing Early Christian architecture we designated a whole set of existential meanings with the word "interiority." According to Christian belief, man's inner life cannot be understood as an abstraction of natural and social phenomena. The divine principles of conduct, which are centred on the concept of *love,* are *revealed* to man. But revealed truth needs to be made visible or "concretized" just as much as empirical truth. Here, again, we return to the fundamental importance of *art.* The function of art as a concretization of truth was understood by the medieval philosophers. John Scotus says that works of art belong to the *materialia* which may represent the *immaterialia.*[23] Romanesque architecture gives the *immaterialia* a secure home on earth; it fulfills the promise of the Early Christian churches, and prepares for the vision of heaven offered by the Gothic cathedral. In the Romanesque church God is still an object of aspiration, he is *Rex tremendae majestatis.* In Gothic architecture he comes down to dwell in his house, and transforms it from within with his divine light.

(21) F. Copleston, *Mediaeval Philosophy* (London, 1952), p. 89

(22) M. Heidegger, "Bauen Wohnen Denken," *Vorträge und Aufsätze* II, p. 23.

(23) H. Sedlmayr, "Die Wende der Kunst im 12. Jahrhundert," *Vorträge und Forschungen* vol. XII (Stuttgart), p. 431.

(1) The new interest is above all due to the positive judgement made by Lewis Mumford. See *The City in History* (London and New York, 1961).

Introduction

In discussing the architecture of the later Middle Ages, the problems of environment and building must be approached more directly than in the previous chapters. In fact, a considerable part of Europe's population still lives in medieval towns and villages, and, although the modern movement of the 1920s wanted to do away with these living records of a past way of life, recently architects and planners have shown a keen new interest in the urban structure and environmental qualities of the dense medieval settlements.[1] The medieval *Altstadt* creates a feeling of being "inside," of being "somewhere," which is lost in the modern town. We have seen that the enclosure is one of the oldest meaningful forms in the history of architecture, but the medieval town is something more than a physical enclosure; it is characterized by an *interiority* which may be compared to the spiritualized space of the Early Christian church. It is as if the existential meaning concretized by the church has been extended to the habitat as a whole. This fact is also emphasized by the central and dominant location of the church.

As the character of the medieval habitat may be understood as an extension of the character previously encountered in the church interior, it implies a new relationship between the church and its surroundings. Whereas the exterior of the Early Christian church was a continuous, enclosing envelope, and the Romanesque church a stronghold, in the Gothic church optical or symbolic dematerialization is replaced by a real dissolution of the wall and it becomes transparent and interacts with the environment. The building is a diaphanous skeleton whose mass is ideally reduced to a network of abstract lines. Fully developed the medieval church no longer appears as a refuge, but communicates with a larger whole, and functions as the centre of a meaningful, spatial organism. It has been said that the Gothic cathedral was built "in spite of the stone," an observation which testifies to the fact that it represented an existential image rather than being an answer to mere practical problems. Basically it was the concretization of a heavenly image, and through its

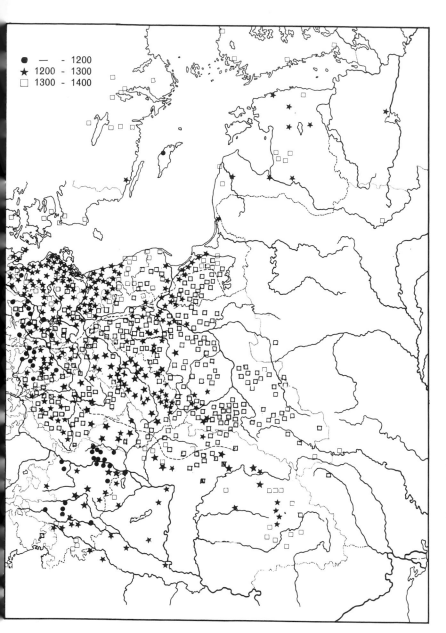

178. *New settlements in central and eastern Europe in the Middle Ages.*

179. *San Gimignano.*

open structure the image was transmitted to the entire community. At the same time transparency offered a new interpretation to Christian light symbolism. In the cathedrals coloured glass transformed natural light into a mysterious medium which seemed to prove the immediate presence of God.[2]

The character of the Gothic church is therefore fundamentally new, and it is not merely a matter of convention to distinguish between the Romanesque and Gothic styles. But as it has already been shown that Romanesque architecture prepared for the Gothic to come, novelty, then, does not imply a break in historical continuity. The Gothic church, in fact, is still based on the fundamental themes of longitudinality and centralization. The growing wish for interaction with the environment gave primary importance to movement in depth, and the nave of the cathedral may be understood as an ideal continuation of the paths of the surrounding settlement, with the portal as a deep, inviting porch.

However, in spite of its longitudinal plan, the Gothic cathedral represented a true centre. Not only was a cathedral centrally placed in a settlement, with its lofty volume and slender spires it is permeated by a general verticality, which makes its status inherent in every part of the structure.

In general we may say that the Gothic age extended the concept of *Civitas Dei* to the urban environment as a whole, with the town conceived as a meaningful organism. The renewed interest in the medieval milieu obviously stems from a conscious or unconscious realization of this fact, but it remains to be seen whether its intimate interiority may be regained without a church at the centre.[3]

(2) When discussing the historical importance of Suger's choir in St. Denis (1140-44), Hans Sedlmayr says: "He did not create a sensation by any technical innovation but by his new vision of God's city of light, a positive assertion of the hereafter in this life." *Die Entstehung der Kathedrale* (Zürich, 1950), p. 235.

(3) Thus Wolfgang Braunfels says: "It is from the cathedral that the towns derive their size, their form, their meaning." *Mittelalterliche Stadtbaukunst in der Toskana* (Berlin, 1953), p. 246.

Landscape and Settlement

In our introductory remarks it is implied that the urban settlement regained its basic importance during the later Middle Ages. From the eleventh century on, a general process of urbanization took place in Western and Central Europe as a result of a considerable growth in population. Old centres from Roman times regained their vitality, small vil-

180. *Aigues-Mortes. Aerial view.*

181. *Carcassonne. Aerial view.*

182. *Cathedral, Ulm. Nave and tower by Ulrich von Ensingen, begun 1392. View from the Danube.*

(4) An important contribution is offered by S. Muratori, *Civiltá e territorio* (Rome, 1967). An important indicator is the ending of towns names, such as -burgh, -wich, -port, and -ford.

(5) Braunfels, *op. cit.*, pp. 46 ff.

lages developed into true towns, and innumerable new settlements were founded. Some of these attained the importance of regional centres, usually because of an interaction of cultural (religious) and economical factors. The process first gained impetus in Italy, especially in Lombardy and Tuscany. From there it spread to Provence and to Northern France and Flanders, where we find a particularly dense concentration of medieval towns, and it was in this region that the Gothic style was born. The towns were connected by a network of roads, but communication was easy only in summer and the medieval towns must therefore be regarded as relatively isolated self-sufficient units. It has been demonstrated that their distribution tended towards a certain regularity, with one day's journey as the standard distance. The more detailed relationship between natural and cultural factors of location has yet to be investigated.[4]

Although they appear irregular and picturesque, the settlements of the later Middle Ages are based on symbolic principles of organization. Regardless of size, they had basic properties in common: enclosure, density, intimacy, and functional differentiation. This last aspect consisted, for instance, in the specialization of streets and quarters for certain purposes, such as types of handicraft. The squares were also specialized in larger settlements. Of particular significance was the city wall which offered the necessary protection to make the town function as a "container," as well as a "magnet," to use Lewis Mumford's words. Thus, the town became a place where a true communal life could develop; in other words, the brotherhood of the monastery was extended to a more comprehensive social unit. In general, the medieval town resembles a living organism, where the wall is the hard shell and the church the delicate core. In between are the dwellings which represent an intermediate character. The city wall, however, was more than a means of protection; it was a symbol of the *civitas,* a domain reigned by law, order and security. In the *civitas* man was free.[5]

The symbolism of the city wall revives important concepts from antiquity, especially as Gothic towns were usually planned in ac-

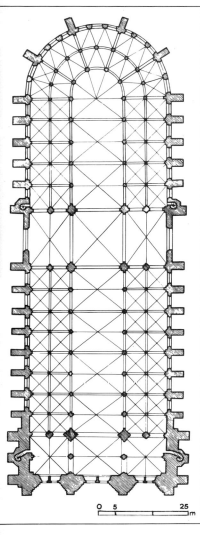

183. Notre Dame, Paris. 1163-1250. Ground plan.

184, 185. Notre Dame, Paris. South side and facade.

186. Notre Dame, Paris. Interior.

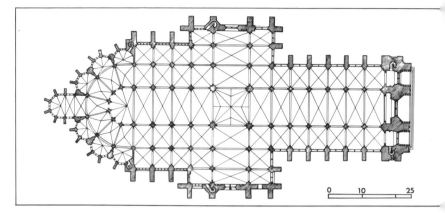

(6)   W. Müller, *Die heilige Stadt* (Stuttgart, 1961), p. 59. In Florence only these streets were paved!

(7)   *Ibid.*, pp. 93 ff.

cordance with the ancient principle of division into quarters by means of two main streets crossing each other approximately at right angles.[6] In the centre, near the main crossing, were the market, the church and the town hall. In many places the town hall came to form a pendant to the church as an expression of the freedom of the burghers. (During the thirteenth century the constitution of many towns, especially in Italy, evolved towards a real democracy.) Although the conscious wish for order brought about a revival of Roman principles of organization in the medieval town, the quadripartite plan was combined with the Christian concept of interiority. As a result, the urban environment is experienced as simultaneously structured and intimate. The quadripartite plan was used in connection with square, rectangular, round or irregular outlines. French towns are usually quadrangular, whereas those of Eastern Germany are round.

The basis of the quadripartite plan was the conception of the town as a representation of an ordered cosmos, where life could take place in an analogously ordered way. Indeed, the whole medieval world was imagined as a quadripartite totality with Jerusalem and Rome forming a double centre. This image was concretized on the most comprehensive environmental levels; at the beginning of the twelfth century Ireland was divided into four provinces, and the German Empire had four defined "corners."[7] The ancient symbolism of the cardinal points was thus revived.

Building

As urbanization developed, the cathedral became the leading building task. The basic function of the cathedral was to illustrate and "explain" the meaningful organization of the medieval world. To achieve this end, architecture, sculpture and painting were unified in a *Gesamtkunstwerk* which remains one of the greatest achievements in the history of mankind.

The plan of the cathedral is based on the organization of the major churches of mature Romanesque architecture. Some have double aisles, there is usually a transept.

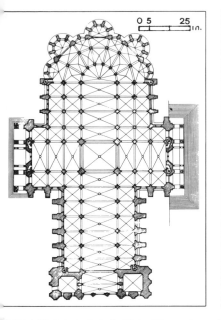

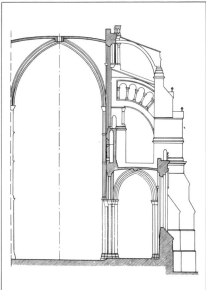

and the chancel with ambulatory and radiating chapels is common. But the Romanesque organism was transformed in characteristic ways, most notably by a conscious wish for spatial and formal integration, and a new, radical interpretation of wall and vault. The spatial and formal integration implies that the different parts of the Romanesque church lost their relative independence. The towers were absorbed by a general verticalism which permeated the whole building, and when a tower was planned, it usually remained a torso.[8] The nave became relatively shorter, the projection of the transept less evident, and the chancel larger. In Chartres and Amiens, thus, the crossing is located almost at the centre of the longitudinal axis. A ribbed-vault made a full geometric integration of the different elements of the plan possible. If we take a look at the plan of Notre Dame in Paris, for instance, it seems composed of a few equivalent units. In general the plan of the cathedral appears as an ideal combination of unity and differentiation. At the same time it unifies the different spatial themes of Early Christian and Romanesque ecclesiastical architecture in complete synthesis. A felicitous solution such as the cathedral of Amiens unites longitudinal movement with a singular expression of general horizontal expansion and vertical aspiration. Like Santiago de Compostela, it combines path and centre in one synthetic form, but the unity has a new assurance. The pilgrimage has, so to speak, become unnecessary, as God is seen as being present in the here and now.

Cathedral exteriors lost any trace of massive enclosure as a result of the desire to transmit the spiritualized space of the interior to the entire habitat. "High Gothic architecture did delimit interior volume from exterior space yet insist that it project itself, as it were, through the encompassing structure."[9] The meaning of the church was no longer enclosed, but had become part of the daily environment.

Cathedrals were built in all the countries of the Western world, and assumed a somewhat different stamp according to local circumstances. Thus in Germany the irrational aspect of Gothic form is more evident than in France, manifesting itself in extraordinar-

(8) The most significant exceptions are found in Germany, where the "fantastic" towers of German Romanesque were continued in tall Gothic steeples.

(9) E. Panofsky, *Gothic Architecture and Scholasticism* (Latrobe, Pa., 1951), p. 44.

(10) P. Frankl, *Gothic Architecture* (Harmondsworth and Baltimore, 1962), p. 1

(11) H. Jantzen, *Über den gotischen Kirchenraum* (Freiburg im Br., 1927).

(12) H. Sedlmayr, *op. cit.*, pp. 235 ff.

192. *Abbey church of St. Denis, near Paris. Begun c. 1135. Ground plan.*

193. *Abbey church of St. Denis, near Paris. Apse.*

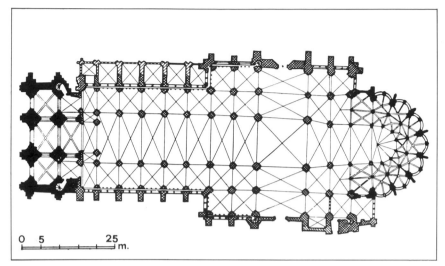

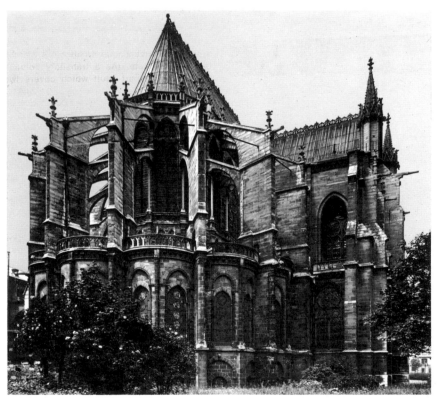

ily tall, pointed steeples (Strasbourg, Freiburg, Ulm, and Vienna), and in interiors o a mystical character, where total effect i more important than logical structure. Thi intention culminated with the Late Gothi hall-churches. In these fascinating interior the spatial elements of the High Gothic ca thedral—nave, aisles, transept, ambulatory chapels—are absorbed by one continuous fluid space, where the piers appear as free standing verticals. Even the bay-structur dissolves into the rich, undulating movemer of complex net-vaults. In some of the mos advanced cases, such as the church at Mos in Bohemia, the space is encircled by continuous, neutral skin, which makes u think of the exterior of the Early Christia churches. The hall-churches, in fact, repre sent a new interpretation of the origina Christian interiority. They stem from a tim when the expansion of medieval civilizatio had come to a halt under the pressure c disease, internal strife and external threat At this time man turned towards introver mysticism and built churches where the opti cal dematerialization of Early Christia architecture had been replaced by irrationa structure.

Articulation

The basic phenomenon of Gothic architec ture is a new interpretation of the wall an the vault. One art historian, Paul Frankl, say that the Gothic style was born "when diago nal ribs were added to the groin-vault,"[1] and another, Hans Jantzen, has pointed ou the fundamental importance of the "diapha nous" wall,[11] but it is futile to try to decide which of the two came first, as the rib-vaul and the diaphanous wall are two aspects o the same total scheme. The driving force be hind both inventions was a new interpreta tion of the meaning of *light*.[12] When Abbo Suger built the new chevet at St. Denis afte 1140, he talked explicitly about the *lux con tinua* and *lux mirabilis* which should deter mine the character of the new construction To gain this end, the wall was designed a a thin shell of stone and glass. Any feelin of mass has disappeared, and the extraor dinarily transparent double ambulatory ap

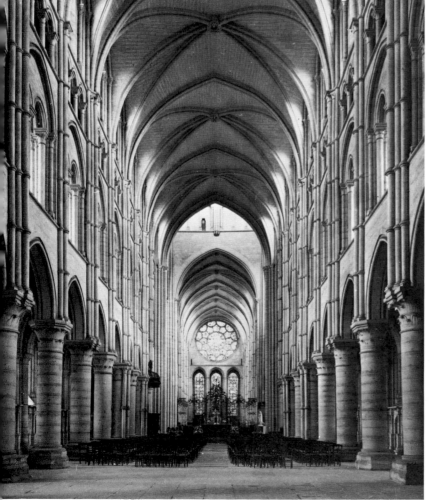

pears as luminous foil around the skeletal apse. The large windows fitted with stained glass produced an unreal, heavenly light which illustrate the words of the hymn sung on the day of consecration: "Your walls are made of gems."

The exterior of this cathedral is really determined from within. Its original construction did not foresee flying buttresses, but with the growing understanding of structural problems during the following decades, a logical system of external buttressing was developed to take care of the concentrated stresses of the Gothic vault and wall.[13]

The skeletal openness of the Gothic wall demanded higher vaults. With the introduction of the diagonal load-bearing rib and the pointed arch, the intermediate cells could be made thinner. The ribs also eliminated certain irregularities resulting from the geometry of Romanesque groin-vaulting.[14] As a pointed arch can be made more or less steeply pointed to suit the different widths of nave and aisles, it was possible to make a vault with a level ridge. The double-bay system of Romanesque architecture thereby became obsolete. (As a transitory solution there is a six-part vault which covers two bays.) Diagonal ribs also implied new spatial directions. Whereas Romanesque space is organized orthogonally, and may be understood as being organized by addition of simple stereometric units, Gothic space is divided by diagonal ribs. The spatial units hence lose their relative independence, and a general integration is achieved. Vertical shafts supporting the ribs are placed diagonally to the other members, and cannot be understood as parts of the wall, but belong to tall baldachins which are surrounded by a continuous luminous boundary. The hall-churches bring this intention to its ultimate conclusion, as the whole structure becomes one large baldachin within a dematerialized skin.

The articulation of the interior wall in High Gothic architecture represents a continuation of the process initiated in the mature Romanesque churches, with the general intention of transforming the mass into a diaphanous structure. In the early cathedrals, such as Noyon (1150) and Laon (c. 1160), the wall still consists of relatively independent

(13) In the Late Gothic hall-churches the buttresses were placed inside a continuous outer skin. They are known as "wall-piers" *(Wandpfeiler)*.

(14) For a thorough discussion of the problem of vaulting see P. Frankl, *op. cit.*, pp. 1 ff.

196. Cathedral, Chartres. Begun 1194. Interior.

197. Abbey church of St. Denis, near Paris. New nave by Pierre de Montereau, begun 1231.

198. Cathedral, Prague. Begun 1344. Interior by Peter Parler, begun 1354.

199. Cathedral, Strasbourg. Façade by Erwin van Steinbach, c. 1277; tower by Ulrich von Ensingen, 1399.

200. Cathedral, Reims. Begun 1211. Ground plan.

201. Cathedral, Reims. Transverse section.

202. Cathedral, Reims. Apse by Jean d'Orbais.

203. Cathedral, Reims. Façade by Jean le Loup, after 1231.

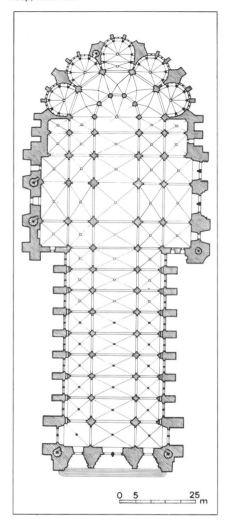

0 5   25 m

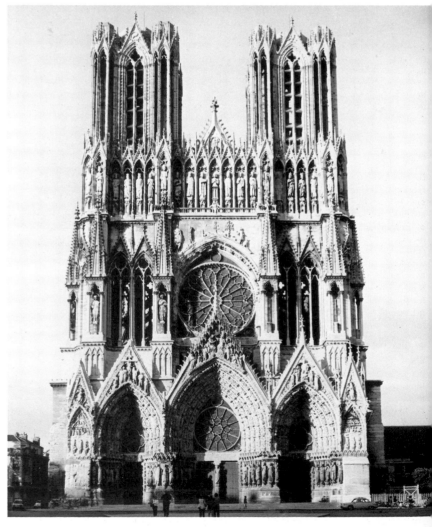

superimposed zones: arcade, gallery, triforium and clerestory. The clerestory windows gradually become larger, the gallery disappears and finally the triforium is united to the clerestory to form one luminous zone above the arcade. The process started in Chartres (1194) and culminated in the new nave at St. Denis (1231) by Pierre de Montereau. At the same time the vertical continuity of the members was stressed, and the columnar piers still present in Notre Dame in Paris (1180) were replaced by dematerialized bundles of thin shafts. This logical differentiation of members according to their particular function produced a characteristically Gothic wall structure: The wall seems composed of several overlapping layers of weblike tracery. The wall, thus, is not only dematerialized by perforation, but by longitudinal division as well. The same principle governs the articulation of the exterior, and is most evident in a façade such as Strasbourg (c. 1277). During the Late Gothic period the wall-tracery was given an irrational, antistructural interpretation which is known as flamboyant style. It is mainly found in France and represents a parallel to the introvert mysticism mentioned above.

Reims

Reims cathedral does not represent the most radical structure among the great French cathedrals, but it possesses a singular overall integrity of style and a pleasing mastery of proportions and detailing which earn it its title of "Queen" among French churches. Construction was started in 1211, probably with Jean d'Orbais as the architect.[15] The twin towers of the west front were never finished, and other towers originally planned for transept and crossing were omitted, with the result that the building appears as a lofty, unified volume. Hardly anywhere else is exterior articulation as uniform as in Reims. Although construction work went on for several decades, the building seems made all of a piece. This is due partially to the repetition of similar buttresses around the whole building, and partially to the repetitive use of decorative motifs, such as the tabernacles containing statues of angels which surmount the buttresses. Moreover horizontal continuity is emphasized by a crowning arcade which runs along the nave and around the chancel. It appears as a diminution of the great King's gallery on the West Front, which most efficiently unifies the tripartite composition. With three deeply embrasured portals and a large sun window, the façade has a strong spatial quality. It represents a transition between exterior and interior, a link between earth and heaven. The composition of the façade is clear and gives a feeling of harmonious proportions, in spite of the heterogeneity of its constituent parts.

The interior has a grandeur and simplicity, but it is not the simplicity of primitive architecture. Here simplicity results from a complex articulation which has given every part its correct position, shape and dimension. The final, convincing result is achieved in spite of a somewhat irregular and old-fashioned plan. The nave is relatively long, and the aisles of the transept considerably wider than the other bays. A regular spatial succession is obtained, however, thanks to continuous vaulting (without any tower over the crossing), and the characteristic *Gestalt* of the piers. These are round with four engaged shafts, corresponding to the transverse arches of nave and aisle as well as the longitudinal arches between them. The shafts belonging to the diagonal ribs of the vaulting rest on the abacus of the piers. A certain orthogonal effect is therefore still present, which contributes to the serene overall character.[16] The triforium is designed as a regular arcade and is not connected with the clerestory, except for a thickening of the central colonnette. However, the clerestory is for the first time conceived as a fully glazed surface between the primary structural members. In Chartres, where the general design is similar, remains of closed walls are still present. Although the triforium and the clerestory form a continuous zone around the interior, the articulation is significantly varied in the chancel where dematerialization and vertical continuity are given particular emphasis. Here the triforium is bipartite, and instead of the plastic colonnettes used in the nave a slender shaft rises up to connect the triforium with the clerestory above. Also significant is the repetition of the shape of the clerestory windows in the aisles, but with a much more plastic relationship to the wall. A vertical increase in dematerialization is thus expressed.

What distinguishes the interior in Reims from the other great cathedrals is the meaningful use of elements which conserve a degree of plasticity. The window niches of the aisles, the round piers and substantial main shafts, and the rather thick colonnettes of the triforium, may be interpreted as a contradiction of the Gothic principle of dematerialization, but it would be more correct to say that they give the idea of dematerialization a deeper meaning. Whereas other cathedrals state the principle as a simple fact, Reims interprets the idea as a peaceful victory of the spirit. In Reims, man experiences a bodily relationship to the plastic members of the lower zone, at the same time as his soul is lifted up and redeemed by the abstract web of the clerestory and vault. Body and soul have become aspects of the same harmonious totality. In Reims, God is no longer understood as *Rex tremendae majestatis,* but as *Deus propinquior;*[17] he is close to man. When we enter the cathedral in Reims we are in fact received by the Virgin with the Child, and angels surround the whole building.

Salisbury

At Salisbury in southern England we find another Gothic cathedral which seems made all of a piece. But what a difference of character! Instead of the unified, lofty volume of Reims, the building is long and low, surmounted with a tall tower over the crossing. The façade looks as if a screen composed of Gothic motifs has been applied to a massive wall, and the interior lacks true verticalism in spite of an abundance of Gothic detail. Reminiscences of Romanesque architecture are present, although the cathedral at Salisbury was erected between 1220 and 1260 on a new site, and is generally considered the purest example of English Gothic.[18] Evidently the English interpretation of the Gothic cathedral differs considerably from the French solution described above.

(15) Frankl, *op. cit.*, p. 86. refers to the church in nearby Orbais (c. 1200) as a "model for Reims." After the death of d'Orbais in 1231, work was continued by Gaucher of Reims, Jean le Loup (façade), and Bernard of Soissons. The total exterior length of the building is about 140 metres (460 feet).

(16) A similar solution is found in Amiens, but there the shafts are thinner and the effect different. In the nave of St. Denis the primacy of the orthogonal axes is no longer felt.

(17) The concept stems from St. Bernard. See H. Sedlmayr, "Die Wende der Kunst im 12. Jahrhundert," *Vorträge und Forschungen* vol. XII (Konstanz and Stuttgart), pp. 438 ff.

(18) The tower with the tall spire was finished about 1330. It reaches the height of 123 metres (440 feet), and the exterior length of the church exceeds 140 metres (460 feet).

(19) P. Frankl, *op. cit.*, p. 96.

(20) H. Jantzen, *Die Gotik des Abendlandes* (Cologne, 1962), p. 117.

Salisbury is the culmination of a long development of the same basic intentions. The large Norman churches built after the conquest in 1066 already possess the typically English plan with an exceptionally long nave (St. Albans 1077, Norwich 1099), two transepts (Canterbury *c.* 1100), and a square east end (Southwell 1114). The first two traits have already been encountered at Cluny III, whereas the square east end was introduced in the severe churches of the Cistercian order. However, in England continental influences were combined to form a new characteristic totality. The plan of the English cathedral is primarily a path with a long, directed nave not leading to any centralized chancel, but continuing through the building without coming to a halt. Even the tall tower over the crossing does not represent a real centre. The fact that the typical English transept is asymmetrical with one aisle only indicates that the tower does not belong to any centralized space, but is rather an emblematic vertical which man carries with him on his wandering. Nor does the second transept serve to create a halt, as in Cluny III, but reinforces the longitudinal movement, as does the subdivision of the nave into continuous horizontal levels. The construction is further distinguished by a feeling for mass. During the twelfth century a series of churches were built where the walls appear immensely thick and the piers of mastodontic dimensions. Finally it is important to notice that the English cathedrals do not form part of an urban setting, but are as a rule isolated within a precinct. In general, they represent a particular interpretation of Romanesque properties. They conserve the "missionary" emphasis given to longitudinal movement, vertical accents and protective mass during the Romanesque period.

How then did the English cathedral adapt to the Gothic style? Evidently it did not undergo a thorough transformation like the great French churches, and all the properties described above are still present in the cathedrals of the thirteenth century, such as Salisbury. The characteristic motif of the screen front offers a key to the problem. Instead of carrying through a real dematerialization of the wall, the English covered the massive core of the building, exterior and

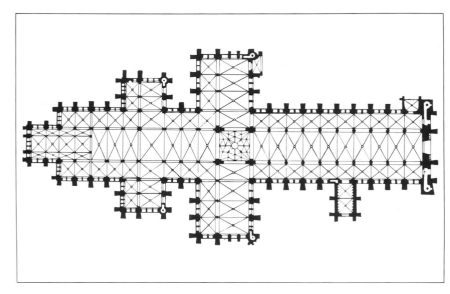

interior, with a purely decorative screen which simulates a skeletal structure. The interiors therefore lack the structural logic found in the French cathedrals. To make the building look Gothic, shafts and profiles are multiplied and made of a material different from the wall behind, such as the Purbeck marble used at Salisbury, without ever dispensing with the massive wall. It is still experienced as the true substance of the building, and makes the Gothic forms appear as mere emblematic motifs. Only towards the end of the period did the screen assume the status of an independent structure, and a few Perpendicular buildings were erected that are fully Gothic and truly English, most important of which is the splendid chapel of King's College in Cambridge (1446–1515).

It would be wrong, however, to dismiss English Gothic as a kind of provincial misconception. Frankl introduces the rather paradoxical term "Gothic horizontalism" to describe the interior of Salisbury.[19] And, in fact, swift horizontal movement is a basic property of the English cathedrals. It is as if the new spiritual assurance offered by the Gothic style had transformed the severe rhythm of the Romanesque path into a dynamic worldly conquest.

Kutná Hora

The development of Gothic architecture came to a splendid conclusion with the hall-churches of Central Europe. The term *Sondergotik* is often used to emphasize their peculiar character. If we take a closer look at the buildings which preceded them, it becomes evident that tendencies which pointed in the direction of unified, "total" spaces were present in Germany already in the thirteenth century. The two most interesting buildings of the period are St. Elizabeth at Marburg (1235) and the Liebfrauenkirche at Trier (*c.* 1240). The former is a hall-church, but the aisles are very narrow and appear as a luminous foil to the wider nave; the hall concept represents a natural consequence of the diaphanous wall.[20] The church at Trier is a centralized building with the cross of a higher nave and transept inscribed.

207. *Peter Parler: St. Barbara, Kutná Hora.*
Begun 1388.

208. *Peter Parler: St. Barbara, Kutná Hora.*
Apse.

(21) G. Fehr, *Benedikt Ried* (Munich, 1961), pp. 36 ff. The schematic west front was added at the end of the nine-teenth century.

Mature Late Gothic architecture developed during the fourteenth century, and is closely connected with the name of Peter Parler from Schwäbisch Gmünd (1330–99). As a young man Peter Parler assisted his father in the construction of the extraordinary church of the Holy Cross in his home town. The building has a fully developed hall choir covered by a net-vault, and the buttresses have become internal wall-piers. In 1354 Peter was called to Prague by the Emperor Charles IV to continue the construction of the cathedral, started in 1344 by Matthias of Arras. A chevet of radiating chapels had already been built, but Peter changed the elevation of the choir. Over a simple, austere arcade he erected a fully glazed, combined triforium and clerestory, which is probably the most beautiful in the history of Gothic architecture. By an ingenious introduction of diagonal elements in the triforium he made the bays unite in a continuous, undulating movement which prepares for the net-vault above.

In 1388 Peter Parler started the construction of St. Barbara in Kutná Hora (Kuttenberg). Here he combined the construction of the choir from Prague with the continuous wall-pier ambulatory already tested in Schwäbisch Gmünd. The intention was to let a diaphanous, spiritualized shrine rise out of a more severe, relatively enclosed space—a Late Gothic interpretation of the theme encountered at Reims. After the death of Parler in 1399, the construction halted, and a hundred years later the choir was finished according to the original design by Matthias Rejsek. In 1512, finally, the nave was begun by the leading architect of the period, Benedikt Ried, who was assisted by Jacob Heilmann. Ried abandoned the basilican layout planned by Parler, and over the severe nave arcade he erected freestanding piers which carry the vault of a complete hall-church.[21] The result is one of the most extraordinary creations of Late Gothic architecture: The web of double curved ribs introduces a continuous, complex movement which creates a unified interior covered by a vault that seems to float in space. Externally, the wish to dematerialize the upper part of the building made the architect abandon the traditional longitudinal roof. Instead we find three con-

209. *Peter Parler: St. Barbara. Kutná Hora. Vaulting by Benedict Ried, 1512.*

210. *Peter Parler: St. Barbara, Kutná Hora. Interior.*

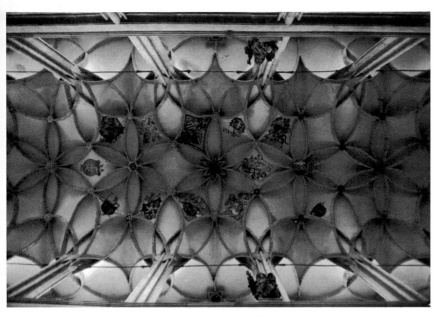

cave tent-roofs surmounted by spires. The original solution gives the church a characteristic Bohemian flavour and represents the last creative variation on the theme of Gothic verticalism.[22]

Because of its complex history, the church at Kutná Hora well illustrates the transition from High Gothic to Late Gothic conceptions. It combines the basilica and the hall-church in a singular synthesis, and shows the inner unity of the Gothic style. The Central European *Sondergotik,* thus, still takes the relationship between light and structure as its point of departure, but instead of logical clarification, it aims at the concretization of a new kind of mystical interiority. This interiority found its last manifestation in the magnificent hall-churches at Annaberg (1515 *ff.*) and Most (Brüx) (1518 *ff.*).[23]

Siena

Innumerable European towns still provide the opportunity to experience the medieval *milieu.* Siena offers a particularly interesting example, as it illustrates how the Gothic style was received in Italy, the country where medieval urbanization originated. Siena is a Gothic town, and because of historical circumstances it has preserved its original character up to the present. During the thirteenth and fourteenth centuries, Siena gained considerable political importance, and the citizens must have possessed an extraordinary civic pride. They were convinced that no other Italian town had more beautiful buildings, streets and squares,[24] and in 1339 began the most ambitious cathedral project in Italy. But in 1348 the great epoch came to an end, when the Black Death killed three quarters of the population.

Siena is a hill town, and although it is generally considered an example of the natural, nonplanned settlement, it is based on a concept of order, even if it does not exhibit a geometrically organized plan. As Siena had the most perfect building code of the Middle Ages, planning probably had much to do with the creation of its admirably unified townscape. Siena even had an office for the embellishment of the town: The *ufficiali dell ornato* controlled every street

(22) Ried repeated the solution in the church of St. Nicolas at Louny (Laun) (after 1517).

(23) See H. Mannlová, *Kostel Nanebevzeti Panny Marie v Moste* (Prague, 1970).

(24) H. Keller, *Italienische Kunstlandschaften* (Munich, 1965), p. 300.

211. *The three principal streets of Siena (dotted lines), dividing the city into thirds. (1) Città (2) Camollia (3) San Martino.*

212. *Piazza del Campo, Siena. Aerial view.*

213. *Siena. A typical street.*

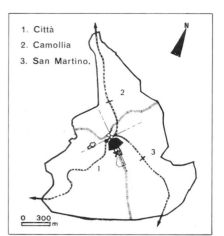

(25) Braunfels, *Mittel-alterliche Stadtbaukunst in der Toskana*, p. 123.

and every house, and secured regularity and order. In 1297 it was ordained that all houses facing the main piazza should have the same windows.[25]

Siena is built on three hills which meet at a central node, to form a Y-shaped system of ridges. Longitudinal streets make the basic pattern visible, and describe the paths which link Siena with the north (Florence), the south (Rome), and the west (the sea). Between the built ridges deep, green valleys structure the landscape. As a counterpoint to the tripartite road system, four monastic churches mark the corners of the settlement. Where the streets meet, at the very centre, is the public square, the great natural bowl of the Piazza del Campo. The cathedral is situated nearby, at the highest point. Both locations are immediately meaningful; the piazza at the point of maximum movement, but separated from the streets as an enclosed place in the real sense of the word, and the cathedral above everything else. The main streets have a strongly emphasized continuity, which expresses their public character, whereas the private secondary streets form an irregular subordinate system. The whole environment is unified by a general use of brick as the main building material, and by a uniform, although varied, articulation. The city wall is of minor importance because of the irregular site.

The Sienese of the Middle Ages were certainly right in considering their Campo one of the most splendid piazzas in existence. Its natural concave shape is surrounded by a continuous row of façades, and a fan-shaped system of lines in the floor concentrates the space on the Palazzo Publico, or town hall (1298). The town hall appears like a screen rather than a volume, and its tripartite Gothic windows establish the basic theme for the wall articulation of the whole piazza. It is capped by an extremely tall tower which is visible from afar, and thus expresses the character of the town as a democratic commune. The single buildings of Siena, thus, do not appear as distinct volumes; the figural character is taken over by the *spaces*, whereby a general interiority is created.

However, the main churches are plastic volumes, and the dome and *campanile* of the

214. *Plan of central Siena.*

215. *Cathedral, Siena. Façade by Giovanni Pisano, 1284-96.*

216. *Siena. View of the tower of the Palazzo Pubblico. In the distance, the cathedral and campanile.*

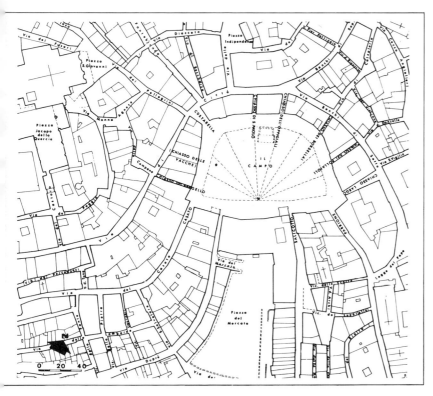

cathedral compete with the civic tower. In the cathedral (after 1230) the Gothic motifs of the houses are concentrated and "explained." The plan is a curious variation on the cruciform basilica with a square Cistercian east end and an inscribed octagonal dome. The interior has throughout a revetment of black and white marble in horizontal layers, which creates a vibrating effect of dematerialization. The most important part of the building is the first order of the façade by Giovanni Pisano (1284–96), where the forms dissolve in a play of light and shadow.

Space Conception and Development

In the Gothic style the intentions of Christian architecture reached their fulfilment. The spiritualized space imagined by Early Christian architecture had finally become, after long development, an immediate concrete presence. From the very beginning the symbol of the basic meaning of Christian space was light and the character of Christian space is primarily determined by the interaction of light and material substance (mass). Being the spiritual element, light transforms natural and anthropomorphic matter; it illuminates the things of our everyday world and gives them a new meaning. We have called the architectural aspect of this process "dematerialization." This dematerialization is always a function of light, and should not be confused with the merely technical dematerialization of modern skeleton construction.

Dematerialization as a function of illumination may be achieved in several ways. The Early Christian churches receive light, but only the interior surface is influenced by it. Slowly, however, the interaction became more profound. By the fifth century the apse was penetrated by windows, and, as time passed, even more of the massive wall was absorbed by light. The semidarkness of the Romanesque church gave way to the Gothic vision of light. At a certain point of this development, when structure became diaphanous, Gothic was born. The process of dematerialization not only made the amorphous, massive wall disappear, but trans-

217. *Ste. Chapelle, Paris. 1243-48. Choir.*

218. *Castle of Hradcany, Prague. Vladislav hall by Benedikt Ried, 1482; new vault, 1502.*

(26) In contrast to the Albertian concept of harmony, that is, that nothing might be added or taken away.

formed it into a differentiated, logical structure where every part expressed its role in the totality. This structure became visible from the outside; the Gothic cathedral transmits the symbolic order which results from the interaction of light and matter to the whole community.

However, Gothic order is not simple and definable in terms of elementary geometric relationships. It is highly differentiated and hierarchical, at the same time as it aims at integration of the single parts. Accordingly a cathedral may very well contain parts from different périods without losing its harmony; its form is in a certain sense open as long as a few general principles are observed.[26] The same holds true for the Gothic town. For example, while the plan of Siena is not based on orthogonal principles of organization, it is still differentiated, hierarchical and integrated. It consists of primary and secondary elements (nodes, paths, domains) and is unified by means of the general principle of continuity. A Gothic town *may* have an orthogonal structure, but that does not make it more or less Gothic. Gothic form, thus, is a living totality rather than a static, eternal image. In this sense the Gothic style is truly Western.

The Gothic wish for formal integration is a function of the experience of the immediate presence of divine truth. Centre and path unify in the "total" plan of the cathedral, and the formerly independent motif of the tower is absorbed by a general verticalism. The different types of churches of the Romanesque period also give way to the one, dominant task: the cathedral, which offers a complete concretization of the late medieval image of the world, and synthesizes the existential meanings of the period. In the cathedral Christendom is no longer on its way; it has settled down and experiences *Civitas Dei* as an accomplished fact.

The development of the cathedral is one of the great themes of the history of Western architecture, and has been illuminated by Frankl, Jantzen, Sedlmayr and Panofsky. It all happened in Île de France within a span of a hundred years, and the church of St. Denis marks the beginning as well as the culmination of the process. A development where every architect is willing to learn from

219. The Church. c. 1220-30. Musée de l'oeuvre Notre-Dame, Strasbourg.

220. The Synagogue. c. 1220-30. Musée de l'oeuvre Notre-Dame, Strasbourg.

his predecessor can be followed from the chevet of Suger to the nave of Pierre de Montereau. Nowhere is there arbitrary caprice; every work represents an interpretation of meaningful common themes, and every work was dedicated to the glory of God.

Meaning and Architecture

Gothic architecture concludes an age in the history of Western culture which may be called "the age of faith." During this era ecclesiastical architecture was of primary importance, and its development expresses the growth of man's understanding of divine revelation and its relation to his everyday world. From the relatively undifferentiated, general intuition represented by the Early Christian church, he arrived at the highly articulate, illuminating system of the Gothic cathedral. As the point of departure was faith, so the end was a full understanding of the meaning of existence. This attitude is expressed in the famous words of St. Anselm of Canterbury (1034–1109): *credo ut intelligam,* "I believe in order to understand." Without bringing God close, no understanding was possible. Romanesque architecture created the strongholds man needed to receive God. In the Gothic cathedral he came close.

How, then, did the cathedral help man to understand the meaning of existence? Basically it happened in two ways. Firstly, the cathedral was the "mirror of the world." Its iconographical programme brought the heavenly and the earthly spheres together in one complex tale, a *Biblia pauperum,* which taught illiterate man the history of the world from the creation, the dogmas of religion, the examples of the saints, the hierarchy of the virtues, the range of the sciences, arts and crafts. "The countless statues, disposed in scholarly design, were a symbol of the marvellous order that through the genius of St. Thomas Aquinas reigned in the world of thought. Through the medium of art the highest conceptions of

theologian and scholar penetrated to some extent the minds of even the humblest of the people."[27] Secondly, the architecture itself represented a manifestation of the ordered Christian cosmos. According to St. Thomas, "Sacred doctrine makes use of human reason, not to prove faith but to make clear whatever else is set forth in this doctrine."[28] In scholastic philosophy the structure of the cosmos was made clear by means of systematic articulation. "The whole was divided into *partes* which could be divided into smaller *partes;* the partes into *membra, quaestiones* or *distinctiones,* and these into *articuli.*"[29] Panofsky has convincingly demonstrated that the Gothic cathedral was organized in an analogous way. This was possible because architectural articulation, like reason, has the power to bind and to dissolve. The systematic subdivision into parts, without losing the vision of the whole, produced a clarification corresponding to the aims of scholastic philosophy. Gothic illumination, thus, means something more than the presence of divine light. It implies clarification and understanding, and is concretized in architectural terms as a logical structure resulting from the interaction of light and material substance. The form of the Gothic cathedral can then justly be characterized as "spiritualized matter." In the Late Gothic hall-church, the logical, open structure of the cathedral developed into a "barnlike shell enclosing an often wildly pictorial and always apparently boundless interior."[30] Thus, High Gothic rationalism had been drowned by a new mysticism.

Because of its visual logic the cathedral was an image of the cosmic order. "In the religious system of the Middle Ages every phase of reality is assigned its unique place; and with its place goes a complete determination of its value, which is based on the greater or lesser distance which separates it from the First Cause."[31] Man, thus, was understood as a fragment only of the total creation, and to find the totality he did not himself possess, he had to accept his place within the Kingdom of God. To achieve this end, faith had to precede reason, and an attitude of humility was imperative. The cathedral, therefore, does not only con-

(27) E. Male, *The Gothic Image* (Gloucester, Mass., 1958); (London, 1961). p. vii.

(28) St. Thomas Aquinas, *Summa Theologiae* I, qu. 1, art. 8. ad. 2.

(29) Panofsky, *op. cit.,* p. 33.

(30) Panofsky, *op. cit.,* p. 43.

(31) E. Cassirer, *The Philosophy of the Enlightenment* (Boston, 1955), p. 39.

cretize the reason of St. Thomas Aquinas but also the virtue of St. Francis of Assisi (1182–1226). Thus God had come close, not only to iluminate man, but to give his existence the meaning of love and charity. From the cathedral the existential meanings of Christianity were transmitted to the human environment as a whole, and the town became the place where the medieval cosmos was presented as a living reality.

221.   Donato Bramante: Tempietto, S. Pietro in Montorio, Rome. 1502.

222.   Filippo Brunelleschi: Sagrestia Vecchia (Old Sacristy) of S. Lorenzo, Florence, Section.

223.   Filippo Brunelleschi: Sagrestia Vecchia (Old Sacristy) of S. Lorenzo, Florence 1420-29. Vaulting.

Introduction

The revaluation of the Middle Ages has produced a change in our attitude to Renaissance culture and the theory of a general rebirth after centuries of darkness is no longer acceptable. But when we look at Brunelleschi's buildings, it is easy to understand why his contemporaries considered them the manifestation of a fundamental break with medieval architecture, even though modern scholars have called attention to the appearance of many of Brunelleschi's motifs in the Florentine proto-Renaissance." Together with the painter Masaccio and the sculptor Donatello, Brunelleschi remains one of the *patres* of the Renaissance style, to use the term of Max Dvořák.

The ends and means of the new architecture are clearly visible in Brunelleschi's first complete major work, the Sacrestia Vecchia of S. Lorenzo in Florence (1420–29). Three properties of fundamental importance can be singled out: an intentional reintroduction of anthropomorphic, classical members, such as Corinthian pilasters, Ionic colonnettes and a fully developed architrave; the exclusive use of elementary geometrical relationships, and a strong emphasis on spatial centralization. It also ought to be pointed out that the primary members are made of dark *pietra serena* and form a figure drawn on a neutral ground, to obtain an immediate intelligibility. In general the differentiated, hierarchical and integrated form of medieval architecture has been replaced by a simple addition of relatively independent spatial and plastic elements. Symmetry unifies the elements to form a self-sufficient whole which obeys Alberti's principle that "nothing might be added, taken away or altered, but for the worse." A new concept of perfection has motivated the architect.

Eighty years forward in time, a building which marks the culmination of Renaissance architecture, Bramante's Tempietto in S. Pietro in Montorio in Rome (1502), still has the same fundamental properties. The main way in which it differs from the earlier work is in a stronger emphasis on the plastic character of the members; whereas the Sacrestia Vecchia still reflected the skeletal

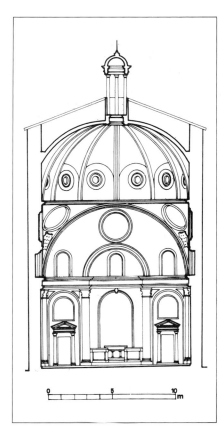

structure of medieval buildings, the Tempietto appears as a plastic body. Although there is no direct prototype in antiquity, these two buildings do reveal a rebirth of important classical properties.

In both examples the spiritualized space of the Middle Ages had given way to a conception of space as a concrete container. This too represents a return to a classical, or more precisely, Roman concept. Renaissance space shows a new wish for homogeneous, geometrical order, concretizing a general belief in harmony and perfection as absolute values. The new intentions manifest themselves on all environmental levels and in connection with all types of building, whether they be ecclesiastical or secular, although not with the same strength. Evidently Renaissance man believed in an ordered cosmos, just like his medieval predecessors, but his interpretation of the concept of order was basically different. Rather than gaining existential security by taking his place within the Kingdom of God, he imagined the cosmos in terms of numbers, and architecture was regarded as a mathematical science which ought to make the cosmic order visible. A new interest in perspective as the means to describe space arose, and the problem of proportion was given primary importance in connection with the question of architectural character. In antiquity proportions were related to the human body, and the Renaissance artists thus found a key to the harmony which is intrinsic to all creation. Their works were experienced as simultaneously cosmic and human. Thus we understand their aversion against Mediaeval verticalism.[2]

Landscape and Settlement

The new image of space manifests itself on the most comprehensive environmental level, that of geography. If we compare medieval maps of the world with maps from the fifteenth century, a significant change is evident.[3] The maps of the Middle Ages did not represent the world as it is, but were illustrations of the Christian image of the world. Usually Jerusalem was placed at the centre,

(1)   M. Dvořák, *Geschichte der italienischen Kunst im Zeitalter der Renaissance* (Munich, 1927).

(2)   See in general R. Wittkower, *Architectural Principles in the Age of Humanism* (London, 1962; New York, 1965).

(3)   See D. Frey, *Gotik und Renaissance* (Augsburg, 1929).

224. *Palma Nova. Plan.*

225. *Francesco di Giorgio: View of an Idea[l]
City. c. 1475-1500. Galleria Nazionale delle
Marche, Urbino.*

226. *Piazza della SS. Annunziata, Florence
1419 and later.*

(4) L. B. Alberti, *Ten Books on Architecture* IV, iii (London, 1738).

(5) See R. Papini, *Francesco di Giorgio architette* (Milan, 1946). The first example of true bastions is, to our knowledge, the fort at Nettuno by Giuliano da Sangallo (1501-3).

and sometimes the earth was represented as the body of Christ with the head in the east, the hands in the north and south, and the feet in the west. Renaissance cartography, in contrast, aimed at a geometrically correct representation, and developed different "projections," which culminated in Mercator's world map (1569). However, this realism did not destroy the general image of a centralized cosmos with the earth as the focus, which was maintained until Copernicus (1543). With its two approaches the Renaissance image of the world unified empirical, homogeneous space and ideal, centralized form.

The image is concretized most strikingly in the notion of an ideal city. Whereas the medieval city was ideal inasmuch as it was a living concretization of the *Civitas Dei,* the Renaissance city aims at ideal form. Scientific studies were made of town design and, although it is not until 1593 that an ideal city was built—Palma Nova, by Savorgnan and Scamozzi—numerous architects published treatises where the problems of the city are analysed with the aim of working out ideal plans. The first and greatest of the theorists, Leone Battista Alberti (1404-72), started with an empirical statement, that "It is certain that the Form of the City and the Distribution of its Parts must be various according to the Variety of Places; since we see it is impossible upon a Hill to lay out an Area whether round or square, or of any other regular Form, with that Ease, that you may upon an open Plain," but arrived at the conclusion that "of all cities the most capacious is the round one."[4] The first plan for an ideal city, Filarete's *Sforzinda* (1464), is in fact based on a circle with a star inscribed, and a piazza with a centralized church in the middle. A treatise by Francesco di Giorgio (1432-1502) offers a multitude of centralized plans for various sites, where the empirical and ideal factors are united. In some of his projects, Francesco di Giorgio also took into consideration the new firearms, and developed better systems of fortifications.[5] The ideal city of the Renaissance no longer expresses a communal form of life, such as the late medieval town, but forms the centre of a small autocratic state. At the centre of the ideal city we therefore

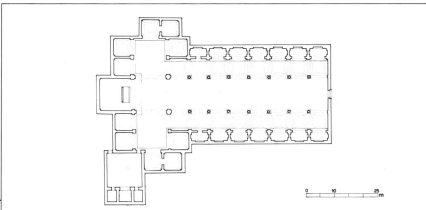

find the palace of the *signore* connected to a large piazza.

Several projects that were realized in part illustrate the Renaissance conception of urban space and the relationship between settlement and surroundings. For example, in the rebuilding of Pienza by Bernardo Rosselino (1459–64), a group of buildings around a piazza is conceived as a single work of art, and the elements are proportionally related to each other. The introduction of a centralized building in the landscape was a normal feature, such as the Bramantesque S. Maria della Consolazione at Todi (1508). The ideal self-sufficiency of the man-made form is here evident; the church could have been located anywhere. Treatment of space in Renaissance architecture led away from the concept of a living urban organism in service of an ideal of pure, formal perfection. The new conception of interior urban space was expressed as a wish for general geometrization, and streets and squares are defined by buildings which seem to consist of the same stereometric units. A programmatic manifestation of the attitude is offered by the famous "cityscapes" by Francesco di Giorgio and Luciano Laurana.

Building

Renaissance architecture is a product of an urban civilization. Like the Gothic cathedral, the leading building types of the Italian *Quattrocento* served the purpose of giving meaning to an urban environment. Renaissance cities no longer embody the concept of an operant *Civitas Dei,* but concretize the image of a mathematically organized universe, and were governed by an autocratic ruler whose residence constituted a new centre of meaning. This does not imply, however, that the church lost its primary importance. The cosmic harmony was still understood as a divine harmony, which was reflected by the centralized state. The church was still the leading building type, but its form had to adapt to the new concept of order.

It has already been suggested that this adaptation consisted in a general geometri-

230. *Donato Bramante: cathedral, Pavia. 1488. Wooden model. Museo del Castello, Pavia.*

231. *Leone Battista Alberti: Malatesta Temple (S. Francesco), Rimini. Presumed plan, 1450.*

(6) After the Sacrestia Vecchia followed Cappella de' Pazzi (1430) and S. Maria degli Angeli (1433, unfinished). The first two are memorials, a fact which should not be forgotten when explaining their centralized form.

(7) Again the centralized plan may be related to the function of the church, as a mausoleum for Sigismondo Malatesta.

(8) For a discussion of the functional problems that arise from centralized and longitudinal plans, see. S. Sinding-Larsen, "Some Functional and Iconographical Aspects of the Centralized Church in the Italian Renaissance," *Acta ad archaeologiam et artium historiam pertinentia,* vol. II (Rome, 1965).

zation, and in a stronger emphasis on centralization, as seen in the pioneer works of Brunelleschi. Brunelleschi did, in fact, build some small churches with a centralized plan,[6] but in his major ecclesiastical buildings, he took the longitudinal basilica as a point of departure. S. Lorenzo in Florence (1421) illustrates his approach: a T-shaped plan of traditional Italian type has been rigorously interpreted in terms of elementary geometrical units, and the three-dimensional articulation serves to translate this plan into an addition of simple stereometric units. A longitudinal aspect is still dominant, as the centralizing effect of the small dome is relatively weak. This design could hardly be satisfying in the long run, and by 1447 Alberti planned to add a Pantheonlike rotunda to the nave of S. Francesco at Rimini.[7] The idea of adding a dominant, centralized space to a longitudinal nave may have been suggested by Florence cathedral where the great dome wanted by Arnolfo di Cambio (1296) and Francesco Talenti (1375) had been executed by Brunelleschi (c. 1420). Quite a long time had to pass, however, before Bramante arrived at a geometrically satisfying integration of longitudinal nave and dominant dome, which he achieved for the cathedral at Pavia (1488). This solution prepared for his magnificent plan for St. Peter's in Rome. At Pavia the width of the dome comprises the nave as well as the aisles. However, the attempts at combining a centralized space with a nave must be considered a concession to practical demands brought forward by the clergy.[8] The interest of the architects above all concentrated on the development of the central plan. This is demonstrated by a series of completed buildings, as well as by numerous projects, such as those of Leonardo da Vinci. The centralized churches of the Italian Renaissance show a much wider range of variation than their Byzantine predecessors. As a result of the new scientific approach to the problem of space, all possible combinations of circular, polygonal and Greek-cross plans with secondary chapels were attempted. The principle of composition used is that of addition; every spatial element conserves a high degree of independence within the whole.

A change in the role of the ruler and the aristocracy produced a new leading building

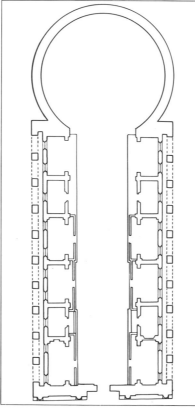

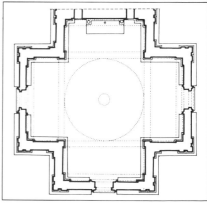

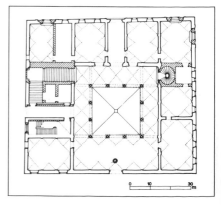

type: the city palace. Whereas the medieval castle had been a stronghold and a symbol of power, the palace of the Renaissance was to be presented in addition as a manifestation of the culture which formed the basis of aristocratic authority. The massive castle of the Middle Ages therefore was geometrized and humanized by introduction of the Classical orders. This process started with Brunelleschi's palaces and culminated with buildings like the Bramantesque Palazzo della Cancelleria in Rome (c. 1489). The fundamental type, developed in Florence during the fifteenth century, can be described as a square, enclosed volume, centred on a *cortile* surrounded by two or three storeys of arcades, and is well illustrated by the Palazzo Medici-Riccardi by Michelozzo (1444–64) and the Palazzo Strozzi by Benedetto da Majano and possibly Giuliano da Sangallo (1489). Basically the city palace was a *family* seat. Through its size and articulation it defined the position of the family in a wider civic context, and was simultaneously enclosed and related to its environment by means of geometrization.

Articulation

As suggested above, Renaissance articulation has two basic aims: geometrization and anthropomorphization. The first aim was satisfied by an exclusive use of elementary geometrical forms and simple mathematical ratios, the second by a reintroduction of the Classical orders. A comparison between a massive, rusticated palace from the *Quattrocento* such as Palazzo Pitti in Florence (after 1457) and the medieval Palazzo Vecchio in the same city (1299–1314)[9] makes the new intentions evident. The later building combines a solid and powerful appearance with the expression of a culture founded on the concept of cosmic harmony. What was a continuous rusticated wall perforated by varied and somewhat irregularly placed windows has become a disciplined, "mathematical" composition. The three storeys of Pitti Palace are individual elements added together, with a succession of large semicircular arches which are perfectly regular. Geometrical discipline prevails, even in the rustication.

The exteriors of palaces of the early *Quattrocento* were not usually subject to the

(9) The Palazzo Vecchio is the work of Arnolfo di Cambio, whereas the Pitti Palace was probably built on a project made by Brunelleschi before his death in 1446. The original project only comprised the seven central bays of the present building. See P. Sanpaolesi, *Brunelleschi* (Milan, 1962), pp. 95 ff.

236. *Filippo Brunelleschi: Palazzo Pitti, Florence. Begun 1458.*

238. *Filippo Brunelleschi: Palazzo di Parte Guelfa, Florence. c. 1420.*

237. *Filippo Brunelleschi: Ospedale degli Innocenti, Florence. Begun 1419, Loggia.*

(10) The idea, however, was not unanimously accepted, as shown by later major palaces such as Pitti Palace and Gondi Palace (Giuliano da Sangallo, 1490). The latter shows a sophisticated differentiation of the rustication of the three storeys which corresponds to the characters of the Classical superim-position.

Classical orders, but anthropomorphic members are found in the *cortile,* as constituent parts of the surrounding loggias. A meaningful distinction is thus made between the somewhat reserved exterior and the more explicitly expressive interior. There are, however, important exceptions to this rule. When Brunelleschi built the Ospedale degli Innocenti in Florence (1419), he gave the building an external loggia of an exceptionally light and elegant character. Considering the public and social function of the building and its urban setting, the solution is natural, as is the use of external (giant!) pilasters in his Palazzo di Parte Guelfa (*c.* 1420). Being the house of a political party, this building had to demonstrate its "content" more directly than the private city palace. Its council hall also shows for the first time in Renaissance architecture the use of Classical pilasters as interior wall articulation. The palace therefore well illustrates the concept of homogeneous, geometrical space.

In about 1450 Alberti superimposed Classical orders on the rusticated façade of the Palazzo Rucellai in Florence, thereby initiating a new phase in Renaissance wall articulation.[10] Underneath, however, the basic design was still a simple accretion of storeys and a regular horizontal succession of bays, but in the Palazzo della Cancelleria in Rome, articulation is varied horizontally as well as vertically. The ground floor serves as a massive basis for two orders of rhythmically disposed pilasters. In spite of the *Quattrocento* restraint which characterizes the façade, it seems to embody a certain organic life when compared to the more schematic and abstract compositions of the early Renaissance. In general, the introduction of the anthropomorphic orders opened up a whole range of expressive possibilities which formed a point of departure for the Mannerist architecture of the following century.

The articulation of churches follows a basically similar development as that of palaces, in spite of the difference in building tasks. Brunelleschi's church interiors are articulated by a regular repetition of classical members which make the spatial geometry visible. The exterior treatment is similar (S. Lorenzo), but relatively less important. Again Alberti made an essential contribution with the invention of the Renaissance basilica

239. *Leone Battista Alberti: Palazzo Rucellai, Florence. 1446-51.*

241. *Palazzo della Cancelleria, Rome. c. 1489.*

240. *Giuliano da Sangallo: S. Maria delle Carceri, Prato. Begun 1484.*

façade in S. Maria Novella in Florence (1456). He did not only use Classical orders and carefully calculated proportions to organize the complex section of the basilica, but introduced volutes to take care of the difficult transition between the lower and upper storeys.[11] Towards the end of his life Alberti also applied the rhythmic articulation mentioned in connection with the Cancelleria palace to the interior of S. Andrea in Mantua (c. 1470). The problem of the church façade received its finest solution with Bramante's introduction of a giant order defining the nave in the parish church at Roccaverano (c. 1510),[12] and in general Bramante's mature work is characterized by a rhythmical and plastic richness unknown to his predecessors.

Renaissance articulation does not usually correspond to the technical structure of the building, as demonstrated by the unfinished S. Maria delle Carceri at Prato by Giuliano da Sangallo (1484), where a massive wall is dressed up with a spurious skeleton. What was aimed at in this building was a typically Renaissance idealization through the use of space, as in the evenly distributed, neutral light of *Quattrocento* interiors.

Santo Spirito

The name of Filippo Brunelleschi has appeared throughout our exposition of the principles of Renaissance architecture. Born in Florence in 1377, Brunelleschi was the first great protagonist of the new style and until his death in 1418 was indisputably the leading architect of his time. After a somewhat unfortunate start as a sculptor, he worked mainly as a military engineer until 1418, when he won the competition for the execution of the dome of the cathedral of S. Maria del Fiore in Florence. Brunelleschi is also credited with the invention of scientific perspective (c. 1415). Traditionally Brunelleschi was considered the first real architect in history: Whereas the architects of the Middle Ages were contributors to a collective work, Brunelleschi was considered the first individual creative genius. Today, knowing that medieval architects were highly educated men possessed with creative genius, we may with good reason maintain that the history of architecture has always been brought

(11) See Wittkower, *op. cit.*, pp. 36 ff.

(12) See A. Bruschi, *Bramante Architetto* (Bari, 1969), pp. 237 ff. The design became the point of departure for Palladio's church façades.

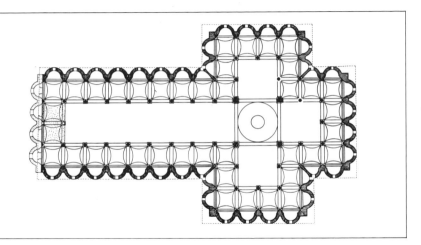

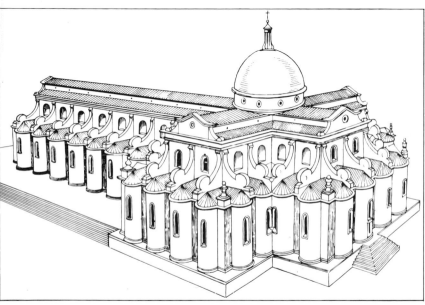

242. *S. Maria Novella, Florence. Façade by Leone Battista Alberti, begun 1456.*

243. *Filippo Brunelleschi: S. Spirito, Florence. Begun 1444. Ground plan of the original project of 1436.*

244. *Filippo Brunelleschi: S. Spirito, Florence. Hypothetical reconstruction of the original project by Sanpaolesi.*

245. *Filippo Brunelleschi: S. Spirito, Florence. Interior.*

forward by creative personalities, and that what Brunelleschi represents is simply a new social role.

Among his works the church of S. Spirito in Florence may be considered the most mature achievement. The project was ready in 1436 (possibly already in 1432), but the construction was begun only in 1444. As a result the finished building is somewhat different from the original design, mainly in the exterior, where the continuous succession of semi-circular apsidioles planned by Brunelleschi has been incorporated in conventional straight walls. Brunelleschi did not intend to give the building a façade of any special significance, but a basilica front with a central portal was added after 1475. On the other hand, the interior was probably executed according to the original design, and only a main altar from 1599 disturbs the exceptionally harmonious effect. The church is of considerable dimensions, having an interior length of 97 metres (318 feet).

S. Spirito is a masterpiece of geometrical planning. The design clearly derives from the earlier church of S. Lorenzo, but represents a decisive step forward. The whole plan is based on a simple square, and, as has convincingly been shown by Luporini, the section of the building is based on the same module.[13] It is shaped as a Latin cross with a dome over the crossing, and with continuous aisles surrounding the whole space. The basic square is repeated in regular succession in these aisles, whereas the crossing, the transepts and the chancel consist of one quadruple square each. The nave comprises four of the larger squares.[14] The aisles are accompanied throughout by semi-circular apsidioles. Except for the longer nave, the plan is perfectly symmetrical around the crossing. In fact, S. Spirito ought to be characterized as an "elongated central building." Its centralization is strengthened by the division of the end walls of the nave, transepts and chancel into *two* bays, which denies the axes of the cross plan the function of paths.

Although the plan of S. Spirito may resemble the disposition of the medieval

(13) E. Luporini, *Brunelleschi* (Milan, 1964).

(14) Unfortunately the aisle along the entrance wall, planned by Brunelleschi, was omitted in the execution, thereby creating a serious break in the regular system.

246. *Leone Battista Alberti: S. Andrea Mantua. Designed 1470. Ground plan.*

247. *Leone Battista Alberti: S. Andrea, Mantua. Tentative reconstruction of the façade (Norberg-Schulz).*

248. *Leone Battista Alberti: S. Andrea, Mantua.*

(15) Sanpaolesi, *op. cit.*, plate D.

(16) A splendid critical edition in two volumes, edited by Paolo Portoghesi, was published in Milan 1966. The English edition by James Leoni (1729) was reissued in London in 1955 with a foreword and notes by Joseph Rykwert.

(17) At the same time the four wide pillars of the crossing on which the dome rests were strengthened, disturbing the continuity of the nave, transepts and chancel. For a detailed discussion of S. Andrea, see C. Norberg-Schulz, "Le ultime intenzioni di Alberti," *Acta ad archaeologiam et artium historiam pertinentia*, vol. I (Oslo, 1962).

(18) In his ninth book Alberti recommends the ratios 1:1, 1:2, 1:3, 2:3 and 3:4, and refers to the theory of musical harmonies.

pilgrimage churches, in particular Santiago de Compostela, the meaning is different. In S. Spirito, the axes do not represent paths of salvation coming from all the four corners of the world, but form part of a centralized, self-sufficient symbolic system. Whereas the church does have a longitudinal nave, this should be seen as a compromise with traditional and functional demands.

Inside the articulation consists in a visualization of the geometrical system by means of members in dark *pietra serena*, which have figural character in relation to the secondary wall surfaces of white plaster. The result is one of the most serene and perfect interiors in existence. The original outside of S. Spirito has been reconstructed by Sanpaolesi.[15] The centralized plan is here expressed by the absence of proper façades, which have been replaced by a continuous encircling row of apsidioles. These prepare for a relatively small dome which is thus related to the wings below, and manages to function as the dominant centre of a harmonious whole. In spite of the additive principle of composition, S. Spirito appears as a unified, profoundly meaningful totality. With admirable skill Brunelleschi managed to create a consummate masterpiece and paved the way for decades of fertile architectural design.

Sant'Andrea in Mantua

Even more than Brunelleschi, Leone Battista Alberti (1404–72) represents the new social role of the artist. (As we shall see later, this role is intimately related to the more general Renaissance image of man as *uomo universale*.) Alberti was not only a creative architect, but also the first theorist of Renaissance art and architecture, a versatile man of letters, and in addition is supposed to have been an athlete with considerable physical capacities. His *Ten Books on Architecture* (*De re aedificatoria*) were written about 1450 and still remain one of the most illuminating and inspiring books on the subject.[16] In these treatises Alberti sought to replace the Classical exposition of Vitruvius with a more thorough and systematic work. His theory was founded on practical insight as well as

an extensive knowledge of the architecture of antiquity, which is also reflected in his architectural projects. His unfinished façade of S. Francesco at Rimini, thus, is inspired by the Roman triumphal arch, and the original façade of S. Sebastiano at Mantua (1460) was derived from late Roman temple façades. As in general Alberti had a more conscious relationship to history than Brunelleschi, and was less involved with the problems of additive geometry, his works are more varied and allow for a wider range of meaningful characterization. However, because of his many activities, his production remained small.

The church of S. Andrea in Mantua was planned in 1470 and construction was started in 1472, shortly after Alberti's death. The exterior was never finished, and is today partly hidden by houses. Alberti can hardly have intended the somewhat confusing interior decoration nor the tall dome which was added by Juvarra after 1732.[17] Wide main spaces without aisles form the Latin cross shape. In place of aisles the nave is accompanied by alternating open and closed chapels which form a rhythmical succession. The rhythm is repeated in transepts and chancel, and the latter is closed off by an apse. All the main spaces are covered by tunnel-vaults, whereas the crossing probably should have had a simple hemispherical dome, like those of the small closed chapels. In general the disposition corresponds to his indications in the seventh book of *De re aedificatoria*, and the proportions also correspond to his theories. Where Brunelleschi had regular repetitions, various ratios constitute a meaningful succession: The intervals of the pilasters of the narthex façade have the relation 1:3; in the nave the tension is somewhat smaller, with a ratio of 1:2. The end walls of the transepts show the ratio 2:3, and in the apse, finally, the tension has calmed down to a "perfect" 1:1.[18] Exterior and interior are thus unified by means of a repetition of the same wall motif, at the same time as the different parts of the building are proportionally differentiated and lead towards the "ideal" articulation of the apse.

In current literature on Renaissance architecture the plan of S. Andrea is usually shown with one narthex only. Undoubtedly the original plan was to have similar entrances

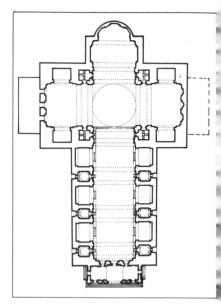

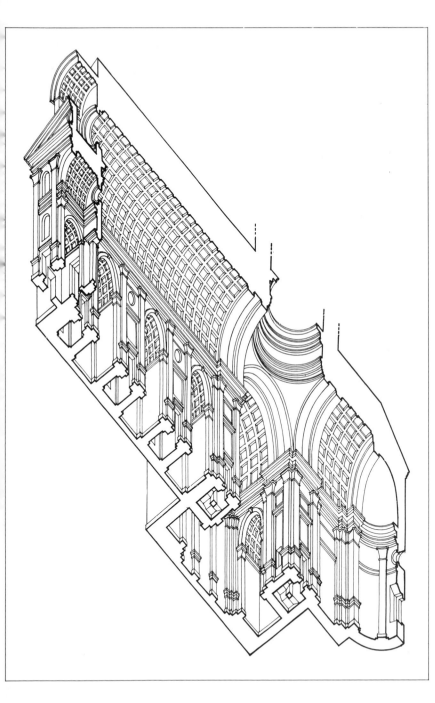

to the transepts as well, and on the northern side there is, in fact, an unfinished narthex and transept façade. From this it appears that the church was intended as an elongated centralized building with three identical façades. S. Andrea thus belongs to the great tradition of Apostle churches, and the use of the form of the Roman triumphal arch for the narthex façades ought to be understood in this context. It is also important to point out that the front, which is usually described as the façade of the church, is only a part of the originally planned elevation. The façade proper is behind the narthex and it was intended to have lateral volutes and a crowning triangular pediment.[19]

In general, S. Andrea represents a Renaissance interpretation of ancient symbolic themes. Centre and path are again brought together, and through its deliberate use of Roman motifs the building is a major example of the rebirth of Classical culture. The idea of using proportions as a means of organization is truly Renaissance. Proportions imply that dimensions are experienced simultaneously, that is, belong to a homogeneous space. Alberti thus adopted Brunelleschi's space concept and made it a flexible instrument of meaningful expression.

San Pietro in Vaticano

Donato Bramante was born in Urbino in 1444 and was active in Northern Italy until 1500 when he moved to Rome. During his Milanese period he rebuilt the church of S. Maria presso S. Satiro (1482), a building which underlines the fundamental importance of centralization in *Quattrocento* architecture. On the narrow site it was impossible to fit in a central plan, but Bramante used perspective illusion to make the T-shaped interior appear as a fully developed centralized church.[20]

In 1503 he was appointed architect to Pope Julius II and directed the planning and construction of the new church of St. Peter's until his death in 1514. This building marks the culmination of the development of the centrally planned Renaissance church.

We possess two closely related plans by Bramante for the church. In both he inter-

(19) The large external vault which today protects the circular window over the narthex is an addition from 1702.

(20) A. Bruschi, *op. cit.*, p. 134.

250. Donato Bramante: drawing for the ground plan of St. Peter's (A20). 1506. Gabinetto dei Disegni, Uffizi, Florence.
251. Donato Bramante: first ground plan for St. Peter's. c. 1506 Gabinetto dei Disegni Uffizi, Florence.

252. Donato Bramante: first ground plan for St. Peter's. c. 1506.
253. Caradosso: commemorative medallion showing the exterior of St. Peter's according to Bramante's plan. 1506.

(21) The *pentyrigion* also appears in a drawing by Filarete.

(22) See O. H. Förster, *Bramante* (Vienna, 1956), fig. 120.

preted the central plan as a *pentyrigion* with towers added at the four corners,[21] and this is how the church appears on the foundation medal of 1506. In both plans a large Greek cross forms the core of a complex spatial organism. The Greek cross is modified by a considerable widening of the crossing, to make the dome function as a dominant centre. In the corners between the arms of the cross for smaller Greek cross units are added. They appear as complete centralized churches, at the same time as their inner arms form a square ambulatory around the main dome. Octagonal sacristies surmounted by tall towers were added between the outer arms of the small units. The main difference between the first and the second project is a general strengthening of the load-bearing piers and the addition of semicircular narthexes around the four apses of the main space. In general the composition may be characterized as a hierarchical addition of complete spatial units. The result is an organism which combines clarity and richness in a more convincing way than perhaps any other project from the history of Western architecture.

It is possible that Bramante planned to add a longitudinal nave to the central plan. Such an addition was possible without disturbing the unity of the design, and consisted in extending one of the arms of the main space, as well as two arms of the small Greek-cross units to form aisles.[22] If a nave was intended, it may be considered a concession to functional demands, or an expression of the new interest for movement in space coming to the fore during the *Cinquecento*.

The interior of Bramante's final project should have been articulated by giant pilasters, and crowned by a great semispherical dome resting on a columnar drum. The serene and monumental space would have been a most convincing concretization of the Renaissance image of cosmic harmony. As in S. Spirito the exterior would not have had any real façade and would have been of secondary importance. The great dome, however, would have acted as a meaningful centre, not only to the city of Rome, but to the Christian as a whole.

It is not necessary to relate here in full the complex history of the further planning of

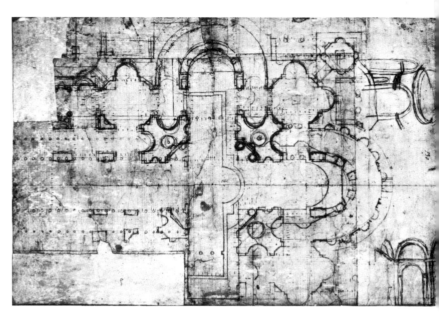

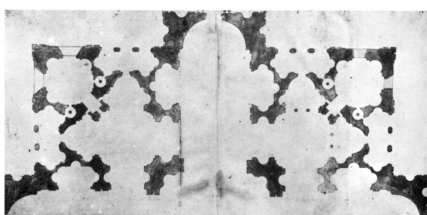

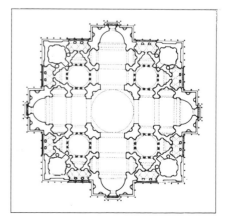

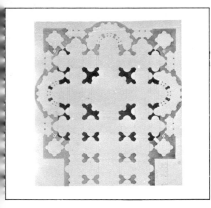

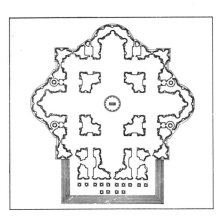

254. *Donato Bramante: second ground plan for St. Peter's (after Förster).*
255. *Michelangelo: ground plan for St. Peter's (redrawn from Dupérac). 1546.*
256. *Etienne Dupérac: section of St. Peter's as designed by Michelangelo. 1569.*
257. *Michelangelo: St. Peter's, Rome. 1546-64; dome completed 1591. Apse.*

St. Peter's after Bramante's death in 1514, beyond noting Michelangelo's changes after he took over as architect-in-charge in 1546. First of all he radically altered the character of the plan by cutting away the outer arms of the small Greek-cross units and the sacristies planned by Bramante. In doing this he transformed the outer boundary of the space into a continuous, enclosing wall, and substituted one coherent "muscular" body for Bramante's relatively independent volumes. Articulation is used throughout to express a conflict between vertical and horizontal forces.[23] The former are stated with vigorous power by means of a continuous series of colossal pilasters surrounding the whole building, and the upward thrust is repeated in the coupled columns of the drum and the ribs of the dome. But the vertical forces are everywhere counteracted by horizontal-circumferential ones. As a result, the harmonious, static Renaissance character intended by Bramante is changed into a dynamic whole permeated by symbolic tensions. The implicit meaning is revealed by Michelangelo's project for the dome, where the upward movement of the interior articulation ends in a *dark* lantern. As shown in Dupérac's section of Michelangelo's project, a thin ceiling should have been inserted between the dome and the upper part of the lantern, thus impeding the divine light from entering the interior of the church.[24]

(23) See R. Wittkower, "Zur Peterskuppel Michelangelos," *Zeitschrift für Kunstgeschichte*, vol. II, 1933.

(24) The interpretation is confirmed by a poem by Michelangelo which reads as follows:

"Squarcia 'l vel tu, Signor. Rompi quel muro che con la sua durezza ne ritarda il sol della tua luce al mondo spenta!"

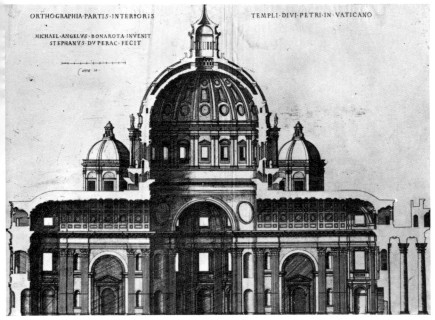

ORTHOGRAPHIA·PARTIS·INTERIORIS — TEMPLI·DIVI·PETRI·IN·VATICANO
MICHAEL·ANGELVS·BONAROTA·INVENIT
STEPHANVS·DV PERAC·FECIT

Ferrara

If we want to experience the urban environment and the general spatial character intended by *Quattrocento* architects, Ferrara is the only grand-scale example existing, and fortunately it represents a very interesting and well-preserved Renaissance milieu. Its origins go back to Roman (and perhaps Etruscan) times. During the Middle Ages it developed into a walled town, extending along a branch of the river Po; to a large extent it has been preserved. Its unified character is due to the frequent appearance of characteristic architectural motifs, as well as the consequent use of brick as a building material. An urban centre is formed by the cathedral (1135 *ff.*), the palace of the *signore*

258. Biagio Rossetti: Palazzo Roverella, Ferrara. c. 1508.

259. Ferrara. Plan.

260. Biagio Rossetti: Palazzo dei Diamanti, Ferrara. 1493. The palace (right) and crossing streets.

261. Biagio Rossetti: Cristoforo alla Certosa, Ferrara. 1498. Interior.

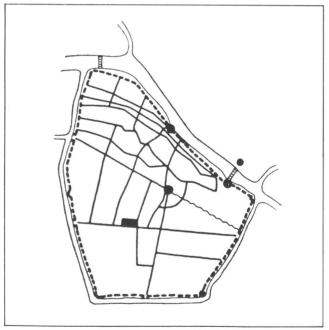

and the market. Close to the centre, on the northern periphery, the grandiose Castello Estense was built after 1385. In 1492 the Duke Ercole I d'Este commissioned a city extension towards the north, the Addizione Erculea. The project was handled by the talented local architect Biagio Rossetti (c. 1447–1516), who served as city planner as well as designer of numerous palaces and churches.[25] He produced an extraordinarily unified cityscape which translates the character of medieval Ferrara into the geometrical language of the *Quattrocento*. It was characterized by Jacob Burckhardt as "the first modern city in Europe."

Rossetti's designs show an interesting combination of ideal plan and empirical accommodation to local circumstances. Instead of conceiving the city extension as a regular geometrical figure, Rossetti followed the natural topographical conditions of the area, and incorporated small suburbs which already existed outside the medieval town. The perimeter of his plan is therefore somewhat irregular. According to contemporaneous theories, a radial street pattern centred on the Castello Estense would have represented an "ideal" solution.[26] However, Rossetti divided the area into four domains by means of two main streets crossing each other approximately at right angles. The north-south axis *(cardo)* leads from the castle to a city gate, whereas the east-west axis *(decumanus)* unites two other gates. Between the main streets, Rossetti introduced another, secondary system of approximately orthogonal streets which joins the new area to the already existing paths of the medieval town. His intention evidently was to make the whole city become one living organism, and the distribution of the main buildings and the new, spacious piazza has to be seen in relation to this intention. However, empirical considerations did not deny the city extension a regular and harmonious character. In spite of the accommodations, the street system is *experienced* as orthogonal, and the main axes form a most efficient means of organization.

The new streets were only in part defined by buildings. Even today large open areas remain within the Addizione. The buildings are therefore secondary to the streets and spaces; the city is conceived as a spatial system. This becomes particularly evident when we consider how Rossetti employed pilasters and balconies on the corners of the adjacent buildings to define the crossing of the streets. Even the most important building of the new town, the Palazzo dei Diamanti (1493 *ff.*), is accommodated to the crossing. The palace as such is a singular case of Renaissance geometrization: The natural symbol of rustication has been transformed into an abstract, ideal pattern of diamond shapes.

Rossetti's versatility is demonstrated when we compare the ideal, aristocratic refuge of the Palazzo dei Diamanti with the elegant arcades around the Piazza Nuova, or with the late Palazzo Roverella (c. 1508) which is situated on the main street between the medieval town and the Addizione. The Roverella Palace is the only building by Rossetti which is articulated by means of a grid of superimposed Classical pilasters; evidently as an accommodation to the public space it faces. The original distribution of windows is inspired by medieval Ferrarese models, at the same time as it points towards the subtle tensions of Mannerist façades. Rossetti's churches, finally, represent interesting variations on *Quattrocento* motifs. In general they are based on the addition of stereometrical units introduced by Brunelleschi, but the interiors are more varied (although less pure), and the articulate exteriors have an active urbanistic function. The consequent use of longitudinal plans confirms Rossetti's empirical approach to design.

Space Conception and Development

To understand the space conception of Renaissance architecture, it is useful to start with a basic aim it has in common with Gothic architecture: the concretization of the cosmic order. Like his medieval predecessors Renaissance man believed in an ordered universe and in divine perfection. But his interpretation was quite different. The visual logic of Gothic architecture is of a functional kind, and the single members can only be understood as parts of a working totality. In the Renaissance we find a different kind of logic: the logic of absolute and eternal geometrical order. Perfection of form replaced functional meaning. According to Alberti the most perfect, and hence most divine form is the circle. Centralization is therefore implicit in the concept of geometrical order. The concept also implies that every part of a building should appear as a clear, easily recognizable and rather independent form. As a result Renaissance space becomes homogeneous, and the buildings of the period static, self-sufficient compositions where "nothing might be added, taken away or altered, but for the worse." In this way the work of architecture became a symbol of the cosmic order. As late as 1570 Palladio wrote: "If we consider this beautiful machine of the world, with how many wonderful ornaments it is filled, and how the heavens, by their continual revolutions, change the seasons according as nature requires, and their motion preserves itself by the sweetest harmony of temperature; we cannot doubt, but that the little temples we make, ought to resemble this very great one, which, by his immense goodness, was perfectly compleated with one word of his."[27]

Homogeneous space is a fundamentally new environmental image, which, for the first time in the history of architecture, allowed for formal integration of the different environmental levels. Whereas the Romans applied the same symbolic motif, that is, the intersecting axes, to all levels without a concept of a homogeneous spatial continuum, Renaissance space is basically the same on all levels. Space was treated as a kind of substance which is structured by means of geometry and described visually by means of perspective. The concept of homogeneous space, however, did not prevent meaningful spatial differentiation. Our examples have shown how different buildings were given different character, according to the private, public or sacred nature of the task. This was achieved by the use of more or less "perfect" forms, and by means of meaningful wall articulation. Without ceasing to be part of a homogeneous space, a building may, for instance, be characterized as more or less enclosed. Alberti was fully aware of the need for meaningful differentiation, and

(25) See in general B. Zevi, *Biagio Rossetti* (Turin, 1960).

(26) For a detailed analysis see *ibid.*, pp. 143 ff.

(27) A. Palladio, *The Four Books of Architecture*, Book IV, Preface (London, 1736).

(28) Alberti, *op. cit.*, IX, viii.

(29). See J. White, *The Birth and Rebirth of Pictorial Space* (London and Boston, 1967).

(30) Sedlmayr characterizes this change with the words Gott*mensch* (Gothic) and *Gott*mensch (Renaissance). See H. Sedlmayr, *Verlust der Mitte* (Salzburg, 1948), pp. 223 ff.

(31) Sedlmayr, *op. cit.*, p. 226.

(32) Alberti, *op. cit.*, VI, ii.

(33) E. Forssman, *Dorish, jonisch, korintisch* (Uppsala, 1961), p. 20.

(34) Alberti, *op. cit.*, VI, ii.

sought to represent a hierarchy of building tasks through a hierarchy of forms. He maintained that the most "perfect" forms should be reserved for the church, and that public buildings in general should be executed in the strictest conformity with his formal principles, recommending deviations from these rules for private houses.[28]

The Renaissance concept of space developed in Florence at the beginning of the fifteenth century.[29] It was anticipated by the so-called "proto-Renaissance" which is distinguished by the use of Classical members and by a general clarity of composition. Byzantine influences have also been invoked to explain the Renaissance ideal of centralized static form. And, in fact, centre, circle and heavenly dome are basic forms in both architectural languages. However, these forms become quite inevitable if one wants to interpret the concept of cosmic harmony in terms of geometry. (It is interesting to note in this context that the architects who "created" Byzantine architecture, Anthemios and Isidorus, were both mathematicians.) Renaissance architecture does not possess the dematerialization and the spiritualized space basic to Byzantine architecture. The boundary-dissolving double-shell structure, thus, was replaced by an addition of clearly defined, self-sufficient volumes, and the shimmering wall surface by substantial, anthropomorphic articulation.

Meaning and Architecture

The first time we encountered the concept of ideal, perfect form was when we related Greek architecture to Plato's theory of archetypes. For Plato "cosmos," "order" and "beauty" were synonyms; and Pythagoras interpreted cosmic harmony with the words "all is number." With its idealistic forms the existential image of the Renaissance was

Platonic as well as Christian—in fact a synthesis of the two. During the Gothic age, God was envisaged as close to man. Only a small step was needed to change the image of the human God into the image of the divine human being,[30] and in the Renaissance divine perfection no longer consisted in the transcendence of nature, but was found in nature itself. Natural beauty was understood as an expression of divine truth, and human creativity was given an importance which approached the creative power of God himself. The self-assurance implicit in the new interpretation of the relationship between man and God actually brought about an enormous liberation of human creativity. Man experienced himself as great, as *uomo universale,* and apotheosis and ascension became main themes of Renaissance iconography. The adaptation of the triumphal arch for the façade of the church (Alberti) is significant in this connection. In general, "this does not signify a paganization of Christianity, but a Christianization of pagan antiquity."[31]

The reintroduction of the Classical orders in architecture has to be seen against this background. As anthropomorphic symbols they no longer represented a natural world which had to be negated by man, but became means to endow buildings with divine beauty. Alberti actually distinguished between two types of aesthetic quality in a building: beauty and ornament.[32] "Beauty" consists in the "harmony of all the parts," and is the result of "proportion and connection"; in other words, of the geometrization discussed above. "Ornament" is something added and means an "improvement to beauty." Wall articulation, such as rustication and Classical detail, belonged to the category of ornament. Alberti himself said that the column is the principal ornament in all architecture, but he did not use the Classical orders for the characterization of different building tasks. Bramante, however, brought back to life the

Vitruvian concept of characters, and chose the Doric Order for his Tempietto which was erected on the spot where the heroic martyr St. Peter is supposed to have been crucified. In so doing he initiated the deliberate Christianization of the iconography of the classical gods.[33] Renaissance architecture thereby received a new psychological dimension which was to become a main preoccupation to the architects of the *Cinquecento.*

In a certain sense the psychological dimension was present from the beginning of the Renaissance epoch, but to start with it only presented itself as a general freedom of choice. Renaissance man was not automatically divine: He had to prove his divinity through moral action. According to Pico della Mirandola man has an indeterminate nature, and may degenerate into the lower brutish forms of life, or he may be reborn into the higher forms which are divine. Choice naturally brings about doubt, but during the *Quattrocento* man still believed in his triumphant, creative powers. This belief in man's ability to conquer the dark side of existence is well expressed by Alberti, who wrote: "Beauty will have such an effect even upon an enraged enemy, that it will disarm his anger, and prevent him from offering any injury: insomuch as I will be bold to say, that there can be no greater security to any work against violence and injury, than beauty and dignity."[34] Alberti considered man's primary aim to be to create beauty and to live a dignified life, and that he was allowed to be proud of himself if he thus realized himself. Culture, therefore, was the primary basis of Renaissance authority—a humanist culture founded on the belief in man's moral and intellectual powers. In this sense it signified a rebirth of Greek antiquity, but the new concept of homogeneous space, however, is not found in antiquity. Here the Renaissance concretized that synthesis of Christianity and Platonism which forms its true core.

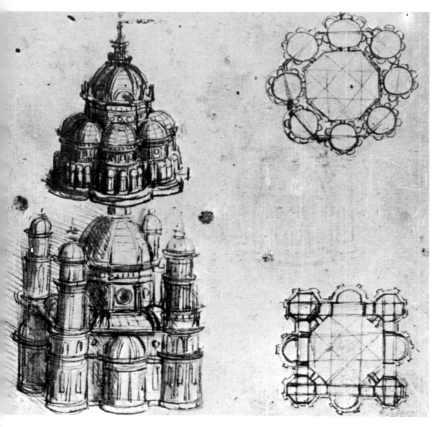

262.   Leonardo da Vinci: architectural drawing.
c. 1490. Bibliothèque de l'Institut de France,
Paris, MS. B. f. 25v.

263.   Raphael Sanzio: The School of Athens.
1509-11. Vatican, Rome.

8. Mannerist Architecture

(1)   After Raphael's
death Antonio da San-
gallo was in charge of
the construction. The
original project is known
from one of his draw-
ings. Less than half of
the originally planned
villa was built. See M.
Bafile, *Il giardino di Villa
Madama* (Rome, 1942).

Introduction

After the serene perfection of the *Quattro-cento,* the architecture of the following cen-tury appears as its antithesis. Harmony and order are gone, and the forms become charged with tension, conflict and experi-ment. Although the same Classical language is used, the existential meanings concretized by the works of art are different. This funda-mental change in intention has already been discussed in relation to Michelangelo's transformation of Bramante's plan for St. Peter's. Whereas the original plan con-cretized a harmonious and unitary image of the world, Michelangelo introduced an at-mosphere of doubt, conflict and tragedy which is hardly found before in the history of art. It seems that man for the first time had become conscious of his existential prob-lem. And, in fact, the basic phenomenon of the sixteenth century is the disintegration of the world order.

During the *Cinquecento* conception of space undergoes a profound transformation. The idea of a general spatial continuity is maintained, but where before there was a static addition of relatively independent, "perfect" units, now there is a dynamic inter-play of contrasting elements. The change be-comes evident if we take a look at the plan for Villa Madama (1517) built on the slopes of Monte Mario in Rome by Bramante's pupil Raphael (1483–1520).[1] Three important in-novations make Villa Madama a truly revolu-tionary project: a deliberate development of a new building type—the *villa suburbana*—a new active interplay between man-made and natural environment, and a new dynamic organization of the interior spaces. The spatial disposition is based on two orthog-onal axes which define the main directions of the site. Where the axes intersect, there is a circular *cortile* which forms the centre of the whole composition. The entrance is situated on the transverse axis. It is flanked by round towers, and gives access to a rec-tangular forecourt. Proceeding along the axis, a wide flight of stairs leads up to a slightly narrower vestibule with aisles and, further on, to a corridor. The space, thus, contracts as we move on, but only to be released again in the great rotunda of the *cortile*. Here we experience a choice: either

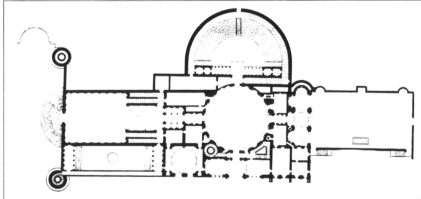

264. *Raphael Sanzio: Villa Madama, Rome.*
Begun 1517. Aerial view.

265. *Raphael Sanzio: Villa Madama, Rome.*
Ground plan.

266. *Raphael Sanzio: Villa Madama, Rome.*
Loggia on the garden.

267. *Raphael Sanzio: Villa Madama, Rome.*

268. *Gianpaolo Pannini:* View of the Farnese
Gardens. 18th-century print.

269. *Giacomo da Vignola: Palazzo Farnese,*
Caprarola. 1559. Aerial view.

to go into nature through the theatre to the left; experience nature as panorama from the *belvedere* to the right; or proceed along the axis to the "tamed" nature of a long *parterre,* which is actively related to the building by means of an open loggia. The static, symbolic space of Renaissance architecture, thus, has been transformed into a dynamic occupation of the environment. It is possible that a series of garden spaces were to join the building along the sloping main axis, as shown in a reconstruction by Bafile.[2]

The new approach to the problems of space encountered in Villa Madama, and in other works by Bramante's successors, was accompanied by a radical transformation of plastic articulation. Articulation was no longer used merely to visualize stereometric relationships, but became a means to express a multitude of interacting and conflicting characters. The reintroduction of the Classical orders made this possible, and they were usually employed together with symbolic rustication, illustrating the problematic relationship between man and nature. The psychological dimension discovered in classical Greece was thus revived, as was the recognition of natural forces and individual places. In general the art of the sixteenth century asks for another kind of human participation. Art becomes an object of emotional experience and is used to express man's situation in the world, rather than an ideal image. In this sense the *Cinquecento* initiated the modern approach to life and art, and we do not need any explanation to grasp the deep human content of the best works of the period.

Landscape and Settlement

For many centuries man had concentrated his attention on the general, cosmic aspects of nature. Accordingly, his settlements represented an ideal image, rather than an interaction with local natural forces. The early Renaissance garden still retained its medieval character as *hortus conclusus,* but was geometrized to express the image of an ideal nature, forming a complement to the ideal city of the period. During the sixteenth century, this concept of static perfection was

(2) *Ibid.,* plates VIII, IX.

270. Domenico Fontana: Villa Montalto, Rome. 1570. From a print of the period.

271. Sixtus V's plan for Rome. 1585. Reconstruction (Giedion).

(3) G. C. Argan, "Giardino e parco," *Enciclopedio Universale dell 'Arte,* vol. VI (Florence, 1958), p. 159.

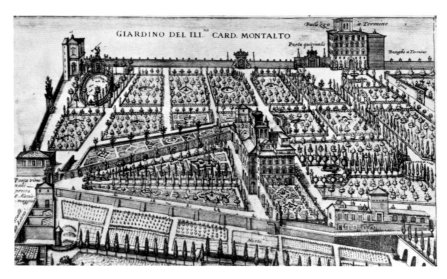

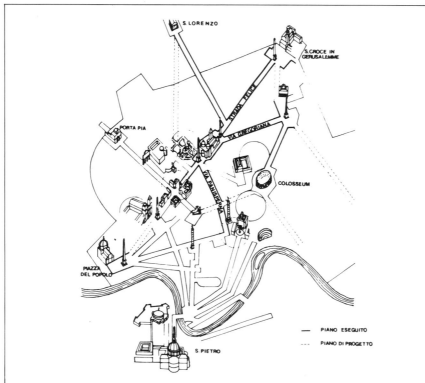

replaced by the idea of a fantastic and mysterious world consisting of a variety of places. "The idea of 'regular' nature was now superseded by that of 'capricious' nature, full of 'inventions' and of the unpredictable. . . . The idea of a garden as a wonderful, fantastic place, perhaps even magical and enchanted, led to the breaking down of walls and fences, and to the transformation of the garden into a group of different places, each designed in relation to human feelings."[3] In several of the villas of the sixteenth century some basic characters began to be established which were to have a fundamental importance for further development: the decorative garden consisting of flower *parterres;* the extension of the function of dwelling in a *bosquet* made up of hedges and other "tamed" elements of nature; and the introduction of free nature in a *selvatico* ("wilderness"). In the Villa Montalto in Rome, built in 1570 by Domenico Fontana for Sixtus V before he became pope, all these elements are present, as well as a new pronounced desire for dynamic spatial integration. From the side entrance near S. Maria Maggiore, a trident branched off to define the *palazzetto* and its lateral *parterres.* The main axis continued through the building, crossing a transverse axis and ending at a distant *point-de-vue.* However, the relationship between the meaningful domains and the system of nodes and paths is still somewhat undecided. As a rule the *villa suburbana* is situated where the public world of the city and the natural world of the garden and landscape meet. The private enclosed palace, thus, is transformed into a spatially active link between the basic domains.

In 1585 Pope Sixtus V introduced a grand plan for the urban transformation of Rome. Its principal aim was to connect the main religious focuses of the city by means of wide straight streets. Main intersections were marked by obelisks which not only introduce a vertical accent, but serve as "axes" for the change of direction of the streets. Sixtus V incorporated the Roman columns of Trajan and Marcus Aurelius in his scheme, topping them with statues of St. Peter and St. Paul. Earlier fragments of regular planning were also integrated in the plan, such as the trident of Piazza del Popolo, where

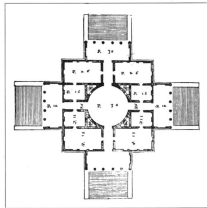

three streets branch out to connect the main city gate with different urban districts. The new streets planned by Sixtus V also structured the large, abandoned areas between the medieval town and the Aurelian wall, and in general, the plan gave a new coherence to the city. The isolated nodes of the past were united to form a network, in which the role of the individual element as part of a general religious system was expressed. Sixtus's plan made Rome the prototype of the basic unit of the Baroque architecture of the following century: the capital city. The whole area of Rome was imbued with ideological value; it became a real *città santa*. Whereas the cities of the Middle Ages and the Renaissance were static and enclosed worlds, the new capital city became the centre of forces extending far beyond its borders.

Exterior space was made expressive and dynamic, and single active elements were gradually integrated into a coherent system. This implies that the space between the buildings became the most important constituent element of the urban totality—a conception which was potentially present in the homogeneous space of Renaissance architecture. It was realized in Rossetti's plan for Ferrara, and dynamically interpreted in the plan of Sixtus V for Rome. The movement, however, is still rather schematic and lacks the organic, pulsating quality found in the plans of the Baroque epoch. Mannerist space is characterized by a simple, directed movement in depth, as demonstrated in the Uffizi palace by Vasari (1560).

Building

The interest in the character of place and the relationship between a building and its surroundings made the villa a building type of primary importance. Whereas the early villas of the *Quattrocento* were relatively enclosed buildings, a fundamentally new type was developed by Peruzzi shortly after 1500.[4] His Villa Farnesina near the Tiber in Rome (1508–10) has an entrance façade with a *cour d'honneur* and an open loggia between the wings, while the garden front is a simple straight wall with an exit in the

(4) The first true villa, as opposed to a medieval country seat, was Villa Medici in Fiesole by Michelozzo (1458-61). The horseshoe-shaped plan was introduced in the villa Le Volte near Siena, possibly by Peruzzi (c. 1500-1505). See C. L. Frommel, *Die Farnesina* (Berlin, 1961).

276. *Palazzo Borghese. Rome. Begun by Martino Longhi the Elder, 1586; continued by Flaminio Ponzio, 1607. Court.*

278. *Rocco Lurago: Palazzo Doria-Tursi, Genoa. Begun 1564. Ground plan.*

280. *Typical plans of baroque churches: centralized longitudinal space and elongated central space. (Norberg-Schulz.)*

277. *Andrea Palladio: Chiesa del Redentore, Venice. Begun 1577.*

279. *Giacomo da Vignola: S. Anna dei Palafrenieri, Rome. Designed 1572. Ground plan.*

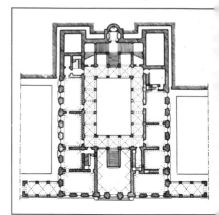

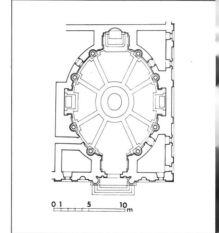

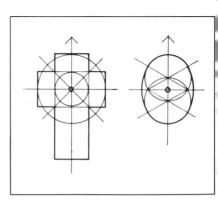

middle. The resulting horseshoe-shaped plan was to become the basic scheme of the villas and great residences of the Baroque period, and in this respect the Farnesina represents a major typological innovation. However, its exterior articulation is still a pure example of Renaissance visualization of proportional stereometry.

The horseshoe-shaped villa was further developed and varied by Andrea Palladio. This architect's oeuvre is particularly rich and includes many types, of which the Villa Rotunda in Vicenza (1570) is especially famous. Here the subordinate spaces of a centralized plan are proportionally related to form a rhythmical group, a scheme which goes beyond the additive repetition of the early Renaissance. The Rotunda's disposition appears conservative, but this was in reality a function of the surrounding landscape, as shown by Palladio's own words: "and therefore, as it enjoys from every part most beautiful views, some of which are limited, some more extended, and others that terminate with the horizon; there are loggias made on all the four fronts."[5] Palladio, in fact, describes his projects in relation to the different sites or situations in question, and thus proves to be a true Cinquecento architect, in spite of his preoccupation with ideal form.

Although the city palace was a more conservative building task than the villa, it was considerably developed during the sixteenth century. The static, self-sufficient volume of the early Renaissance was gradually opened up, and the interior more actively related to its environment. The first step was to join the cortile to a garden behind and to a spacious vestibule in front, whereas the closed street façade was retained. A characteristic example is offered by Palazzo Doria-Tursi in Genoa by Rocco Lurago (1564). Here a splendid vestibule leads to an elongated cortile which is not closed at the back, but connected to the garden above by means of a free flight of stairs. Very impressive is the cortile of Palazzo Borghese in Rome, where the three-storey wings of the building are connected by a two-storey transparent loggia, a design attributed to Flaminio Ponzio (1607). The emphasis on the longitudinal axis which joins the building to an ideal landscape be-

hind implies an extension of the private domain, rather than an interaction between the building and the urban environment.[6]

The aim of spatial integration and continuity manifested in the villa and the palace of the Cinquecento also produced an important change in the approach to the planning of the church. The centralized plan of the Quattrocento was not well suited to meet liturgical demands, and after the Council of Trent (1963) a more pronounced negative attitude towards the centralized plan became general, so as to strengthen tradition and to abolish the "pagan" forms of the Renaissance. A new ideal of a congregational church with a longitudinal cross plan was deliberately established by St. Charles Borromeo (1577), and the major churches built during the last decades of the Cinquecento followed his advice. But interesting attempts at an integration of the central and longitudinal schemes were also made—a problem most naturally solved by means of the oval. The oval as such appears in projects by Peruzzi and Serlio, but the first churches with an oval plan are due to Vignola. In S. Andrea in Via Flaminia (1550) a rectangular space is covered by an oval dome, and in the more important S. Anna dei Palafrenieri (1572) the whole space has become oval. The prototype became very important for the Baroque development. In general, the Cinquecento developed two basic types of plan: the centralized longitudinal plan for larger churches, and the elongated central plan for smaller churches and chapels. Both types express the new need for participation in an extended spatial system.

Articulation

During the sixteenth century the Classical characters were transferred to sacred as well as profane buildings. Serlio, a sixteenth-century commentator, said: "The ancients dedicated these Doric temples to Jove, Mars, Hercules, and to others among the mighty, but after the incarnation of Our Saviour, we Christians were obliged to follow other orders: having to build a church in honour of Jesus Christ Our Redeemer, St. Paul, St. Peter, St. George, or similar saints whose

courage and strength led them to expose their lives for the faith of Christ, it is fitting to adopt this Doric Manner."[7] It was generally assumed that the three Classical orders were capable of expressing all basic characters, as they comprise two extremes and a mean. The Tuscan and Composite Orders were added for further differentiation. A particular role, however, was assigned to rustication. Rather than being an order, expressing a human content, rustication was considered to represent nature itself, as something unformed and raw existing as a dialectical opposite to the works of man. Serlio thus calls rustication "opera di natura," while the orders are "opera di mano." These basic characters were still valid during the Baroque epoch.

The style of a building was determined not only by a choice between the orders but also by the way they were employed. In Renaissance architecture the Vitruvian principle of superimposition was reintroduced, whereby the lighter orders rested on the heavier, and the whole system on a rusticated basement. In certain works of the Mannerist period a fundamental doubt in this humanist expression arises. Raphael's Palazzo Caffarelli-Vidoni (after 1500) has a row of double engaged columns on the piano nobile, which rests on a heavily rusticated ground floor, expressing thus a tension between dialectically opposed forces. In the façade of Palazzo del Tè at Mantua by Raphael's pupil Giulio Romano (1526), the tension has become an open conflict between two interpenetrating systems, and other details in the same building show the Classical orders undergoing a process of disintegration. The conflict between the forces of nature and the work of man found its most typical manifestation in the cortile of the Pitti Palace in Florence by Ammanati (1560). Here the superimposed orders are covered by rustication; only the bases and capitals remain free.

A particularly interesting juxtaposition of orders and rustication is found in Peruzzi's famous Palazzo Massimo in Rome (1532).[8] The traditional relationship between opera di natura and opera di mano is turned upside down, as the order carries a tall rusticated wall. The weight of the upper part is

(5) Palladio, The Four Books of Architecture, II, 3 (London, 1736).

(6) The idea of introducing a longitudinal axis in the city palace stems from Michelangelo's transformation of Antonio da Sangallo's Palazzo Farnese in Rome (1546). See C. Norberg-Schulz, Baroque Architecture (Milan and New York, 1971), pp. 239 ff.

(7) S. Serlio Tutte l'Opere d'Architettura, IV, Preface (Venice, 1537).

(8) See H. Wurm, Der Palazzo Massimo alle Colonne (Berlin, 1965).

281. *Baldassare Peruzzi: Palazzo Massimo alle Colonne, Rome. Begun 1532. Façade.*

282. *Baldassare Peruzzi: Palazzo Massimo alle Colonne, Rome. Court.*

(9) In Palladio's earlier works Mannerist tendencies are strongly felt. A particularly important example is offered by his Palazzo Thiene (1545). See in general R. Pane, *Andrea Palladio* (Turin, 1961).

emphasized by its treatment as a continuous surface, and by the row of windows on the *piano nobile* which rests heavily on the entablature of the ground-floor order. The members are doubled to support the symbolic weight, creating a tension which is intensified towards the centre of the façade where freestanding columns take the place of the traditional massive basement, thus giving rise to the popular name "Palazzo Massimo *alle colonne.*" The entrance portico and the axial disposition of the plan indicates a more active relationship between the building and its urban environment, as does the curved façade, which is a function of the setting. The traditional self-sufficient palace is thus transformed into a subordinate, although intensely expressive, part of a larger whole.

Towards the end of the *Cinquecento* the tensions and conflicts of Mannerist articulation made way for deliberate attempts at formal integration and powerful simplification. This is evident in the church fronts, where the idea of an increase in plastic intensity towards the middle of the façade is introduced to express the new importance of the longitudinal axis. A particularly beautiful example is offered by Palladio's Redentore (1576), where a giant order unifies the central part of the façade and transforms it into a great "gateway." Palladio also sought a similar unification of palace façades, as shown by his Palazzo Porto-Breganze (1570) and Loggia del Capitanio (1571), both unfinished.[9] These works possess a new self-assurance which was to have a profound influence on architectural development in large parts of Europe.

Biblioteca Laurenziana

Sixteenth-century achitectural intentions were most profoundly expressed in the works of Michelangelo (1475–1564). Although Michelangelo did not consider himself an architect, and referring to his "incompetence" refused the commission as architect-in-charge for St. Peter's in Rome, he contributed more than anybody else to the development of the psychological dimension of architectural expression, characteristic of the *Cinquecento*. Michelangelo combined an

283. *Raphael Sanzio: Palazzo Caffarelli-Vidoni, Rome. 1515. Façade.*

284. *Bartolomeo Ammanati: courtyard of the Palazzo Pitti, Florence. 1560.*

285. *Giulio Romano: Palazzo del Te, Mantua. Begun 1526.*

286. *Andrea Palladio: Loggia del Capitanio, Vicenza. 1571.*

(10) See R. Wittkower, "Michelangelo's Biblioteca Laurenziana," *Art Bulletin,* vol. XVI, no. 2, 1934, pp. 123 ff.

287. *Michelangelo: Biblioteca Laurentiana (Laurentian Library), Florence. Wall of the vestibule.*

288. *Michelangelo: Biblioteca Laurentiana (Laurentian Library), Florence. Begun 1524. Vestibule and stairway.*

extraordinary sensibility with a meaningful, general conception of human existence, and his works belong to the few truly fundamental creations of mankind.

In 1524 Michelangelo initiated the construction of the Biblioteca Laurenziana in Florence, which is situated next to Brunelleschi's church of S. Lorenzo.[10] The library was built over a monks' dormitory, and could only be reached by means of a separate vestibule on a lower level, the so-called *ricetto.* At the other end of the library proper, Michelangelo planned a *piccola libreria* for particularly valuable books, which was unfortunately never built. This layout formed a succession of three spatial units, a square, a rectangle and a triangle, in which each unit was treated as a "place" with a pronounced individual character. The most striking feature of the *ricetto* is its unusual wall articulation. Although it is based on a distinction between a primary structural system in *pietra serena* and secondary, white wall surfaces between which was traditional in Florentine architecture, the effect it made was entirely novel. Coupled columns and superimposed pilasters are placed in deep niches, making the wall areas between them seem to break into interior space with a powerful plastic force. Michelangelo characterized the body as the prison of the soul, and symbolically the Classical order appears to be imprisoned in the amorphous mass of the wall. The conflict motif of the wall articulation is intoned *fortissimo,* and as it is repeated without interruption around the relatively narrow space, the *ricetto* becomes an unendurable place. The only escape is the large staircase which almost fills the space, but this too is a hostile element, a resistance which has to be overcome if we want to reach the library above. Its steps seem to well out from the library door like a cascade, and make the visitor tumble back. But when he has succeeded in mounting them, he may finally enter the calm and harmonious world of the library. Here conflict is gone; a regular succession of simple pilasters creates a rhythm which recalls the symbolic spatial geometry of early Renaissance architecture. In the *piccola libreria,* finally, the composition would have found

289. Michelangelo: Biblioteca Laurentiana
(Laurentian Library), Florence. Interior.

290. Michelangelo: Biblioteca Laurentiana
(Laurentian Library), Florence. Ground plan of
the piccola libreria.

its conclusion in a self-sufficient, centralized space.

The subdivision of a whole into three interrelated "domains" is also found in others of Michelangelo's works, such as the original project for the tomb of Pope Julius II, the ceiling of the Sistine Chapel, and the Medici Chapel (1519). In all these projects, the first, lower zone represents the conflicts of earthly existence, the fight of the individual soul for existential meaning. In St. Peter's this fight is interpreted as hopeless; the light of heaven is forever excluded from this earth. In the Medici Chapel liberation is attained through death, as indicated by Michelangelo's own words: *"La morte e'l fin d'una prigione scura,"* and in the Biblioteca Laurenziana the calm harmony of the library suggests a solution through the intellect. In all these works the third, higher zone symbolizes divine wisdom (in the Biblioteca represented by particularly selected, rare books). The general theme is the relation between man and God, interpreted as a conflict between soul and body, spirit and matter. The *Civitas Dei* of the Middle Ages and the harmonious cosmos of the Renaissance had thus ceded to the experience of human existence as an individual psychological problem. Michelangelo has shown, however, that this problem has a common, interpersonal structure. He thus posed for the first time the fundamental problem of modern man, and therefore his works are still experienced as as deeply meaningful as when they were created. Wittkower, in fact, characterizes the Biblioteca Laurenziana as "the most influential building of the sixteenth century."

Piazza del Campidoglio

The Capitoline hill occupies a special position among the great squares of Italy. Whereas other squares are joined to the urban network of paths and nodes, the Capitol is situated above the city. As a result, a particular kind of expectation is engendered when moving up the long entrance ramp, and this is not disappointed; the unified spatial composition seems to concretize a highly significant content.

The square as it appears today is by and

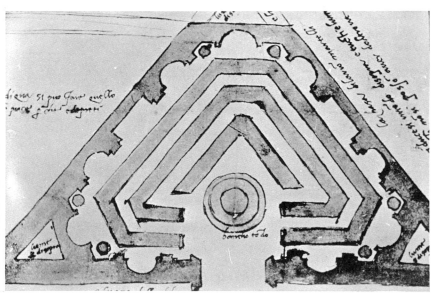

291. Michelangelo: plan for the Campidoglio, Rome (shown in an engraving by Dupérac). c. 1544.

292. Etienne Dupérac: the Campidoglio as designed by Michelangelo.

(11) For a detailed history of the project see H Siebenhüner, *Das Kapitol in Rom* (Munich, 1954). Also J. Ackerman, *The Architecture of Michelangelo* (London, 1961).

large the result of a project by Michelangelo. Michelangelo settled in Rome in 1537, and in 1539 he was asked to give advice on the placing of the equestrian statue of Marcus Aurelius on the Capitoline hill. Although the Capitol served as a political centre to Rome during the Middle Ages, it did not have any clearly defined architectural form. A building for the senate was erected on the ruins of the ancient Tabularium in 1144, and about 1400 another structure was built to house the conservatori. The first building imitated the North Italian communal palaces with corner towers and a high *campanile*. The square lacked pavement, and was used as a kind of deposit for classical sculpture. In 1537 Pope Paul III took the initiative to give back to the ancient focus of *Roma aeterna* its original splendour. The act of placing a Roman emperor at the centre of the new composition obviously had a symbolic meaning, and formed the point of departure for Michelangelo's plan, which must have been produced some time before 1544.[11]

The two existing medieval buildings had to be incorporated in the new scheme, and as they were placed at an oblique angle to each other Michelangelo gave the new piazza a trapezoid form. The narrow side of the trapezoid is open towards the city below, whereas the opposite side is occupied by the symmetrical Palazzo dei Senatori, and on the other two sides by two similar buildings, the Palazzo dei Conservatori and Palazzo Nuovo. Space was the primary object of the architect's attention, in a sort of "urban interior." As shown in the engraved plan and perspectives by Duperac after Michelangelo's design, the palaces were originally intended as shallow "screens" around the square. The engravings further show that Michelangelo wanted to treat the three buildings as parts of one continuous spatial boundary; in the execution by his successors the continuity has been weakened, whereby the axial aspect of the composition is emphasized. The powerful order of pilasters, and the clear articulation of the lateral palaces by means of primary and secondary members were, however, executed according to Michelangelo's design. Within the trapezoid space defined by the buildings, Michelangelo placed an oval which is sunk into the surrounding floor, at

the same time as it rises convexly towards the equestrian statue at the centre. Unfortunately, the circumference of the oval was broken in four places towards the end of the nineteenth century, to allow carriages to enter the central part of the piazza. The radiating star-shaped pattern which articulates the oval part of the pavement was designed by Michelangelo, but executed only in 1940.

In general the plan is based on the tension between the enclosing trapezoid and the expanding oval. It actually looks as if the dynamic oval *breaks through* the surface of the piazza. Tolnay has interpreted the convex oval as representing the curve of the terrestrial globe, and has concluded that the solution in general symbolizes the *caput mundi*.[12] Furthermore Ackerman has pointed out that the star-shaped floor articulation is a cosmic symbol connected with the *omphalos* in Delphi. The Romans brought the navel of the world to the Forum Romanum, and medieval legends associated it with the Capitol. Michelangelo intended to symbolize the meaning which throughout the centuries had been connected with the particular place he had to shape. As *cosmocrator* the emperor is placed at the very centre of the composition. But the Capitol is more than a particular case of symbolic architecture. Because of the *simultaneous expansion and contraction* of the space, it becomes one of the greatest concretizations of the concept of place ever created by man. At the Capitol we are at the centre, not only of the world, but of the departures and returns which give our own individual life meaning and content. Here man experiences his existence as a meaningful, although problematic, relationship between his individual self and the world he belongs to.

Villa Lante

The new interest of the *Cinquecento* in the character of place is closely connected with a new relationship to nature. In nature man originally discovered characters which reflected the basic properties of his own psyche, and the Mannerist emphasis on the psychological dimension again brought the natural characters to the fore. We have al-

(12) C. de Tolnay, "Michelangelo architetto," *Il Cinquecento* (Florence, 1955).

295. *Giacomo da Vignola: Villa Lante, Bag-*
naia. Begun 1566. Ground plan.

296. *Giacomo da Vignola: Villa Lante, Bag-*
naia.

(13) See a. Cantoni, *La Villa Lante di Bagnaia* (Milan, 1961).

(14) Bagnaia consists of a medieval settlement and a *Cinquecento* extension which related the medieval core to the villa by means of a trident.

ready mentioned how the architects of the period conceived their buildings in relation to a particular site. In contrast to the ancient Greeks they did not consider the individual place as an independent unit, but aimed at a unification of the different places into a system of interdependent characters. This is especially evident in the *villa suburbana,* where the public and private domains of the *civitas* interact with nature.

Among the Italian villas of the *Cinque-cento,* Villa Lante in Bagnaia near Viterbo is a particularly beautiful and well-preserved example. Built as a summer residence for Cardinal Gambara, who was nominated bishop of Viterbo in 1566, it consists of two *palazzine,* one to the west built between 1566 and 1578, and one to the east which was added by the new owner Cardinal Montalto in 1578–89.[13] A complete project existed from the very beginning, as indicated by the bird's-eye view painted in the garden loggia of the first *palazzina.* The execution, how-ever, is not entirely faithful to the painted prospect, and several weak details indicate the participation of a hand other than that of Vignola (1507–73, active in Viterbo and Caprarola), who is believed to be its archi-tect.

The villa is situated where the slope of Monte Cimino meets the cultivated land around Viterbo. Its location under the moun-tain recalls some of the characteristic sites of Greek antiquity, but the planning is Roman. Different zones are disposed as a series of interconnected terraces along a sloping axis. The primacy of space is proved by the fact that the *casino,* which naturally would form the focus of a layout of this kind, has been split into two separate *palazzine* that flank the longitudinal axis. In Villa Lante the axis is more than an abstract line of symmetry; it is the real backbone of the composition, and is concretized as a stream of water which runs through the whole villa, some-times disappearing and then reappearing. The stream starts from a spring in a grotto within the *selvatico* at the top of the villa. After being "displayed" in a fountain, it con-tinues as a brook formed as a chain of stone. A new fountain flanked by statues of river-gods marks the entrance into the main *bos-chetto,* where a stone table with a water

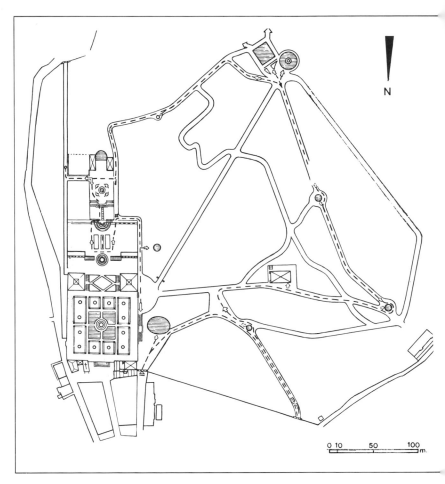

297. *Giacomo da Vignola: Villa Lante, Bagnaia. Garden.*

298. *Giacomo da Vignola: Villa Lante, Bagnaia. Garden.*

channel in the middle allowed for meals among the trees. Another circular fountain composed of a convex and a concave half to form a "water staircase" marks the transition to the civilized domain of the *palazzine* and the large, concluding *parterre*. From the *parterre* a monumental gateway leads to the main axis of the village of Bagnaia below the villa.[14]

In Villa Lante nature and culture are no longer separated, but interpenetrate in various ways. In the *selvatico* nature dominates, whereas the geometrized *parterre* with its large island-shaped fountain symbolizes man's conquest of the natural forces. The composition may also be read the other way around: as a return to nature from the confused and difficult world of the human habitat, an idea already contemplated by Alberti. The symbolic interaction of nature and the man-made world implies a new kind of consciousness which centres on the experience of varying characters. Man's environment, thus, loses its ideal *Quattrocento* character, and becomes more directly alive. The process may be indicated by the word "phenomenization," that is, every phenomenon, every situation, is now experienced as having its own expressive content. In terms of architecture this means that the *genius loci* again gains primary importance. But Villa Lante is more than a particular place; its united composition tells a universal tale, which makes us better understand man's problematic position between culture and nature. In Villa Lante the *palazzine* have in fact a similar symbolic location.

Il Gesù

Sixteenth-century phenomenization and participation led to a profound transformation of ecclesiastical architecture. The church was not now conceived as a static symbol of the cosmic harmony, but became a place where the drama of redemption is enacted, and this drama does not take place in a refuge characterized by interiority and "otherness," like the Early Christian church, but happens in the present as a deeply felt human problem. The sixteenth century, in fact, was the time of the Reformation and Counter-

299. *Giacomo da Vignola: Il Gesù, Rome. Begun 1568. Ground plan.*

300. *Giacomo da Vignola: Il Gesù, Rome. Section (after Dupérac).*

(15) *Canons and Decrees of the Council of Trent*, Session XXV, Tit. 2. Quoted from A. Blunt, *Artistic Theory in Italy 1450-1600* (Oxford, 1956), p. 108.

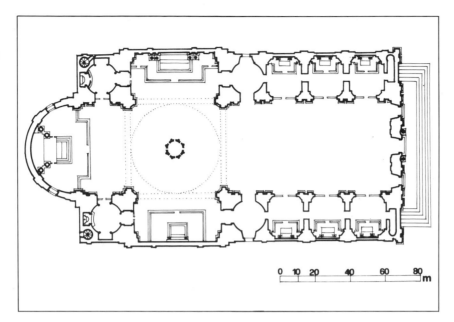

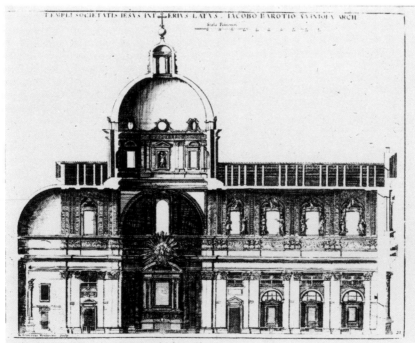

Reformation. During the period of religious schism, the Church became highly dependent upon persuasion. Realization of this motivated St. Ignatius Loyola to write his *Spiritual Exercises* which were first written in the language of the common man and which aim at an imitation of Christ by means of imagination and empathy. Later the Roman church came to give particular importance to the visual images as a means of persuasion. "And the Bishops shall carefully teach this, that, by means of the Stories of the Mysteries of our Redemption, portrayed by paintings and other representations, the people are instructed and confirmed in the habit of remembering, and continually revolving in mind the articles of faith."[15]

In Il Gesù in Rome (1568 *ff.*) Vignola satisfied the new ideal of a congregational church which would allow a great number of people to participate in the liturgical functions. Michelangelo had already made a longitudinal plan for the church of Gesù (1554), and his basic disposition was taken over by Vignola. Vignola's project for the façade, however, was rejected, and in 1573–75 Giacomo della Porta added the present front. Today Il Gesù has a rich Baroque decoration. As planned by Vignola it should have been simpler, but it still corresponded to the general wish for persuasive splendour expressed by St. Charles Borromeo.

Il Gesù gives a new active interpretation to the two traditional motifs: the path of redemption and the heavenly dome. It has a longitudinal plan which shows a strong wish for spatial integration. There are no aisles, only chapels accompanying the wide nave. The movement in depth is emphasized by a straight entablature and is given persuasive power by coupled pilasters. Whereas the chancel gains depth by the addition of a spacious apse, the transepts are short and do not have independent spatial value. However, a relatively large dome dominates the church, and its symbolic form accompanies the movement along the main axis. A tall drum gives emphasis to the vertical axis of the dome and makes it form an expressive and persuasive contrast to the horizontal path. In illuminating the interior the architect has discarded the evenly distributed light of the Renaissance, and revives the Early Christian

*01. Giacomo da Vignola: Il Gesù, Rome. In-
erior.*

*02. Giacomo da Vignola: Il Gesù, Rome.
acade by Giacomo della Porta, 1573-75.*

contrast between a relatively dark inferior zone and large clerestory windows, which here cut through the lower part of the tunnel vault.

Della Porta's façade is the first example of a strongly emphasized increase in plastic intensity towards the middle of the wall. This is achieved by having engaged columns instead of the central pair of pilasters, by a gradual stepping forward of the plane of the façade, as well as by a richer plastic decoration towards the middle. The façade also well illustrates the end of additive Renaissance composition; here the wall units can no longer be interpreted as independent, self-sufficient elements. Every detail has become a function of the whole, and the composition in general appears as a great gateway which emphasizes the main axis and integrates the building with its urban environment.

Il Gesù answered the needs of the Jesuits well, and many scholars have maintained that the order used it as a general model. Later research has demonstrated that this is not the case, and that the churches of the Counter-Reformation movement are based on a much more complex typology and show many local variants. Il Gesù, however, expresses many of the basic intentions of Baroque church building, and a considerable number of buildings derived from it, starting with the later works of Giacomo della Porta, such as Madonna dei Monti (1580) and S. Andrea della Valle (1591).

Space Conception and Development

Mannerist architecture is based on the Renaissance concept of homogeneous space, but in a certain sense contradicts it. Whereas the *Quattrocento* stressed the aspect of isotropic, static order, the *Cinquecento* developed the possibility of differentiated, dynamic spatial succession. Qualitatively different, interacting places and domains were defined within the general extension of space. Space was, in other words, conceived as a means of "direct" expression, and became an object of emotional experience. The basic constituent fact of Mannerist architecture is actually the phenomenization of abstract,

(16)   For the general development of military architecture, see. C. Norberg-Schulz "La fortezza di Porto Santo Stefano e l'architettura militare," *Acta ad archaeologiam et artium historiam pertinentia,* vol. II, (Rome, 1965).

(17)   See H. Sedlmayr, *Verlust der Mitte* (Salzburg, 1948), pp. 187 ff.

(18)   E. Gombrich, "Zum Werke Giulio Romanos I," *Jahrbuch der Kunsthistorischen Sama62ge VIII,* 1934, p. 99.

(19)   Palladio's influence on the Protestant North probably stems from the fact that he won Palladio's ambiguity without subscribing to the rhetoric of Counter-Reformation architecture.

(20)   Michelangelo was called both "il divino" and "il terribile."

(21)   See M. Weber, *The Protestant Ethic* (Tübingen, 1920; New York, 1930).

symbolic space. Space thus regained its concrete, phenomenal character and was understood in terms of individual places. In a certain sense, this meant a rebirth of the Greek approach to reality, but the experiences of the Middle Ages and the Renaissance were not forgotten in the *Cinquecento,* and the concept of place was combined with the idea of an environmental continuum.

Mannerist conception of space was concretized in certain recurring ways. In relation to landscape and settlement it produced an opening up of the enclosed stronghold, which so far had represented the basic image of the human habitat. The engirdling city wall was replaced by a system of bastions, which, although they did not bring the surrounding land physically closer, implied a more active spatial relationship between the civic and natural domains.[16] In the villa a direct contact between dwelling and landscape was established by means of axes which, in some cases, did not lead to any particular goal, but indicated a new concept of general extension. In Sixtus V's plan for Rome, axes were used to relate the urban nodes and to transform the city into a dynamic system.

In general the axes manifest a new interest in movement in space. Space is no longer simply a "container," but something which ought to be conquered by action. Spatial continuity is not an invention of the *Cinquecento,* but the succession of significantly related spaces which have a different character is a typical creation of the century (hence the fundamental importance of the Biblioteca Laurenziana). Different characterization was achieved by means of articulation, as well as variations in space, form and proportion, and new dynamic forms such as the oval were used in answer to the wish for spatial interrelation.

During the first half of the sixteenth century designs expressed contrast, tension and conflict. Mannerist works of art have been characterized as "cold" and "sinister," and Mannerist spaces as having an "unendurable" atmosphere.[17] Sometimes the forms are shown in a state of disintegration or as unfinished. This "disturbed" form was in general used to arrive at a more intense expression. *Opere di mano* were seen as the result of a fight with the forces of nature which

might also end with a catastrophe, as in the *Sala dei Giganti* in Giulio Romano's Palazzo del Tè.[18] In this respect Mannerist form is dualistic: It is based on contradictions, and concretizes the meanings inherent in unresolved conflicts. It is usually disturbing, but may transcend the sphere of conflict and become truly tragic, as in the works of Michelangelo.

The conflict and tragedy of Mannerist architecture is always expressed by means of the Classical orders, and it may be said that the dualistic form was a result of the reintroduction of anthropomorphic members. The problem of geometrization was easily solved by *Quattrocento* architects, but the problem of anthropomorphization was attended by the question of man's relation to nature and to God. During the first six decades of the *Cinquecento* there was thought to be a profound split between body and soul. The third session of the Council of Trent (1562–63), where religious art was discussed, marked an official turning point, and during the last decades of the century a new wish for unambiguous form came to the fore. A colossal, dominant order and a new goal-oriented spatial dynamism came to be used; these tendencies were present in certain aspects of the works of Michelangelo, Vignola and Palladio, and were given primary importance by Giacomo della Porta.[19]

Meaning and Architecture

In the sixteenth century fundamental aspects of existence were felt to be problematic: the relationship of man to other men; to nature; to culture; to God; and even to himself. "Divine" man was replaced by a man who doubts and fears, and who is split internally by the problem of choice.[20] The belief in freedom of choice implicit in Renaissance humanism naturally led to this situation, as it implied that the eternal values no longer were directly revealed to man, but had to be conquered through creative action. But the Renaissance belief in man's moral and intellectual powers did not last long. Erasmus and Luther expressed doubt in the purpose of freedom and in the "dignity of man," to use Pico's expression, and Copernicus de-

clared that the earth was not the centre of the universe. The political foundation of Renaissance civilization broke down, and the division of the church ratified the disintegration of the unified and absolute world. Above all, the new situation was experienced as a psychological problem; modern man, who wants to substitute for authority personal conscience and responsibility, was born during the sixteenth century. His world is a problematic and divided world, and he himself is a suffering and alienated man. Never before had the quest for meaning been felt more intensely.

The problem of meaning was solved in different ways by Protestants and Catholics. As the Protestant believed he was entirely dependent upon Divine Grace, his actions could not help him, and culture hence became unnecessary and useless. Protestantism therefore came close to denying the value of religious art altogether, and wanted to reduce symbolism to a meagre minimum. For the Protestant, the world was essentially meaningless, that is, it did not manifest any divine truth, and his space was neutral and without "qualities." Protestantism thus solved the human crisis by negating traditionally important existential meanings. The "technocratic" society and secularized man of our time is a natural outgrowth of the Protestant approach to reality.[21]

For the Catholic, truth reveals itself in the world, and history is man's path towards redemption. On his way man is guided by the Church. One of the first aims of the Counter-Reformation, therefore, was to deny the right of the individual to settle his problems using his own reason. The leaders of the Counter-Reformation wanted to reinstate ecclesiastical authority, which had been weakened by Renaissance humanism. The concept of perfect form and beauty was therefore given up, and religious art was turned into a means of persuasion and propaganda as has already been discussed in connection with Il Gesù. The general process of phenomenization which took place during the sixteenth century thus suited the purposes of the Church well.

Persuasion has participation as its goal, and, to meet this end, there grew up in addition to the reforms introduced by the Council

of Trent organizations whose aim was to adapt the Catholic faith to the needs of the day.[22] Of primary importance were the Jesuits, who aimed at making religion appeal to the emotions. As a result, a popular antiintellectual kind of religion came into being, which was propagated to the whole Catholic world during the following two centuries, and which was made visually manifest by saturating the landscape with religious elements, such as road-crucifixes, chapels and sanctuaries.[23] Pilgrimage again became a living factor in the life of the Church, and the monasteries regained some of the cultural importance they had during the Middle Ages.

The main reason for the emphasis on persuasion and propagation evidently was the fact that the Catholic Church no longer represented the only system of meanings available to Western man. From now on the Church was only one among many religious, political and philosophical systems. Not being all-comprehensive, its propagation was essential and a dynamic, centrifugal character became general. In architecture the restless forms of Mannerism were thus taken over and transformed into the goal-oriented, assuring dynamism of the Baroque epoch. So far, the human crisis had been overcome by giving up the Renaissance idea of human freedom.

(22) For a good introduction to "The Council of Trent and Religious Art," see Blunt, *op. cit.*, chapter VIII.

(23) An early example of the new sacred landscape is offered by the aspiring vertical of Vittozzi's Cappucini al Monte at Turin (1584 ff.).

303. *Michelangelo: New Sacristy of S. Lorenzo, Florence, 1519. Interior.*

304. *Michelangelo: New Sacristy of S. Lorenzo, Florence. Vaulting.*

305. *Giovanni Battista Piranesi:* Basilica and Piazza of St. Peter, Rome. *18th-century print.*

306. *Paris. Plan.*

307. *Giovanni Battista Piranesi:* View of the Piazza del Popolo, Rome. *18th-century print.*

(1) This hold true for Baroque art in general. We may for instance point out the dynamic systematization which characterizes the music of the epoch.

(2) See d'Alembert's "Discours préliminaire" to the French *Encyclopédie* (1751), where he distinguishes the interest in the system as such from the scientific *esprit systématique* of his own century.

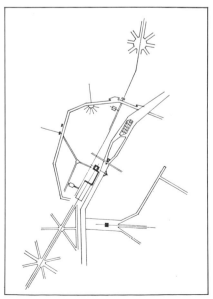

9. Baroque Architecture

308. Place Dauphine, Paris. *18th-century print.*

309. Place Vendome, Paris. *17th-century print.*

Introduction

Baroque architecture is essentially a reflection of the great systems of the seventeenth and eighteenth centuries, especially the Roman Catholic Church and the political system of the centralized French state. The purpose of Baroque art was simultaneously to symbolize the strict organization of the system and its persuasive power, and Baroque architecture therefore appears as a singular synthesis of dynamism and systematization.[1]

Although Baroque buildings are characterized by plastic vitality and spatial richness, close study always reveals an underlying systematic organization. The two seemingly contradictory aspects of the Baroque phenomenon, systematization and dynamism, form a meaningful totality, for persuasion and propagation only become meaningful in relation to a centre representing the basic axioms of the system. The religious, scientific, economic and political centres of the seventeenth century were focuses of radiating forces, which, seen from the centre itself, had no spatial limits; they had an open and dynamic character. Departing from a fixed point they could be infinitely extended. In this infinite world movement and force are of primary importance. The resulting absolute but open and dynamic system was basic to the Baroque age. Already d'Alembert talked about the *esprit de système* of the seventeenth century.[2]

The Baroque world may also be characterized as a great theatre where everybody was assigned his role. However, participation presupposes imagination, a faculty educated by means of art, so art was of central importance in the Baroque age. Its images were a means of communication more direct than logical demonstration, and furthermore accessible to the illiterate. The most splendid of the Baroque "theatres" is undoubtedly the centre of the Roman Catholic world, the Piazza San Pietro in Rome, built in 1675-77 by the great master of Baroque persuasive art, Gian Lorenzo Bernini (1598-1680). First of all the piazza has a symbolic basis, as expressed in

149

(3) *Codice Chigiana* H. II, 22.

(4) G. C. Argan, *L'Europa delle Capitali 1600—1700* (Geneva, 1964), p. 106.

(5) A. Cavallari-Murat, *Forma urbana ed architettura nella Torino barocca* (Turin, 1968).

(6) Its prototype is the Capitoline square by Michelangelo, which is again derived from ancient Roman models.

(7) For a detailed discussion of the Baroque squares of Paris see C. Norberg-Schulz, *Baroque Architecture* (New York, 1971), pp. 64 ff.

(8) See E. DeGanay, *André Le Nostre* (Paris, 1962).

Bernini's own words: "for since the church of St. Peter's is the mother of nearly all the others, it had to have colonnades, which would show it as if stretching out its arms maternally to receive Catholics, so as to confirm them in their faith, heretics, to reunite them to the Church, and infidels, to enlighten them in the true faith."[3] Bernini went on to realize his programme in a way which makes St. Peter's Square one of the greatest urban spaces ever conceived. The main oval space is simultaneously closed and open. It is clearly defined, but the oval shape creates an expansion along the transverse axis. Instead of being a static, finished form, the square interacts with the world beyond, an intention also expressed by the "transparent" colonnade. The space really becomes the "meeting-place of all mankind," at the same time as its message radiates to the entire world. The obelisk has an important function as the node where all the directions meet and are connected with the longitudinal axis which leads to the church. An ideal synthesis of concentration and longitudinal direction towards a goal is thereby created. The theme is repeated within the church where the movement finds its final motivation in the vertical axis of the heavenly dome. St. Peter's Square is a supreme example of space composition, worthy of its function as the principal focus of the Catholic world. At the same time, Bernini has succeeded in concretizing the essence of the Baroque age with a singular simplicity. Better than any other example, St. Peter's Square shows that the basis of Baroque art is found in general principles rather than in exuberant detail.

In Baroque architecture the importance of *space* as a constituent element which was suggested by Mannerism is fully realized. In contrast to a construction of plastic members, the Baroque building is made up of interacting spatial elements which are modelled according to outer and inner forces. We have certainly talked about space in connection with Renaissance architecture, but then as a uniform continuum which is subdivided by the geometrically disposed architectural members. Baroque space cannot be understood in this way. Argan says: "The great innovation was the idea that space does not surround architecture but is created by it."[4]

Landscape and Settlement

During the seventeenth century there is for the first time in history a truly large-scale transformation of the natural landscape. So far nature had been firmly kept outside the *civitas.* A map of Paris and its environs from 1740 shows that the whole landscape has been transformed into a network of centralized systems, which, ideally, have an infinite extension. Most of them stem from the seventeenth century. In a still larger context, Paris formed the centre of an analogous system, comprising the whole of France, and if a magnifying glass were trained on the same map, it would show that the single elements, the buildings, are organized on similar patterns; it appears that the world was understood as a series of geometrically ordered extensions. Each system is focused on a "centre of meaning." In relation to this focus Man's existence became meaningful. In spatial terms the meanings were expressed as a set of converging paths. At the very centre of the systems we find the capital city. In general Rome served as the prototype. During the seventeenth century, however, Rome's urban system was not further developed, and attention instead concentrated on subordinate focuses, such as St. Peter's Square, or on particular monumental buildings. Instead one has to turn to Paris and Turin for the most important city developments during this period.[5]

The development of Paris during the seventeenth century took a very different course from that of Rome. Instead of starting with a system, Paris was built up as a series of monumental episodes, which gradually came together to form a coherent, systematic structure. After his entry into Paris in 1594, Henri IV restored and strengthened the monarchy, and during the last years of his life he wanted to transform his capital city into a worthy expression of the new system. Whereas Sixtus V could take as his point of departure urban focuses already in existence, Henri had to start afresh. In answer to this need he created a new element, the *place royale,* an urban space centred on, and developed around, a statue of the sovereign.[6] Surrounded by dwellings, it concretizes a new relationship between the sovereign and his people.

The first of Henri's projects, the Place Dauphine, is of particular interest because of its relationship to the city as a whole. He developed a square of triangular form between the Pont Neuf and the Île de la Cité, with an equestrian statue of the sovereign where the axis of the square crosses the bridge. The main axis of the scheme corresponds to the landscape axis of Paris, which is the Seine, and in fact the Place Dauphine makes the river an essential part of the architecture of the city. Later, Henri had the Place des Vosges built in a square shape and planned the Place de France, which was not executed, like a star. During the long reign of Louis XIV, two more royal squares were created, the circular Place des Victoires (1682–27) and the rectangular Place Vendôme (1699–1708), both designed by Jules Hardouin-Mansart (1646–1708).[7] At Place Vendôme uniform façades were erected without houses behind them to secure the systematic integration of the cityscape. In addition to the new internal structure given Paris by its royal squares, a ring of boulevards and centrifugal axes created a new open relationship to the environment.

The ideas behind these innovations stem from garden architecture. Here the great innovator was André Le Nôtre (1613–1700). In spite of their infinite variety, his gardens are based on a few simple principles. The main element, naturally, is the longitudinal axis. It forms the path which leads the observer towards his goal: the experience of infinite space. All the other elements are related to this axis: a palace which divides the path into two different halves; arrival from man's urban world through an open courtyard; and departure into infinity defined as a gradual passage through the still "civilized" world of *parterres;* the "tamed" nature of a *bosquet;* and the "natural" nature of a *selvatico.* Transverse axes and radiating patterns are introduced to indicate the general open extension of the system. The programmatic work here was the garden of Vaux-le-Vicomte (1656–61).[8]

The sacred landscape of the Baroque epoch is not organized in any integrated geometrical system, but rather consists of a saturation of the environment with sacred elements. Particularly important are the great

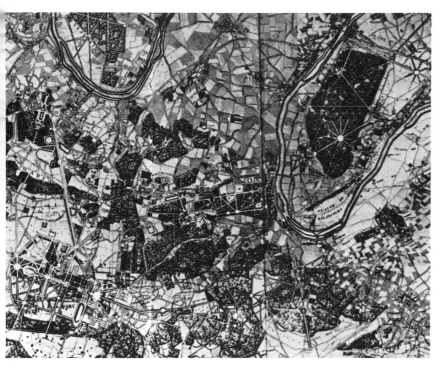

monasteries of the eighteenth century in Central Europe, which were usually given a high and dominant location.[9]

Building

The dispositions of Baroque churches are variations on the basic types of centralized longitudinal plan and elongated central plan, popular during the last decades of the sixteenth century. Developing from these layouts spatial integration was especially emphasized, and the Baroque church in general served as a testing ground for the development of advanced spatial ideas.[10] The crucial step was taken by Francesco Borromini (1599–1667) who deliberately introduced space as the constituent element of architecture. His spaces are complex totalities given *a priori* as indivisible figures. This character is stressed with all the means at his disposal, above all by the continuity of the bounding walls. A good example is his cloister in S. Carlo alle Quattro Fontane in Rome (1635–36), where Borromini succeeds in creating a unified spatial element with the simplest possible means. The cloister is surrounded by a continuous system of rhythmically placed columns. There are no corners in the usual sense of the term, as the smaller bay of the wall system is carried on in a convex curve where the corners would have been. The space is intended as a unit, which may be articulated but not decomposed. In an unfinished little church S. Maria dei Sette Dolori (1642), Borromini made a first attempt at making several spatial units mutually interdependent. About the same time François Mansart introduced the idea of spatial interpenetration in the church of the Visitation in Paris (1632), where oval chapels on the main axes are interpenetrated by the circular main space so as to break up their forms.

In the works of Guarino Guarini (1624–83), the general principles proposed by Borromini are systematically worked out. Guarini composed complex plans with interdependent or interpenetrating cells, and produced energetic forms that resemble pulsating organisms, which give the Baroque ideas of extension and movement a new dynamic and

(9) Particularly important examples are Melk (1700 ff.) by Jacob Prandtauer and Göttweig (1719) by Lucas von Hildebrandt.

(10) For a thorough discussion see Norberg-Schulz, *op. cit.*, chapter III, as well as Norberg-Schulz, *Late Baroque and Rococo Architecture* (New York, 1972).

312. *Francesco Borromini: S. Carlo alle Quattro Fontane, Rome. Begun 1635. Cloister.*

313. *Francesco Borromini: S. Carlo alle Quattro Fontane, Rome. Interior.*

(11)   In fact, Guarini considered the pulsating, undulating movement a basic property of nature, saying, "The spontaneous action of dilation and contraction is not governed by any principle, but is present throughout the whole living being." (*Placita Philosophica,* Paris, 1665).

(12)   See C. Norberg-Schulz, *Kilian Ignaz Dientzenhofer e il barocco boemo* (Rome, 1968).

(13)   For a thorough discussion of the Late Baroque church see Norberg-Schulz, *Late Baroque and Rococo Architecture.*

(14)   See Norberg-Schulz, *Baroque Architecture,* p. 285.

vital interpretation.[11] A particularly interesting example is offered by S. Lorenzo in Turin (1668), where a centralized plan is developed around an octagonal space whose sides are convexly curved towards the inside. A transverse oval presbytery is added to the main axis, according to the principle of interdependence or "pulsating juxtaposition." On the transverse axis similar spaces could have been added, but they have been omitted. In principle the system is open, but Guarini has only used some of the possibilities for adding secondary spaces, thereby creating what has been called a "reduced centralized building." Guarini's general approach could be applied to large and small centralized and longitudinal churches as an *ars combinatoria,* and his basic achievement consists in the development of open spatial groups. His ideas were of fundamental importance for the Late Baroque architecture of Central Europe, and he found a worthy successor in Kilian Ignaz Dientzenhofer (1689–1751) who built innumerable "open" and "pulsating" churches in Bohemia.[12] Towards the end of this period a more static centralized plan, defined as a double-shell structure, became usual, notably in the many Piedmontese churches of Bernardo Vittone. The late Baroque church thus ended as a receptacle of Divine Light.[13]

In France, where the church was of relatively minor importance, it was the palace which came to the fore. The city-palace and the villa *(château)* tended to be treated in the same way, and as a result both came to have the horseshoe-shape as their basic structure. Moreover, both were generally situated at the meeting point of habitat and nature, where the *villa suburbana* would be located. The great residences of the seventeenth and eighteenth centuries follow these general principles. At the same time inner organization became more differentiated and comfortable, especially with the introduction of the *appartement double* which made the rooms independent of each other and gave them privacy.[14] The main addition of the eighteenth century was the great staircase, which received its most splendid treatment at the hands of Balthasar Neumann.

This development took place mainly in France, due to the work of DeBrosse, Mansart and LeVau. The latter's masterpiece,

314. Francesco Borromini: S. Carlo alle Quattro Fontane, Rome Vaulting.

315. François Mansart: church of the Visitation, Paris. Begun 1632. Vaulting.

Vaux-le-Vicomte (1657–61), shows a fully mature solution of the problems of the palace as a product of exterior and interior needs. Differences in ways of life and social structures were expressed in the buildings of different countries.[15] The inhabitants of the French *hôtel* with its withdrawn *corps de logis* did not participate in the civic milieu, but they were still subject to the dominated space on which their courtyard opened, and became parts of the general system. The Italian *palazzo*, on the other hand, usually maintained its private, centralized *cortile;* at the same time the inhabitants could follow civic life from their dwelling over the street.

Articulation

The most conspicuous property of Baroque exterior wall articulation is the abolition of the conflict motifs of Mannerist architecture. Again the *opera di mano* rises with full self-assurance over a rusticated base, but now is dominated by a colossal order. Towards the middle of the façade plastic intensity increases, relating the articulation to the primary, longitudinal axis of the spatial composition. A straightforward example is offered by Bernini's Palazzo Chigi-Odescalchi in Rome (1664–67), whereas his first project for the Louvre (1664) is a more magnificent variation on the basic themes. In France the feeling for plastic values was less strong, probably due to the Gothic tradition of the dematerialized, diaphanous wall. As a result the classical members were used to compose elegant and relatively light skeletons, where tall french windows almost entirely occupy the remaining wall surface. In spite of the Gothic tradition of vertical continuity, the colossal order is usually avoided, probably because a correctly proportioned colossal member would have received an excessive plastic force. Instead, superimposed orders are the normal solution. French wall articulation is particularly sophisticated in the works of François Mansart (1598–1666), among which his masterpiece is the Château de Maisons near Paris (1642–46), where steep Gothic roofs are used. About the same time LeVau invented the broken, so-called mansard roof which became a characteristic

(15) · The horseshoe-shaped plan which was used by Peruzzi in the Farnesina was taken over by Maderno in Palazzo Barberini in Rome (after 1625), but it did not have any considerable following in Italy.

316. *Francesco Borromini: S. Maria dei Sette Dolori, Rome. Begun 1642. Ground plan.*

317. *Guarino Guarini: S. Lorenzo, Turin. 1668-80. Ground plan.*

318. *Guarino Guarini: S. Lorenzo, Turin. Interior of the dome.*

319. *Guarino Guarini: plan for S. Filippo Neri, Casale Monferrato. 1671.*

320. *Kilian Ignaz Dientzenhofer's method of composition. (Norberg-Schulz.)*

321. *Carlo Maderno and Gian Lorenzo Bernini: Palazzo Barberini, Rome. After 1625. Ground plan.*

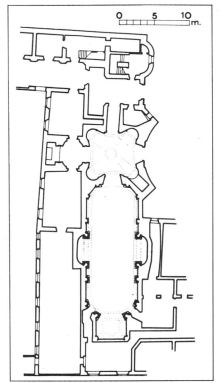

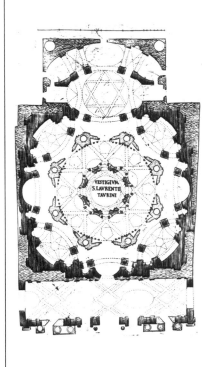

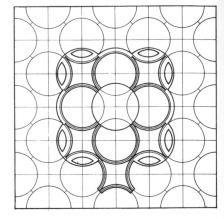

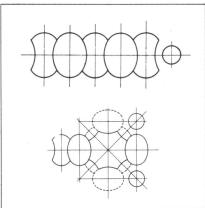

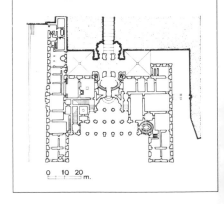

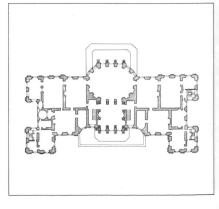

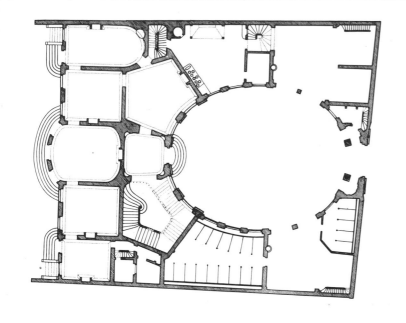

322. Louis LeVau: Château de Vaux-le-Vicomte. 1656-61. Ground plan of the palace.

323. Germain Boffrand: Hôtel Amelot, Paris. 1710-13. Plan of the ground floor.

324. Francesco Borromini: S. Carlo alle Quattro Fontane, Rome. Façade, 1665-67.

feature of Late Baroque architecture, giving the buildings an almost sensual voluminosity. The development of the transparent, skeletal structure culminated with the works of Jules Hardouin-Mansart, and then ceded to the Rococo treatment of the wall as a continuous, perforated skin.

In ecclesiastical architecture the problems of wall articulation are somewhat different, due to the different spatial organism and the traditionally more intimate contact with the environment. The most important development was the "undulating wall," introduced by Borromini as a revision of the interaction that was first developed in Il Gesù.[16] In his S. Carlo alle Quattro Fontane the façade (1665–67) appears to result from the interaction of interior and exterior forces.[17] The undulating wall was later applied to the open spatial groups of Guarinesque architecture, where it appears as a continuous enveloping skin, as in a chapel in Smiřice in Bohemia (1700) by Christoph Dientzenhofer. Another solution was adoption of the Gothic wall-pier system, also used in Smiřice where the interior walls were transformed into neutral, secondary surfaces between the vertical members of a primary system of large baldachins. Smiřice's plan derives from S. Lorenzo in Turin, but the use of wall-piers makes the Guarinesque space truly open. Christoph Dientzenhofer's innovation was developed and varied by his son Kilian Ignaz, who extended the spatial group along the lines of the complex double-shell structures of medieval architecture. Medieval double-shell spaces and diaphanous walls are also sources of inspiration for the splendid sanctuary In der Wies (1746 ff.) by Dominikus Zimmermann, where tall wall-piers are combined with a relatively simple, oval plan.

In Baroque art the phenomenization initiated during the sixteenth century was further developed. Architects of this time were exceptionally sensitive to the effects of texture, colour and light, as well as water and other natural elements, and were capable of giving their spaces any desired character. At the same time, then, it is possible to find such different variations on the Baroque "theatre" as the persuasive, "miraculous" church interiors of the brothers Asam and the light, gay and sensuous Rococo *salons*

(16) The term was introduced by S. Giedion in *Space, Time and Architecture* (Cambridge, Mass., 1941).

(17) For a spatial analysis see. P. Portoghesi, *Borromini* (Milan, 1967), p. 295.

325. Gian Lorenzo Bernini: first plan for the principal facade of the Louvre. 1665. Louvre, Paris.

326. Francois Mansart: Château de Maisons, 1642-46.

327. Jules Hardouin-Mansart: Grand Trianon, Versailles. 1687.

328. Christoph Dientzenhofer: palace chapel, Smirice. Begun 1700. Ground plan.

329. Christoph Dientzenhogfer: St. Nicholas on the Kleinseite (Malá Strana), Prague. 1703-11. Interior.

330. Dominikus Zimmermann; Die Wies pilgrimage church (Upper Bavaria). Interior.

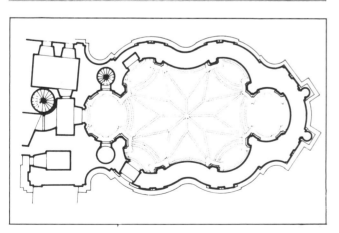

31.   Filippo Juvarra: Palazzo Madama, Turin.

32.   Filippo Juvarra: Palazzo Madama, Turin.
718-21. Grand staircase.

333.   Johann Bernhard Fischer von Erlach:
Karlskirche, Vienna.

334.   Johann Bernhard Fischer von Erlach:
Karlskirche, Vienna. Begun 1715.

335. *Versailles. Plan.*

336. *André Le Nôtre: gardens, Versailles.*
1661-68. Principal axis.

(18) His book *Entwurff einer historischen Architektur* (1721) starts with Stonehenge and ends with his own projects.

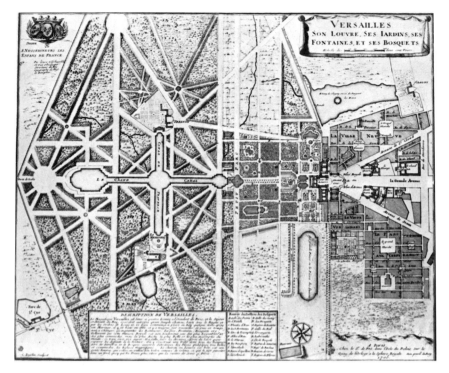

of François de Cuvilliés. There is also the deliberate pluralism of expression developed by the great Italian architect Filippo Juvarra. In his work every building and every space within the building has got its appropriate character: the exterior of Palazzo Madama in Turin (1718) is defined in terms of representative monumentality, whereas in the interior the forms become plasticly alive to accompany the festive movement of the splendid stairs.

In general, phenomenization led toward a dissolution of the archetypal characters of the Classical tradition, and also prepared the way for motifs and forms from other styles, in particular the Gothic. The resulting "historical architecture" found its first major manifestation in the Karlskirche in Vienna (1715) by Fischer von Erlach. The Karlskirche represents a singular synthesis of Roman splendour, Gothic verticalism and Baroque persuasive power. Fischer, in fact, considered his own works the natural conclusion to the history of architecture.[18]

Versailles

Our short sketch of Baroque urbanism demonstrated how the basic ideas of centralization, integration and extension were concretized in the capital cities of Rome and Paris. Some characteristic themes were of particular importance, such as the symbolic square, the directional street, and the uniform district. In most cities of the period, however, these elements appear without real systematic integration. Idealized plans were executed in only a few places, on a smaller scale. The most famous, and most typical, is Versailles.

The urban development of Versailles started in 1661 with the extension of the Royal Palace by Louis LeVau (1612–70). The gardens were planned by Le Nôtre who supervised the works for more than thirty years, and the total scheme may be considered the result of the simultaneous or successive contributions of LeVau, Le Nôtre and Hardouin-Mansart. The palace occupies the very centre of the plot and its long wings divide the area into two halves: gardens on one side and town on the other. Both halves

are characterized by infinite perspectives centred on the palace: The town is structured by three main avenues radiating away from the centre, the Avenue de Paris, the Avenue de Sceaux, and the Avenue de Saint-Cloud, with secondary streets and squares planned on an orthogonal grid; the layout of the gardens is based on a system of radiating paths and *rond-points*. The entire surrounding landscape falls under the seemingly limitless system. To make the extension still more effective, natural topography is transformed into a series of flat terraces, and large surfaces of reflecting water contribute to the experience. To mark the centre, Hardouin-Mansart planned to crown the palace with a dome to glorify the "Monarch by divine right." Versailles represents the very essence of the seventeenth-century city: domination and definition, but also dynamism and openness. It is therefore something more than an expression of absolutism; its structure has general properties which give it the capacity to receive other contents.

After his success with Vaux-le-Vicomte, LeVau was commissioned to rebuild the palace at Versailles for Louis XIV in 1664. He was ordered to preserve the old hunting lodge built for Louis XIII in 1624, and in 1669 it was decided to envelop the old *château* in a new building which left the original court exposed. The result was an immense, almost square block with two wings attached to form a very deep *cour d'honneur*. The *bel étage* was articulated by Ionic pilasters and columns carrying a tall entablature and an attic. Long transverse wings were later added by Hardouin-Mansart, repeating the same wall system at a total length of over four hundred metres. Evidently, extension as such is the basic theme, and accordingly the building has been transformed into a simple repetitive system, consisting of a transparent skeleton where the intervals between the pilasters are entirely filled in by large, arched windows. Versailles accordingly has the character of a glass house, and links the transparent structures of the Gothic period and the great iron-and-glass buildings of the nineteenth century. Another property that prefigures certain modern conceptions is the "indeterminacy" of its extension.[19] Seen in this context, the unusual "Italian" roof

(19) The intentions of Hardouin-Mansart culminated with the Grand Trianon at Versailles (1687). Here the very long one-storey wings consist of a uniform system of pilasters which carry a straight entablature. The continuous rhythm is emphasized by arched french windows, and the flat roof contributes to the effect of indeterminate extension.

(20) See Norberg-Schulz, *Late Baroque and Rococo Architecture*, chapter III.

(21) The importance of the wall in Borromini's works was first pointed out by Sedlmayr in *Die Architektur Borrominis* (Berlin, 1930).

also becomes meaningful. As an expression of centralized extension, Versailles concretizes the basic intentions of the Baroque age, intentions that were particularly connected with absolute monarchy and which one would expect to be expressed here more than anywhere else. Versailles is a true symbol of the absolute but open system of seventeenth-century France.

The basic properties of Versailles were repeated in many of the Late Baroque "residence-cities" of the eighteenth century. In Mannheim, Stuttgart and Würzburg the palace was not situated in the middle of the city proper, but acted as a focus for a larger whole which comprised an ideally "open" landscape. The most perfect example of this concept is Karlsruhe (1715). Here the tower of the palace is placed right in the centre of a system of thirty-two radiating streets. One quarter of the circle is filled in by the regularly planned town, and the other three quarters are given over to nature. The persuasive Baroque dynamism which was based on tensions between centres and directions has almost disappeared, and is replaced by a nostalgic manifestation of a world which already belongs to the past. The development of the Baroque palace culminated with the projects of Balthasar Neumann, notably the Residenz in Würzburg (1719 ff.).[20]

Sant'Ivo alla Sapienza

In 1642 Borromini began what is generally considered his masterpiece, the church of S. Ivo in Rome's old university, the Sapienza. The situation here demanded a centralized structure inserted at the end of the existing courtyard. Borromini, however, was not satisfied with adopting one of the traditional schemes, such as the octagon or the Greek cross, and invented one of the most original organisms in the entire history of architecture. S. Ivo indeed justifies his proud words: "I would not have joined this profession with the aim of being merely an imitator."

The plan is developed around a hexagon, and shows an alternation of apses and convex recesses. The complex shape which results is unified by continuous wall articulation and an engirdling entablature. The six

corners of the hexagon are characterized as being of primary structural importance, having double pilasters, while the apses and recesses have single ones. And, in fact, over these corners ribs rise vertically to carry the ring of the lantern, while the other ribs only form large frames around the windows of the dome. The basic invention of S. Ivo, however, is the idea of attaining vertical continuity by carrying the complex shape of the ground-plan without interruption into the dome. The dome, therefore, has lost the traditional character of static enclosure. It seems to be undergoing a process of expansion and contraction, a process that gradually comes to rest towards the circular ring under the lantern. In spite of its novel and rich shape, the interior of S. Ivo is one of the most unified spaces in the history of architecture.

The exterior is in general complementary to the interior space. The six structural corners appear in the drum as bundles of pilasters, while the walls between them have the character of expanding membranes, contrasting with the concave exedra below. The concave sides of the lantern form another contrast to the dome and the spiral that ends the dynamic vertical composition. In total the exterior synthesizes dome and tower, and thus expresses a new unity of cosmic symbolism and aspiring religious faith. More than other work, S. Ivo must have inspired Borromini's contemporaries to consider him a "Gothic" architect.

Borromini's real contribution did not lie in the development of new types, but in the invention of a *method* of handling space. By this method he was able to solve the most varied tasks, creating buildings that are particular and general at the same time. Basically his method is founded on the principles of continuity, interdependence and variation. His spaces, therefore, have the character of a dynamic field determined by the interaction of outer and inner forces, and the wall becomes the critical zone where these forces meet.[21] These forces also have psychological implications. The changing inside-outside relationships represent psychic processes, just as the fusions and transformations of the traditional anthropomorphic forms make the static psychological categories of the past break down. Bernini felt

339. Francesco Borromini: S. Ivo alla Sapienza, Rome. Begun 1642. Section.

340. Francesco Borromini: S. Ivo alla Sapienza, Rome. Ground plan.

341. Francesco Borromini: S. Ivo alla Sapienza, Rome. Isometric drawing.

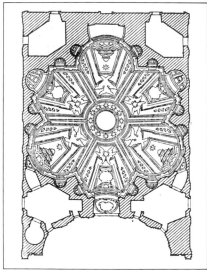

342. *Francesco Borromini: S. Ivo alla Sapienza, Rome. Vaulting.*

343. *Francesco Borromini: S. Ivo alla Sapienza, Rome. Court.*

this when he called Borromini's works "chimeric." Borromini thereby also intended a historical synthesis of a particular kind. His wish for unity does not only concern the spatial, but also the temporal dimension. While Bernini's space is "a stage for a dramatic event expressed through sculpture," to use Wittkower's words, Borromini made space itself a living event, expressing the everchanging situation of man in the world.

Borromini's conception of space was present from the very beginning of his career.[22] The plan of S. Carlo alle Quattro Fontane (1634) is still based on the traditional models of longitudinal oval and elongated Greek cross, but the two forms are fused rather than combined, and are concealed within a continuous, undulating boundary. Vertically the conventional point of departure is more evident, as we easily recognize the usual elements of arches and a superimposed ring which carry the dome. Anyhow, the wish for continuity and transformation is strongly felt. Borromini's spatial integration culminated with the diaphanous, skeletal structure of the Cappella dei Re Magi (after 1660), where a colossal order of pilasters is connected with a net of diagonally disposed ribs to create a complete "Gothic" system.

Vierzehnheiligen

The development of the Baroque church culminated with the great sanctuaries and monastic churches of Central Europe from the eighteenth century. Here all the basic themes of the history of Christian architecture are unified in a last magnificent synthesis made possible by Borromini's introduction of the unified spatial element, by the *ars combinatoria* of Guarini, and by the Late Gothic wall-pier system, which was employed by builders and architects trained within the local tradition of building technique.[23] The decisive step of combining the wall-pier system with the spatial groups developed by Guarini led to the creation of a fascinating series of buildings and projects. There is not space to discuss here the rich oeuvre of Christoph, Johann and Kilian Ignaz Dientzenhofer,[24] but instead we will examine the crowning achievement of the epoch, the great

(22) It is in fact evident in the Cappella del SS. Sacramento in S. Paolo fuori le mura, which was planned by Maderno in 1629 and executed by Borromini.

(23) The first to realize its importance was Hans Alberthal, who was active during the first three decades of the seventeenth century. Later the wall-pier became a main expedient of the Vorarlberg school.

(24) See Norberg-Schulz, *Kilian Ignaz Dientzenhofer e il barocco boemo.*

344. Balthasar Neumann: plan for Vierzehnheiligen pilgrimage church (near
Bamberg). 1743-72.

345. Balthasar Neumann: Vierzehnheiligen,
pilgrimage church (near Bamberg). Isometric
drawing.

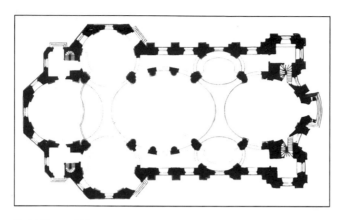

sanctuary of Vierzehnheiligen in Franconia (1744 ff.) by Balthasar Neumann (1687–1753).

This pilgrimage church has a beautiful position over the river Main. Its restrained exterior is in the form of a Latin-cross basilica with an impressive twin-tower façade which fuses Baroque rhetoric and medieval verticalism. Its convex central part gives an indication of the rich and dynamic interior. Within a seemingly infinite, luminous space a series of oval baldachins are organized according to the Guarinian principle of spatial interpenetration in a complex composition structured by a regular skeletal system of colossal columns and pilasters. A large main altar in the presbytery emphasizes the longitudinal axis, but equally strong is the oval centre marked by the splendid Rococo altar of the fourteen saints.

Analysis shows that two systems have been combined in the layout: a biaxial organism, already tried by Neumann in the Hofkirche in Würzburg (1731), and a conventional Latin cross. As the centre of the biaxial layout does not coincide with the crossing, an exceptionally strong spatial syncopation results. Over the crossing, where traditionally the centre of the church ought to be, the vault is eaten away by the four adjacent baldachins. The space defined by the groundplan is thereby transposed relative to space defined by the vault and the resulting syncopated interpenetration implies a spatial integration more intimate than ever before in the history of architecture.[25] This dynamic and ambiguous system of main spaces is surrounded by a secondary, outer zone, derived from the traditional aisles of the basilica. The relatively simple enveloping wall is perforated by numerous, large windows, which create a general diaphanous effect.

Vierzehnheiligen unifies all the great themes of ecclesiastical architecture. It contains the dominant centre, the longitudinal path, the cross, the basilican section, as well as the diaphanous double-shell structure which represents the most convincing interpretation of Christian light symbolism and spatial extension. The aisles and the superimposed galleries form a kind of two-storey ambulatory around the main oval—a conscious or unconscious reference to the medieval pilgrimage church. Moreover, the succession of ovals indicates a movement in depth which is related to the diagonal directions of High Gothic interiors. The articulation is both skeletal and plastic, as the colossal columns form part of an integrated system without losing their anthropomorphic character. The space is both differentiated and integrated, infinite and contained.

In his last major work, the Benedictine church at Neresheim (1747), Neumann returned to a simpler, unambiguous combination of dominant centre and longitudinal path, and a large double-shell rotunda placed in the middle of a longitudinal axis was, in fact, to become the major theme of the last great churches of the Central European Baroque. It is found in Dominikus Zimmermann's project for Ottobeuren (1732), in Kilian Ignaz Dientzenhofer's project for Kutná Hora (1735), and in Peter Thumb's cathedral at St. Gall (1756). It is also found in the splendid church at Rott am Inn (1759) by Johann Michael Fischer, in whose works the exterior is usually rather neglected, indicating a return to an interiority which also characterizes the works of the contemporaneous Bernardo Vittone. This marks the end of Baroque development with a desire to turn away from persuasive rhetoric.[26]

Belvedere

The great Late Baroque palace architecture of Austria was born when the Turks were defeated outside Vienna in 1683. The Austrian victory was a decisive turning point in the history of the country, which then assumed the role of a primary power in Europe. In architecture, this meant that the artistic programme of the Austrian Baroque had a political basis, which involved outdoing the art of their French rival, Louis XIV. In 1690 Fischer von Erlach (1656–1723) produced a magnificent project for the "Austrian Versailles" Schönbrunn. Unfortunately the project remained on paper. If built as originally planned, Schönbrunn would have been a culminating synthesis of basic experiences of Western architecture, comparable in scope to the great visions of Leibniz.[27] Whereas Leibniz's philosophy was directed towards the future, the Staatskunst of Fischer, however, belonged to a world concept which was approaching its end.

It was Fischer's rival Lucas von Hildebrandt (1668–1745) who was to carry out the most accomplished garden palaces of the Austrian Baroque. Gifted with an extraordinary artistic sensitivity, he may in many respects be considered a true follower of Borromini, and during his youth in Italy he certainly made acquaintance with the Turin churches by Guarini, which are reflected in some of his early ecclesiastical projects.[28] Hildebrandt's career culminated with the magnificent Belvedere palace in Vienna, built for Prince Eugene of Savoy whose position in the Austrian Empire made him the Emperor's equal. The extensive layout consists of two parts, the Lower Belvedere and the larger Upper Belvedere. In about 1700 Hildebrandt worked out a plan for the gardens and incorporated a general project for the lower palace, which was finally built between 1714 and 1716. The larger building on the top of the hill was erected in 1721–22. The result is a very original organism, where the infinite perspective of the Baroque garden has been transformed into an enclosed space. The elements of parterre and bosquet are still there, but they now form part of a more intimate world. At the same time the upper palace dominates the surrounding space like a medieval castle. The whole is a synthesis of local tradition, foreign importation and the new eighteenth-century approach to space.

The lower palace is based on a conventional cour d'honneur plan. Its basic aim is simultaneous differentiation and integration. The main rooms are contained within a relatively small ressaut which has a double-height salon in the middle. This ressaut is integrated with the extended wings by means of an ingenious interpenetration of volumes. As a result the flanking rooms of the ressaut have the same roof as the wings.

In the upper palace the same characteristics appear splendidly enriched and varied. From a distance the palace appears as a flat surface with a richly modelled silhouette. On the entrance side a large water basin blocks the longitudinal axis and forces the visitor to approach the building obliquely, drawing attention to the rich interplay of volumes: the

(25) The principle was suggested by Guarini in his project for S. Filippo Neri in Casale Monferrato (1671) and fully developed by Christoph Dientzenhofer in St. Nicholas in the Little Town of Prague (1703-11).

(26) The development of the Catholic church thus aimed at a solution which has a certain affinity to the typical centralized Protestant church.

(27) For a thorough analysis see H. Sedlmayr, Johann Bernhard Fischer von Erlach (Vienna, 1956).

(28) In 1699 Hildebrandt began the church at Gabel in Bohemia which repeats the scheme of S. Lorenzo in Turin, and which might have been a source of inspiration for Christoph Dientzenhofer.

348. *Lucas von Hildebrandt: Upper Belvedere, Vienna. 1721-22.*
349. *Lucas von Hildebrandt: Upper Belvedere, Vienna. Garden façade.*
350. *Lucas von Hildebrandt: Upper Belvedere, Vienna. Principal façade.*
351. *Lucas von Hildebrandt: Upper Belvedere, Vienna. Lateral façade.*

transparent vestibule in the middle, the flanking three-storey apartments and the towerlike corner pavilions. These various volumes are united by a continuous, although differentiated, wall. A similar treatment characterizes the garden façade. Because of the sloping land, what was a basement on the other side has become a ground floor, and the three-storey wings are united with the protruding central *ressaut* to form a majestic front. The sloping land also allowed for an ingenious treatment of the inside distribution of spaces. From the entrance a flight of stairs leads only half a storey down to the *sala terrena,* and another flight half a storey up to the main salon. This "split-level" disposition gives a feeling of spatial continuity hardly found in any other Baroque palace.

The upper Belvedere palace may be considered the greatest single achievement of Late Baroque secular architecture. Here Hildebrandt united all the basic intentions of the period into a highly original synthesis. The volumetric integration and the skinlike outer wall are related to contemporary French designs, but the articulation is different. It is neither characterized by French restraint nor by Italian plasticity, but is an entirely new invention: a vibrating, seemingly alive surface where the forms appear, disappear, disappear and change like the characters of a fairy tale.

Space Conception and Development

Baroque architecture is an architecture of inclusion. It does not exclude any aspect of the total architectural experience, but aims at a great synthesis. Both the systematic organization of Renaissance space and Mannerist dynamism are integrated. The transcendent quality of the Middle Ages and the anthropomorphic presence of antiquity are absorbed. The only property shunned is conflict, for a true synthesis does not allow for doubt. Baroque architecture, therefore, expresses assurance and victory, and testifies to a recovery of the existential foothold lost during the first decades of the *Cinquecento.* This new state of affairs is expressed through the basic properties of Baroque space: domi-

352. S. Susanna, Rome. Façade by Carlo
Maderno, 1597-1603.
353. Johann Bernhard Fischer von Erlach:
National Library, Vienna. Begun 1722. Court.

nant centre; infinite extension and persuasive, plastic power. The latter aspect is particularly strong in the Roman south, where the anthropomorphic tradition was still alive, whereas extension really became infinite in the French layouts of the *grand siècle*. The dominant centre is common to all Baroque systems because it represented the axioms which made the system meaningful.

As Baroque architecture is synthetic, it is characterized by simultaneous formal differentiation and integration. Baroque compositions are rich and complex, but they also possess a grand, comprehensive design. They therefore demand much from the observer, and are not easily appreciated by a period which lacks the human grandeur typical of the Baroque age. Baroque inclusion may also be understood as a synthesis of opposites: space and mass; movement and rest; enclosure and extension; proximity and distance; power and gentleness; dignity and delicacy; illusion and reality; *opera di mano* and *opera di natura*. This naturally is related to the general process of phenomenization described above, and in the works of certain artists, such as Borromini, the characters fuse or undergo a metamorphosis, as if to predict a new and deeper understanding of the human psyche.[29] We have also seen that phenomenization allowed for a differentiation of character according to the building task, and how it opened the way for architectural historicism.

Of particular interest are those formal properties which became "constituent factors" for the architectural development of the following centuries.[30] Although Baroque architecture concretized the systems of the period, it also represents an important contribution to the growth of general architectural experience, that is, to the universe of "possible" meanings. In this context the concepts of infinite extension and the related open form should be mentioned, as well as the methods developed to concretize these concepts, above all Guarini's spatial *ars combinatoria* based on interdependence and interpenetration of cells, and the undulating wall developed by Borromini to express the new fundamental importance of space. Finally, the environmental character could be differentiated within an all-inclusive homogeneous space, a concept which prefigures

(29) Bernini, instead, uses sculpture in relation to architecture to attain an analogous end. He therefore was, more than anybody else, the creator of the Baroque *Gesamtkunstwerk*.

(30) The problem was taken up for the first time by Giedion in *Space, Time and Architecture*.

165

(31) The case of Descartes is particularly illuminating. Having found that everything can be doubted, he concludes that his own doubt being a thought represents the only certainty! On the basis of this certainty he proceeds constructing a comprehensive system of "facts."

modern pluralism.

Baroque architecture started in Rome as an expression of the new self-assurance achieved by the Church through the Counter-Reformation movement. The first true protagonist was Carlo Maderno, and the further development is mainly due to Bernini, Borromini and Pietro da Cortona. The concept of dynamic system was soon adopted in France, where DeBrosse, Mansart and LeVau developed the clear and sensitive style known as "French Classicism." The Counter-Reformation and political aspects were unified by the Austrian Baroque, which is mainly due to the genius of Fischer von Erlach and Hildebrandt. In the works of the latter we also feel the nostalgic intimacy of the French Régence and Rococo. The Rococo is a style of transition which is rooted in the Baroque, but also assimilates the new empiricism and sentiment of eighteenth-century Enlightenment. In German Late Baroque architecture all the previous experiences are brought together to form a last great synthesis, above all in the comprehensive works of Balthasar Neumann. Whereas the Renaissance mainly was an Italian phenomenon, the Baroque became an international style based on a common general attitude to the problem of existence.

Meaning and Architecture

It may seem strange to talk about a "common general attitude" in connection with an age characterized by diversity and a certain freedom of choice. We have, however, indicated the reason in referring to d'Alembert's term *esprit de système*. The Baroque world may be called "pluralistic" in so far as it offered man a choice between different alternatives,

be they religious, philosophical, economic or political. But all the alternatives had in common the aim of arriving at a complete and secure system based on *a priori* axioms or dogmas. Man wanted absolute security, and he could find it in the tradition of the restored Roman Church, in one of the schools of Protestantism, which were all based on the belief in the absolute truth of the Biblical word, in the absolute monarchy "by divine right" or in the great philosophical systems of the age. The attitude was most natural; in fact, it represented different but analogous attempts at establishing a substitute for the lost medieval cosmos.[31]

In the long run the *esprit de système* could not satisfy man's need for a secure existential basis. The possibility of choice between different systems soon led critical minds to the conclusion that systems have a relative rather than an absolute value. But something had to replace the lost certainty, and the solution was found in the liberation of reason from the fetters of preconceived ideas. People suddenly realized that the conclusions ought to come at the end of an investigation, instead of being stated at the beginning! The new empiricism which resulted formed the basis for a new concept of existence, fundamentally different from the Baroque *esprit de système*.

Baroque architecture concludes a period in the history of Western culture which is usually called the "age of humanism." During the period people were still predominantly Christian in Europe, but they now wanted to integrate faith with the understanding of nature and human character inherited from antiquity. The process of solving this problem underwent three characteristic phases. During the Renaissance only the divine aspects

of man and nature were considered. Divine perfection was found in the human body, and in the rest of nature as well. As a result man felt safe and consummate, and in harmony with the great cosmic order. Renaissance architecture is therefore characterized by spatial geometrization by means of the Classical anthropomorphic orders. Mannerism represents doubt in this simple solution by exclusion. The dark side of man and nature was again experienced as a threatening reality. Rather than an expression of divine beauty, man felt his own body as a prison of the soul, and as a result he became subject to fear and alienation. Mannerist architecture is therefore characterized by conflict between the natural *ordine rustico* and the anthropomorphic members. More often than not, the latter are swallowed by the former. Nature, thus, was experienced as a multitude of acting forces, whereas the cosmic aspects were forgotten. During the Baroque age, finally, the totality of natural and human aspects were considered. Body and soul were now understood as parts of an inclusive, dynamic whole, and the experience of meaning was often connected with a state of ecstasy. In general we may say that the Baroque solution to the problem of body and soul consisted in participation. The art of the period concentrates on vivid images of situations, real or surreal, rather than on absolute form. "The charm of fables awakens the mind," Descartes said. Baroque architecture is therefore characterized by active participation of the anthropomorphic members in a dynamic spatial system. Participation, however, implied that man became more conscious of his own existence, and in the long run what should have made the system secure, therefore, led to its disintegration.

354.   *Gian Lorenzo Bernini: Throne of St. Peter.*
1657-66. St. Peter's, Rome.

10. Enlightenment

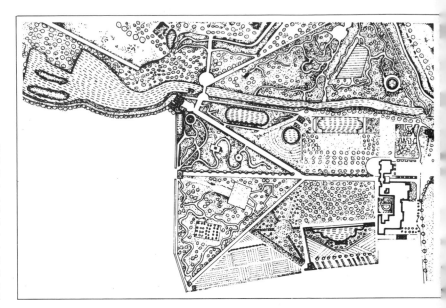

(1) For a significant discussion of the cultural problems of the nineteenth century, see H. Sedlmayr, *Verlust der Mitte* (Salzburg, 1948).

(2) For a discussion of the landscape garden, see F. Hallbaum, *Der Landschaftsgarten* (Munich, 1927).

Introduction

After the great Baroque systems had lost their impetus and self-confidence around 1750, a fundamentally new situation came into being. The industrial and social revolutions confirmed the decline of the old world, but so far they did not bring forth a new order that could satisfy man's quest for an existential foothold. Three symptoms characterize the new situation: the loss of identity of the old integrated settlements; the creation of numerous new building tasks; and the arbitrary use of architectural forms borrowed from the styles of the past. As a result the nineteenth century is usually considered to be an age of confusion and decline. The symptoms, however, may also be interpreted as attempts at concretizing new meanings to replace the traditional symbolic forms of walled town, church, palace and significant motif,[1] and during the second half of the century a new kind of architecture related to the new industrial technology became ever more important.

It is significant to note that the attempts to give architecture a new identity started with a new conception of landscape. As early as 1709 Lord Shaftesbury wrote that "the genuine order of nature" ought to replace the "mocking of princely gardens," but the English "landscape garden" only became a reality two decades later thanks to the genius of William Kent.[2] Kent aimed at a slightly stylized nature which would look more natural than nature itself. His basic intention was to return to an original paradisiac condition, throwing overboard the artificial systems of the Baroque period. "Classical" buildings were put into the new landscape representing "enlightened" man who places himself as a spectator in front of the natural world of the garden. Seen together, the landscape garden and the Neo-classical buildings concretize a general longing for a golden age when man lived in close contact with nature and was guided by his natural faculties. Shortly after 1750 the French theorist Laugier went back to the primitive hut to rediscover the "true" and "natural" elements of architecture—column, entablature and pediment—and he maintained that the Greek

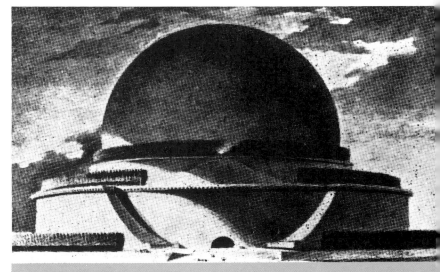

temple had inherited the simple logic of the primitive hut.[3] Somewhat later de Fournay approached the same problem from another angle, demanding that "architecture ought to regenerate through geometry"; and in contemporary projects cube, pyramid, cone, cylinder and sphere were legion.[4]

The new building tasks also represented different attempts to find "true" and "original" values. They did not have the power, however, to constitute new centres of meaning, and were absorbed by a new pluralism of tasks. Some architects, such as Schinkel, showed a true understanding of the characters of historical styles, but in general they were no more than a mask covering the real structure of the edifice. During the great epochs of the past certain forms had always been reserved for certain tasks. When, during the nineteenth century, the same forms were transferred to new types of buildings, a devaluation of the forms resulted.[5] The truly creative works of this period are the great utilitarian structures of iron and glass, where the Baroque concept of an open and dynamic space is given a new interpretation.[6] Protests against historicism were expressed from time to time, and towards the end of the century the dissatisfaction became general. Already in 1826, however, Schinkel, deeply impressed by the new industrial buildings he had seen in England, had asked, "Should we not try to find our own style?" In 1827 he designed a *Kaufhaus* which prefigures the straightforward forms of the technological architecture of the second half of the century.

Landscape and Settlement

In discussing the environment of the nineteenth century it is important to distinguish between the real conditions and a new ideal image which became manifest in many projects. Without the traditional city wall, and left to the uncontrolled play of economic forces, the organic settlements of the past gave way to a new kind of limitless agglomeration where the main elements were "the factory, the railroad and the slum."[7] Whatever was left over from a more meaningful past also underwent a process of gradual erosion. The new typical urban plan was the

(3) See W. Herrmann, *Laugier and Eighteenth Century French Theory* (London, 1962), pp. 49 ff.

(4) See Sedlmayr, *op. cit.*, p. 97

(5) See S. Giedion, "Napoleon and the Devaluation of Symbols," *Architectural Review*, no. 11, 1947.

(6) The importance of Baroque concepts of space for the development of modern architecture was first pointed out by S. Giedion in *Space, Time and Architecture* (Cambridge, Mass., 1941).

(7) L. Mumford, *The City in History* (London and New York, 1961), p. 458.

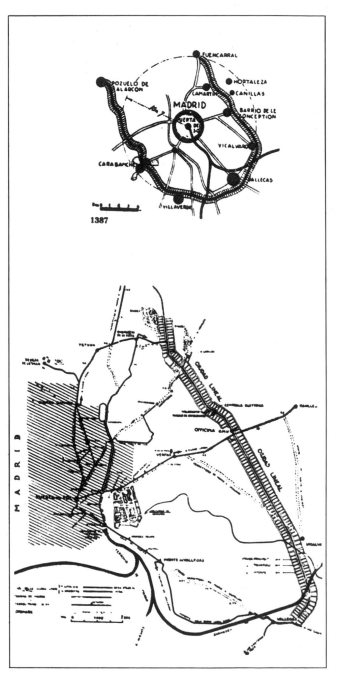

orthogonal grid, with similar building lots which could be treated as a mere economic commodity. Meaningful growth and planning in terms of places, paths and domains was thus replaced by the introduction of a neutral coordinate system, where the content and the corresponding environmental character were entirely determined by arbitrary individual enterprise. As Lewis Mumford says, "At the very moment that cities were multiplying in numbers and increasing in size all throughout Western civilization, the nature and purpose of the city had been completely forgotten."[8]

In certain projects of the period, however, we encounter ideas which contrast with the normal haphazard urban development and indicate the rise of a new environmental image. The project by Hector Horeau for the international exhibition in Paris 1867 shows the exhibition building to be conceived as a visually unbounded part of a limitless space, symbolized in the perspective drawing by a continuous horizon. In this design Horeau transforms the goal-oriented extension of Baroque layouts into a general openness, which may be understood as a concretization of the new global situation. A contemporary description of an executed building by Krantz confirms this interpretation: "To take a walk round this hall, which is round like the equator, is literally to take a trip round the world. All peoples are represented: Enemies live in peace side by side."[9]

The most important urban projects from the nineteenth century are based on this general image of an open space, at the same time as they seek a solution of the social problems created by the urban squalor and sprawl. The Spanish engineer Soria y Mata planned a linear city around Madrid (1882), which is based on the idea of open, but ordered linear growth, and on a new active interrelationship between settlement and nature. He made his intentions known: "The medieval idea of the walled city ought to be replaced by the idea of the open and rural city." The concept of the Garden City reached maturity with Ebenezer Howard, who published his ideas in 1898 under the title "A Peaceful Path to Real Reform." Howard squarely approached the problem of giving the open city identity and structure, introduc-

360. Tony Garnier: project for an industrial
city. 1901.

(8) *Ibid.*, p. 419

(9) S. Giedion, *Bauen
in Frankreich, Eisen,
Eisenbeton* (Leipzig,
1928), p. 41

361. Ebenezer Howard: diagram of a garden city. 1898.

362. Contamin & Dutert: Galerie des Machines, World Exposition of 1889, Paris.

363. Decimus Burton and Richard Turner. Palm House, Kew Gardens, London. 1844-48.

364. Decimus Burton and Richard Turner. Palm House, Kew Gardens, London. Interior.

365. Decimus Burton and Richard Turner. Palm House, Kew Gardens, London. Transverse section and structural details.

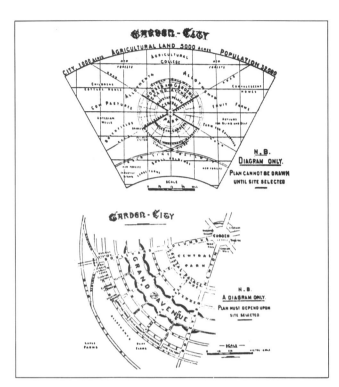

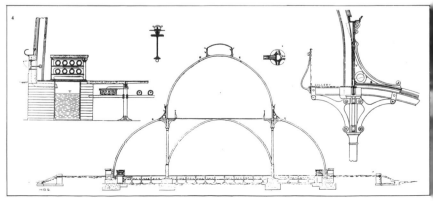

366. *Karl Friedrich Schinkel: Altes Museum, Berlin. 1822-30. Main staircase.*

367. *William Le Baron Jenney: Fair Store, Chicago, under construction, 1890.*

ng ideas of zoning, differentiated street system and urban centre. The latter he conceived as a central park containing town hall, theatre, concert hall, library, museum and hospital. About the same time Tony Garnier concretized similar ideas in his architecturally rich and articulate project for a *Cité Industrielle* (1901).

The basic problem for settlements in the industrial age was how to combine openness and flexibility with a meaningful spatial order. To achieve this, the pioneers of modern city planning aimed at a new interpretation of the fundamental concepts of place (centre), path (linear continuity) and domain (zoning). The general image of a garden city stems from the dream of a return to nature and a natural kind of life, originally represented by the landscape garden. It is important to stress that a pioneer like Howard envisaged the city as a living organism, for many of his successors evaded the real problem and created green, but lifeless suburbs.

Building

The new general situation created by the industrial and social revolutions produced a multitude of new building tasks. The church and the palace lost their importance as leading tasks, and during the nineteenth century the monument, the museum, the dwelling, the theatre, the exhibition hall, the factory and the office building in turn took over their role. Each of these tasks, as well as their temporal succession, indicates the rise of a new form of life based on new existential meanings. The monument represented a wish for a return to original archetypal forms, that is, the basic meaning concretized was the experience of eternity. Thus Chesterton said, "Eternity, the largest of the idols, the mightiest of the rivals of God."[10] The museum was conceived as an "aesthetic church," where all the works of man were brought together, as the manifestation of a new kind of art pantheism. In the dwelling the small and commodious space of the private world was understood as a symbolization of truth. Baroque phenomenization, thus, was given a new intimate interpretation in the *Kleinkunst* of the Biedermeier. Appositely Sedlmayr

(10) Sedlmayr, *op. cit.*, p. 31. Our discussion of the new building tasks follows Sedlmayr's exposition.

173

368. *Frank Lloyd Wright: Isabel Roberts House, Chicago, 1908.*

369. *Frank Lloyd Wright: Isabel Roberts House, Chicago. Plans of the first and second floors.*

370. *Antonio Gaudi: Casa Milá. Barcelona. 1905-10.*

(11) Thus Wagner wrote that the *orchestra* is " a garden of endless, general sensitivity, out of which the individual sensitivity of each performer can grow to perfection." Sedlmayr, *op. cit.*, p. 45.

points out that bourgeois society substituted the fairy tale for myth and religion. In contrast to the Apollonian world of the museum and the intimate world of the house, the theatre represented the Dionysian aspect of existence. Especially in the *Gesamtkunstwerk* of the opera, human feelings found their dramatic manifestation.[11] The exhibition, finally, represented the economic values of the new capitalist society, and the factory and the office building its productive forces. In general, the multitude of building tasks shows how the integrated and hierarchical forms of life of the past had given way to a pluralism of equally valid meanings which interacted in various ways.

It is important to point out, however, that a new spatial image developed mainly in connection with some of the new tasks, which therefore obviously had a particular significance. After the middle of the nineteenth century, the large hall (for production, exhibition and distribution), the office building, and the individual house became the leading tasks which determined the character of man's environment. The hall developed mainly in Europe when iron and glass were adopted for the construction of large exhibition buildings, railway stations, department stores and factories. A splendid example was offered by the Galerie des Machines at the Paris exhibition of 1889 by Contamin and Dutert. The immense main space measured 420 by 115 metres (1378 by 377 feet) and was accompanied by aisles and galleries. The **main structure consisted of twenty-three hinged arches which rested on small joints,** creating a revolutionary effect of dynamic lightness. With its continuous walls of glass, the Galerie des Machines realized Horeau's vision of a limitless, luminous space.

Whereas the hall may be defined as a unitary space into which secondary elements are freely placed, the office building was conceived as a repetitive, orthogonal structure, which may be extended horizontally as well as vertically. The basic design is due to William Le Baron Jenney, who played an important role in the reconstruction of Chicago after the great fire in 1871. His Home Insurance Building of 1884 was the first great structure in fully developed skeleton construction. Here the outer wall, although archi-

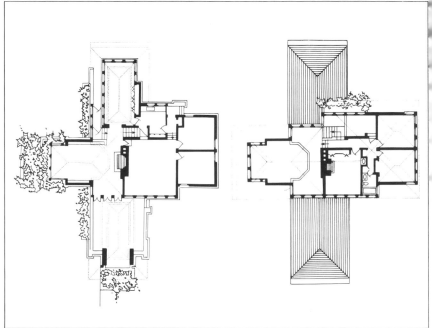

371. Victor Horta: Maison du Peuple, Brussels. 1896-99.

372. Giuseppe Calderini: Palazzo di Giustizia, Rome. 1883-1910.

tecturally immature, had been transformed into a curtain carried by the primary structure. This technique made the development of the skyscraper possible.[12] The third basic building type of the later decades of the nineteenth century, the one-family house, was fundamentally reinterpreted by Frank Lloyd Wright, who destroyed the traditional box to achieve a dynamic interaction of interior and exterior space. Directions and functional domains were defined by means of a juxtaposition of horizontal and vertical planes, usually related to a large, vertical chimney at the centre. In general, the hall, the vertical office building and the house, as conceived by Frank Lloyd Wright, represent contributions to a functional, formal and technical concretization of the basic image of open space.

Articulation

The multiplicity of new building tasks implied a range of characters that could not be expressed within the limits of one style of the past. It is no wonder, then, that architects started to experiment with forms taken from several styles. This approach cannot be condemned as basically wrong, as was usually done during the period of strict functionalism. The styles represent a cultural heritage of possible meanings, and the phenomenization which culminated in eighteenth-century architecture indicated a freer use of their expressive potential. One of the ideas of the nineteenth century, thus, was to select for each task the style which suited it best. Churches were usually built in Gothic style, whereas museums and universities (as "museums of knowledge") were Classical. However, very often architects only copied superficial motifs without understanding their basic character, and the general borrowing of forms produced a lessening of the ability to articulate in the sense of a more general unification and subdivision of surfaces, masses and spaces. Most of the official buildings of the second half of the nineteenth century, therefore, show a lack of correspondence between the general layout and the detailing. Architectural members and details are applied without any convincing relationship to the whole, and it is difficult or

(12) See C. W. Condit, *The Chicago School of Architecture* (Chicago and London, 1964).

(13) See S. Giedion, *Space, Time and Architecture,* 5th ed. (Cambridge, Mass., 1967), p. 293. Characteristic examples of the rhetorical architecture of the later decades of the nineteenth century include Poelaert's Palais de Justice in Brussels (1866-83), and Calderini's Palazzo di Giustizia in Rome (1883-1910).

373. *Claude—Nicolas Ledoux: project for La Saline de Chaux, Arc-et-Senans. 1775-79.*

374. *Claude-Nicolas Ledoux: La Saline de Chaux, Arc-et-Senans. Aerial view.*

375. *Claude-Nicolas Ledoux: La Saline de Chaux, Arc-et-Senans. Workers' houses.*

impossible to distinguish between primary and secondary parts. In the rhetorical buildings that resulted, every part is given the same emphasis, and the meanings implied counteract each other rather than constituting a coherent message. It is hardly surprising that Henri van de Velde described the situation around 1890 as a *moral* problem: "The real forms of things were covered over. In this period the revolt against the falsification of forms and against the past was a moral revolt!"[13]

Together with the pluralism of styles, however, went a continuous search for true characters and principles. The first important contribution is offered by the French revolutionary architects Ledoux and Boullée, who were active during the last decades of the eighteenth century. Their works are characterized by the use of simple stereometric volumes and undecorated surfaces, and in important respects they prefigure the elementary character of Functionalist buildings in reinforced concrete. With the introduction of iron-and-glass construction, it became possible to build such articulate structures as had been envisaged in the fictitious skeletons of the past. Towards the end of the nineteenth century this possibility was exploited by talented architects such as Hector Guimard and Victor Horta, and led to the creation of the sensitive and versatile Art Nouveau where modern technology, the new building types and the basic desire for open space are united with a fine understanding of the quality of natural and human phenomena. As a result a synthetic new art came into being which represents a fine culmination of the intentions of the epoch. The best works of the Art Nouveau have a truly organic character, and, in fact, Pankok defined its aim as "the transformation of dead matter into an organic being." We might add that it also represented a humanization of modern technology.

In America Art Nouveau is paralleled by the articulate and sensitively ornate architecture of Louis Sullivan. Basically the Art Nouveau was an outgrowth of the Nordic feeling for dematerialized structure and transparent space. In the works of the Spanish architect Antonio Gaudí, the organic quality of the Art Nouveau is given a different plastic interpretation, but with a sound (and

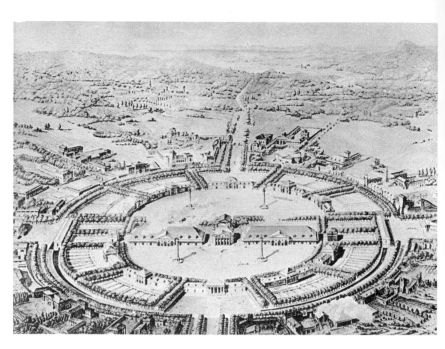

376. *Claude-Nicolas Ledoux: La Saline de Chaux, Arc-et-Senans. Design for the wheel factory.*

377. *Claude-Nicolas Ledoux: project for an agricultural lodge, Maupertuis.*

Coupe.

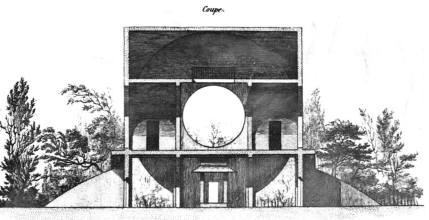

imaginative) technical basis to his sculptural forms.

In the works of Frank Lloyd Wright, finally, there is a new grammar of spatial articulation. The façade hardly matters any more in his houses. For the first time in history architecture had become a truly three-dimensional problem, and for the first time in history the most advanced architectural ideas were used to solve the problem of the dwelling for everyman. In his works the nineteenth century ends with the promise of a new meaningful human environment, where everybody may find his place within an open totality.

Chaux

The first ideal city of the industrial age, and certainly the most fascinating, is La Saline de Chaux between the villages of Arc and Senans near Besançon in eastern France. In 1774 Claude-Nicolas Ledoux (1736–1806) received the commission, and a part of his comprehensive project was built between 1775 and 1779. The layout indicates cosmic implications, and is related to the plans of ideal cities from earlier periods. Ledoux himself explained its circular shape as "as pure as that described by the sun on its daily round,"[14] and moreover the layout incorporates two main paths which cross at right angles and define the cardinal points. But the content makes Chaux different from the ideal cities of the past. It is really conceived as a "ville sociale," with the work of the community at the centre of the symbolic plan. Two long buildings for salt production, with the director's house between them, are placed along the transverse axis, and symmetrically face the visitor who enters Chaux through the main entrance to the south. They are surrounded by a circle of workers' dwellings (of which only the southern half was built), with gardens attached. Another, outer circle was to have been occupied by more freely placed buildings for various common purposes. The general character is that of a garden city, in spite of the basically formal disposition. Ledoux wished to symbolize a new kind of reconciliation between man and nature, created by man's purposive labour, and he wrote, "It is the work of people that

(14) See Y. Christ, *Projets et divagations de Claude-Nicolas Ledoux* (Paris, 1961), p. 44.

(15) *Ibid.*, p. 42.

(16) A project by Durand and Thibault from 1803 shows a monumental "assembly area for meetings of all the citizens of the commune, so as to practise some religion there."

(17) See E. Kaufmann, *Von Ledoux bis Le Corbusier* (Vienna, 1933), p. 65.

(18) P. Beaver, *The Crystal Palace* (London and New York, 1970), p. 17.

(19) The Crystal Palace was in fact moved to a new site in 1852, and re-erected on a somewhat different and much larger plan. In 1866 the northern wing burned down, but the building did not lose its basic formal quality. In 1936 the structure was destroyed by fire.

(20) Beaver, *op. cit.*, pp. 40 ff.

tends and brings to fruition all the seed that nature, in its unspoken contract with man, has promised to make fertile."[15]

That there was a pantheistic-functional philosophy behind the layout of Chaux becomes evident in the different *"édifices sociaux"* planned by Ledoux. At the very centre, over the director's home, he built a sanctuary dedicated to a general *"Etre supreme,"* an idea typical of the revolutionary age.[16] Public buildings along the periphery were planned to serve all conceivable functions: *bourse;* hospital; market; baths; houses for merchants, artisans and artists; a *"maison d'Union"* dedicated to the cultivation of moral values; a *"temple de Mémoire"* dedicated to the glory of women; buildings for education and recreation; and even a "temple of Love" which should have had a phallus at its centre. In all buildings Ledoux aimed at expressing the function by means of an *architecture parlante*. This meant that, for example, the house of the wheelwright should have had circular façades, although the section shows a more conventional interior disposition of orthogonal rooms. The cemetery is particularly interesting; it was conceived as a sphere with a diameter of 80 metres (262 feet), half sunk into the ground and surrounded by catacombs. Ledoux explained that the sphere should symbolize eternity. As it was lit from a circular opening at the top, it also incorporated the ancient concept of the *axis mundi* running from the world of the dead to heaven above. All these building tasks were given the same architectural attention; Ledoux said. "The Great belongs to every kind of building."[17]

Ledoux's formal articulation is based on the use of simple stereometric shapes, and he explicitly says, "The circle and the square, these make up the alphabet used by authors in the fabric of the best works." A characteristic feature is his use of interpenetrating Classical members and rustication, but he does not make of them any expression of conflict. The large dimensions and basically static forms concretize instead the image of a new kind of synthesis, that is, the reconciliation of man and nature already mentioned above. In general, Ledoux's works reveal a fascinating attempt to use archetypal characters to give meaning to a multitude of new building tasks. He thereby introduced one of the fundamental problems of modern architecture, and may indeed be considered a revolutionary architect.

Crystal Palace

The year 1851 marks a turning point in the history of modern architecture. The first large-scale world exhibition was organized in London, and the Crystal Palace built by Joseph Paxton to house it was the first great official building which omitted all references to past styles. Paxton (1801–65) was a gardener who had made a career in the service of the Duke of Devonshire. His inventive genius is well illustrated by the story of how he hit upon the design for the famous greenhouse at Chatsworth for the huge lily Victoria Regia (1837). "One day, to test the buoyancy of the leaves, he placed his little daughter on one of them and noticed that it took her weight without the least distortion. He then studied the underside of the leaf—the radiating ribs strengthened by cross-ribs—and decided to use the Victoria Regia as a pattern for the lily house. The result was a light airy structure with a glass roof supported by light wooden beams which were hollowed out into gutters. These beams were supported in turn by light tubular columns of iron which also acted as drains for the roof. The result was charming and most economical to build."[18]

A competition for the exhibition building was held in 1850, but none of the two hundred and forty-five plans submitted was accepted for construction. Shortly afterwards, Paxton, who had not participated in the competition, was asked to work out a project, and in nine days he drew up the plans for a building 560 metres long and 137 metres wide (1837 by 449 feet). His scheme, described in detail in the official guide, was a masterpiece of standardization. Iron columns, girders and glass panels were made with coordinated dimensions, and were prefabricated in three months. Afterwards it took another three months to erect the immense structure, and the finished plan was received with great acclaim. After the opening *The Times* (London, May 2, 1851) wrote enthusiastically: "Above the visitors rose a glittering arch far more lofty and spacious than the

vaults of even our noblest cathedrals. On either side the vista seemed almost boundless."

The form of the building represented a fundamentally new conception, a realization of the open extension suggested in Hardouin Mansart's Grand Trianon. It was based on a recurrent iron skeleton of extreme lightness and delicacy. An arched transept was introduced during planning to allow for the preservation of some elm trees on the site. Walls and roofs were made entirely of glass, the number of panes amounting to 293,655! The size of the Crystal Palace may be defined as indeterminate, rendering obsolete Alberti's dictum that nothing might be added or taken away.[19] Instead of a static equilibrium of interrelated parts, coherence was created by means of a repetition of the same structural system throughout. In this way the new technical possibilities set architecture free to frame new functions and forms of life.

The Crystal Palace was spontaneously recognized as a manifestation of a new kind of architecture, which proved the general belief in scientific and industrial progress. Sentiments of an almost religious kind were evoked by the great, luminous space. Queen Victoria recorded the impression as "magical" and felt "filled with devotion," and Alfred Tennyson wrote about the opening of the Great Exhibition as the moment "when Europe and the scattered ends of our fierce world did meet as friends and brethren in her halls of glass."[20] The building gave rise to an era of iron-and-glass construction. Les Halles in Paris by Baltard (1853) represented another important early manifestation of the new open architecture, and during the following decades crystal palaces were built in many European and American cities. Even in the anonymous dwellings of the period large surfaces of glass became usual, giving testimony to the symbolic importance of the transparent material which so convincingly concretized the existential space of the new world.

Guaranty Building

Whereas the Crystal Palace represented an ideal image, and was received with almost

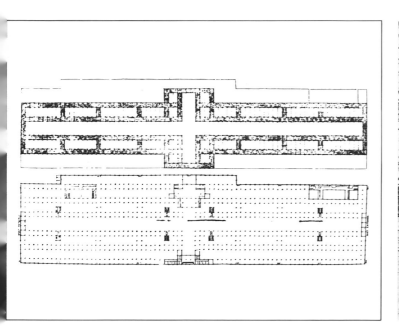

378. Joseph Paxton: Crystal Palace, London.
1851. Ground plan.

379. Joseph Paxton: Crystal Palace, London
Interior.

380. View of the Crystal Palace in a 19th-century engraving.

(21) V. Scully, *American Architecture and Urbanism* (New York, 1969).

(22) L. Sullivan, *Kindergarten Chats* (New York, 1947), p. 44.

(23) *Ibid.*, p. 49.

(24) *Ibid.*, p. 202.

(25) *Ibid.*, pp. 187-8.

381. Louis Sullivan: Guaranty Building, Buffalo. 1894-95.

382. Louis Sullivan: Guaranty Building, Buffalo. Detail of the exterior.

religious reverence, the American skyscraper from the beginning had a more concrete character. That does not imply that it did not possess symbolic significance, but that it was intended as a constituent element of a new townscape. The skyscraper was something more than a manifestation of repetitive skeleton construction; primarily it expressed a new kind of continuous interior volume and, secondly, it functioned as a pointmarker in exterior space. It therefore belongs to the new fundamental class of buildings which concretize the existential image of open space. As has been pointed out by Scully, the basic principles were already present in the Marshall Field Warehouse in Chicago by Henry Hobson Richardson (1885–87), where the exterior of an Italian *Quattrocento palazzo* is expanded to make the new conception of space manifest.[21] A further step towards the expression of continuous open space was taken in Richardson's second Ames Building in Boston (1886–87). In comparison, Jenney's Home Insurance Building (1884–85), where the skeleton frame of iron and steel was introduced, shows a more conventional addition of stories. However, Jenney's invention made a fully consequent definition of the character of the new building type possible, and prepared the way to the important solution produced by Louis Sullivan (1856-1929).

Sullivan was a man of extraordinary sensitivity and creative power, receptive equally to the wonders of nature and to the dynamism of the growing metropolis. He is usually credited with the invention of the slogan "form follows function," but a study of his writings and buildings shows that he interpreted the words "function" and "form" liberally. When he introduces the concepts he explains that they comprise *life* as a whole, and concludes: "American architecture, will mean, if it ever succeeds in meaning anything, American life."[22] The building, therefore, ought to be an organism where the pressure of a living force is made manifest and operative. "The pressure, we call Function: the resultant, Form." Thereby architecture becomes "the manifest consummation of existence."[23] In an essay entitled "The Tall Office Building Artistically Considered" (1896) he applied his ideas to a concrete

383.   *Louis Sullivan: Carson Pirie Scott Store, Chicago. 1899-1904.*

example and asked, "How shall we impart to this sterile pile, this crude, harsh, brutal agglomeration, this stark, staring exclamation of eternal strife, the graciousness of those higher forms of sensibility and culture that rest on the lower and fiercer passions?"[24] To answer the question he gave the first true analysis of a building type as a functional organism, describing the technical purpose of the basement, the public character of the ground floor (offering "great freedom of access"), the mezzanine connected with the ground floor, the *indefinite* number of storeys of offices above, and finally the attic which completes the "circulatory system" of the building.

The validity of Sullivan's analysis is proved by his fine Wainwright Building in St. Louis (1890–91), and by the masterly Guaranty Building in Buffalo (1894–95). Here the differentiated openness of ground floor and mezzanine is convincingly expressed, whereas the office storeys above are unified to indicate the indeterminate vertical extension. Particularly convincing is the upper conclusion of the Guaranty Building which grows organically out of the structure below. By means of ornamentation the "strong athletic and simple form" is "clad in a garment of poetic imagery." "That is to say, a building which is truly a work of art is in its nature, essence and physical being an emotional expression."[25] Sullivan's understanding of architectural character becomes still more evident in a comparison with his Carson-Pirie-Scott department store in Chicago (1899–1904). Here vertical continuity is suppressed to express the horizontal extension of the large sales areas, and the building thus comes to participate actively in the busy longitudinal movement of the adjacent streets. Vertically, as well as horizontally, Sullivan's buildings therefore give scale, structure and meaning to the townscape, and indicate the rise of an open and dynamic urbanism.

Robie House

In the houses of Frank Lloyd Wright (1869–1959) the concretization of open space was brought down to the intimate scale of per-

(26) F. L. Wright, *The Natural House* (New York, 1963; London, 1972), p. 33.

sonal place. The existential problem he had to face was a combination of rootedness and protection with a new sense of freedom and mobility, and he solved it through a new interpretation of the house. Traditionally, the house has been an enclosed space, an inside, a refuge for the individual and the family. In the Baroque palaces this elementary character was combined with a desire for expansion and dominance. Wright, however, wanted openness without dominance; his ideal was always an "architecture of democracy." Thus he destroyed the box and created a new, general interaction between inside and outside. The concept of inside changed from that of a refuge to become a fixed point in space, from which man could experience a new sense of freedom and participation. In this point in space Wright placed a great fireplace with a vertical chimney, commenting, "It comforted me to see the fire burning deep in the solid masonry." Man does not therefore place himself at the centre of his world, as was the case in Versailles. Rather we find at the centre an element which symbolizes the forces and order of nature—a reminder that the new open world should not make us forget the basic meanings of existence. When writing about his concept of the dwelling, Wright, in fact, entitled the book *The Natural House.*

The most important early "prairie" houses by Wright, such as the Ward Willitts House (1902) and the Isabel Roberts House (1908) have a characteristic cruciform plan. Spaces extend along the main axes from the central chimney stack, and seem to dissolve gradually into the surroundings by means of terraces and porches. The traditional perforated wall has been replaced by unbroken planes which are separated from the roof above by continuous bands of windows. The wall thus is no longer used to enclose space, but it is there "to bring the outside world into the house and let the inside of the house go outside."[26] The house still appears as a sheltered place, thanks to the treatment of the roof, which Wright saw as a determinant of the character: "An idea that shelter should be the essential look of any dwelling put the low spreading roof, flat or hipped or low gabled, with generously projecting eaves

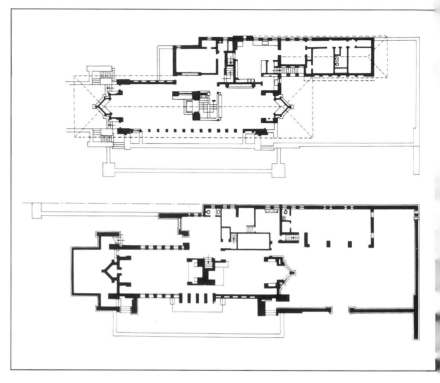

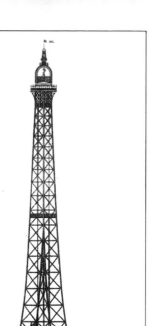

over the whole."[27] The cruciform plan with a centrally placed chimney and the porches which connect the house with its surroundings and had been used before Wright, but he was the first to relate these forms to the general image of open space. Continuity of space and form thus became the distinguishing principle of his organic architecture. Finally, his use of materials should be mentioned, which were always treated according to their nature, be they old or new. Wright also fully realized the importance of glass as "a resource to liberate the new sense of space."

Wright's basic ideas were developed around 1893, and his early period culminated with the Robie House in Chicago from 1909. The house was built on a narrow site, and does not possess a fully developed cruciform plan, but the strongly emphasized longitudinal direction is still maintained by the transversely placed mass of the chimney and by the top floor attached to it. Although it does not appear as a closed box, the lower part of the house is firmly attached to the ground, and the hovering horizontals of balconies and roofs simultaneously define a place and suggest infinite extension: "planes parallel to the earth . . . make the building belong to the ground: I see the extended horizontal line as the true earth line of human life, indicative of freedom."[28] The Robie House therefore fulfils Wright's idea of a dwelling which both protects and liberates. The great impact of his achievement consists in his having given the most fundamental meanings of existential space a modern interpretation. In America, the New World, archetypal meanings were thus rediscovered and taken as the point of departure for a truly democratic architecture. With pride Wright said, "I was born an American child of the ground and of space."[29]

Space Conception and Development

When discussing the architecture of the nineteenth century, we have repeatedly used the term "open space" to indicate the image of a limitless and continuous environment where man may act and freely move about—

not for the sake of movement as such, but as an expression of a new freedom of choice, that is, the freedom to search and create one's own place. The new image, then, is the opposite to the Baroque. Whereas Baroque space represented an integrated system, the open space of the nineteenth century expressed a new ideal of human freedom. (This does not contradict the fact that open space was formally derived from the continuous and dynamic, but differentiated Baroque space.) Open space was concretized in various ways. In the large halls of iron and glass it appears as a "total," transparent and luminous milieu, which has lost the traditional character of "interior." In the repetitive web of Chicago construction it is interpreted as an open growth, which gives the horizontal and vertical dimensions a new meaning. In Wright's houses it appears as a fluid medium which may be directed, dilated and contracted. In some works it is only a vague intuition, in others an accomplished articulate fact.

The image of open space underwent a characteristic development. Its first manifestation, the landscape garden, negates the Baroque systems, at the same time as expressing a wish for a return to a natural situation. Although the landscape garden dates back to the eighteenth century, the meaning it represents is still of real importance. The large halls of iron and glass stated the new spatial image in a general and visionary way, and approached a definition of some of its basic properties, such as transparency and dissolution of the mass. Contemporary reports indicate that the halls in fact were experienced as visionary images. The tall office building and related types gave the concept of open space a concrete interpretation on the urban level, and the best examples, such as the works of Sullivan, offered the promise of articulate environmental character. (Thus Scully writes: "Sullivan brought into the mass metropolis a dignified image of human potency and force."[30] Frank Lloyd Wright, finally, created the modern house, so as to solve the architectural problem of expressing personal identity in an open and mobile world. He achieved this by defining qualitatively different zones within the general spatial continuum by means

(27) *Ibid.*, p. 16.

(28) *Ibid.*

(29) *Ibid.*

(30) V. Scully, *Modern Architecture* (New York, 1961), p. 19.

of a new interpretation of roof, wall and opening. His success was such that his works were of decisive importance for the functionalist phase of modern architecture in Europe.

The first phase of the modern development thus proceeded from a general image to a more precise definition of environmental character, a development which is natural and in accordance with the creative process as such. The failure of historicism can be understood against this background. The eclectic architecture of the nineteenth century took the particular motif as its point of departure, and tried to organize the borrowed forms by means of abstract, academic rules of composition. Several creative artists of the period recognized the impossibility of this inverse approach, and maintained that the particular character has to be abstracted from a comprehensive vision of modern life. A general vision, however, requires an exceptional inner freedom. If he lacks this, by and large man finds existential security in the known motif, and as a result the totality of nineteenth-century architecture became a collection of these. Its most conspicuous product of the nineteenth century; accordingly, is a confusion of styles.[31] However, it should also be pointed out that the interpretation of past meanings in the new form of life was a real and necessary problem, but the failure of historicism has shown that it could not be solved at the outset of the modern development. Only today, after the basic spatial properties and characters of the new architecture have been defined, the more particular meanings of the past return to form part of a more comprehensive and articulate totality.

Meaning and Architecture

The basic intention behind the new image of space was the wish for a liberation from the systems of the past. Enlightened man did not want to accept any *a priori* axiom or dogma. Thus Voltaire wrote: "We must never say: Let us begin by inventing principles according to which we attempt to explain everything. We should rather say: Let us make an exact analysis of things."[32] It was thought reason should be applied to the phenomena themselves, rather than to the deduction of facts from *a priori* axioms, making of reason the tool of a new empiricism or *esprit systématique*. Even earlier Locke had said, "Whence has it [the mind] all the materials of reason and knowledge? To this I answer one word, from *experience*."[33] On this basis natural science was led away from the arbitrary and fanciful assumptions of the past to a new method of observation and analysis, with its great protagonist, Newton. His importance was immediately recognized, as is proved by one of the grandest and most typical architectural projects of the late eighteenth century: Boullée's Cenotaph for Newton (1784), where Newton's sarcophagus is surrounded by a sphere representing the universe. Newton's empiricism, however, did not imply that he rejected philosophy and religion; he regarded these subjects as the end of human knowledge, rather than the foundation on which it must be built.

The new scientific outlook was closely related to a new idea of freedom. Enlightenment philosophy opposed the power of convention, tradition and authority, and the centralized and the hierarchic systems of the Baroque age gave way to a multitude of interacting, equal elements. The slogan *liberté, égalité,* *fraternité* defines the new ideal well. A profound psychological change resulted. While the Baroque attitude may be characterized by the word "persuasion," the enlightened man concentrated on sensation. Accordingly the illusive, allegorical image was replaced by the natural, "true" image, in science as well as in art. Rationalism and romanticism are therefore two different manifestations of the same basic attitude.

In this way enlightened man thus found existential foothold for himself as a participant in the general evolutionary process. Although this reduced him to a tiny atom, the nineteenth century preserved the belief in natural harmony and in man's ability to discover its laws. And, in fact, the scientific and technological progress of the age gave him reason to maintain this belief. Purposeful activity and work, therefore, came to represent a basic existential meaning, and the self-made man is a characteristic product of the perod. Paxton may be mentioned as an example, and the story of the lily house at Chatsworth illustrates the approach of the empirically minded genius.

However, as already intimated, there was a discrepancy between the ideal image of the nineteenth century and the actual conditions. Marx maintained that the social con- ditions prevented man from realizing freedom through his work, and that instead he became alienated from his own self. Marx's criticism is valid and significant, and implies that a healthy society forms an integral part of an open world. Unfortunately, however, his explanations and proposals for improvement were based on dogmatic thinking, and represented a relapse into the *esprit de système*.[34] Marxian philosophy has propagated the dominance of those who put the conclusion at the beginning.

The new architecture of the nineteenth century concretized the ideal of *liberté, égalité, fraternité,* and it naturally gave prime importance to the building tasks connected with work and dwelling: The exhibition was understood as an expression of a new kind of brotherhood, and Wright wanted with his houses to create an "architecture of democracy." This provides the reason why modern architecture was not accepted by the totalitarian movements of the twentieth century. This fact is profoundly significant, and shows that the new image of space from the outset possessed a fundamental symbolic meaning. Considering the discrepancy between ideal image and harsh reality, it should, however, be asked whether the idea of freedom was a mere illusion.

(31) S. Giedion has pointed out the need of the self-made man of the nineteenth century for a "humanistic alibi" to prove his good taste. See 'Napoleon and the Devaluation of Symbols."

(32) Voltaire, *Traité de Métaphysique*, quoted after E. Cassirer, *The Philosophy* of the Enlightenment (Boston, 1955), p. 12.

(33) J. Locke, *An Essay Concerning Human Understanding*, 1690.

(34) See R. Tucker, *Philosophy and Myth in Karl Marx* (Cambridge and New York, 1967).

388. J. M. W. Turner: Rain, Steam, Speed. 1844. National Gallery, London.

11. Functionalism

(1) H. R. Hitchcock and P. Johnson, *The International Style* (New York, 1932).

(2) W. Gropius, *The New Architecture and the Bauhaus* (London, 1935), pp. 21, 32.

(3) *Ibid.*, p. 18.

Introduction

Between the two world wars the architectural scene was dominated by the International Style.[1] This term is suitable in that it indicates that the variety and apparent confusion of the nineteenth century had given way to a uniform and easily recognizable approach to design. The "modern" buildings of the period are distinguished by a few characteristic properties: they are usually derived from simple stereometric shapes; they appear as unitary volumes wrapped up in a thin, weightless skin of glass and plaster; and they show a puritan lack of material texture and articulating detail. Walter Gropius described the buildings as "transparent structures" and "sharply modelled designs in which every part merges naturally into the comprehensive volume of the whole."[2] In their basic properties they relate to the general image of a new architecture born during the nineteenth century, and develop further the concepts of transparency and spatial continuity. At the same time there is a return to the elementary shapes and geometric relationships introduced by the revolutionary architects of the late eighteenth century.

In general the period between the wars was characterized by a search for a secure common basis, that is, for principles. The word "Functionalism" is indicative of its attitudes and aims; in architecture, it is a rationalization of the general approach introduced by Sullivan and Wright. While American architecture after the turn of the century was involved in a new wave of historicism, Wright's works were published in Germany in 1910, and exercised a decisive influence on European development. Following him, European architects sought basic principles in the belief that the new architecture was "the inevitable logical product of the intellectual and technical conditions of our age,"[3] and those who shared this belief considered themselves exponents of a "modern movement," which was confirmed when the Congrès Internationaux d'Architecture Moderne (CIAM) was founded in 1928. With the aid of this organization and its indefatigable general secretary, Sigfried Giedion, the search for principles was coordinated and directed towards dealing with practical tasks,

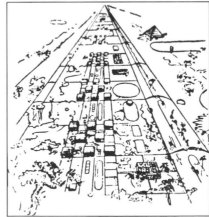

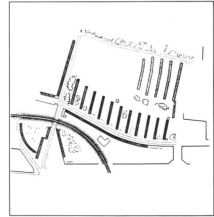

389. *Ludwig Mies van der Rohe: Weissenofsiedlung, Stuttgart. 1927. Aerial view.*

390. *Miljutin & May: plan for the city of Magnitogorsk. 1930.*

391. *Walter Gropius: Siemensstadt, Berlin. 1929. General plan.*

392. *Ludwig Mies van der Rohe: Illinois Institute of Technology, Chicago. 1940. Plan.*

393. *Reinhard & Hofmeister: Corbett, Harrison & MacMurry; Hood, Godley & Foui-houx: Rockefeller Center, New York. 1930-40. Aerial view.*

394. *Le Corbusier: plan for Nemours. 1934.*

such as the social dwelling and the urban environment.[4]

The modern movement thus took as its point of departure the belief in scientific analysis, and aimed at the definition of standards which might secure a "polite and well-ordered society."[5] This does not mean that its leading exponents were blind to the purpose and value of art. Le Corbusier's famous statement in *Towards a New Architecture* (1923) indicates awareness of this: "Suddenly you touch my heart, you do me good, I am happy and I say 'This is beautiful.' That is Architecture. Art enters in."[6] Over and over again Le Corbusier returned to man's need for beauty, which he explained in two ways: as a result of the use of elementary forms and proportional geometry, and as a result of functional appropriateness. "When a thing responds to a need it is beautiful,"[7] and he also believed that architecture is "a thing which in itself produces happy people."[8] Here we touch upon the very core of the Functionalist creed: that the social and human problems of our time are to a large extent the products of a false and deficient environment, and that man's condition may be improved through a new architecture which reconquers true and fundamental meanings. In fact, Le Corbusier asked at the beginning of his programmatic book: "Architecture or revolution?", and answered at the very end, after an enthusiastic homage to architecture: "Revolution can be avoided."

The elementary forms and strict principles of Functionalist architecture may be interpreted as a protest against what the architects considered to be the devalued motifs and academic compositions of historicism, but first of all Functionalism had a positive aim based on a strong belief in man and in architecture. As such it possessed the significance and power to become an international movement.

Landscape and Settlement

Functionalism was deeply concerned with man's condition, and therefore paid considerable attention to the problems of the human settlement. It is, then, appropriate that the major manifestation of the International Style,

(4) The aims of CIAM are summed up in J. L. Sert, *Can Our Cities Survive?* (Cambridge, Mass., 1944).

(5) Gropius, *op. cit.*, p. 27.

(6) Le Corbusier, *Towards a New Architecture* (London, 1927; London and New York, 1960), p. 141.

(7) *Ibid.*, p. 102.

(8) *Ibid.*, p. 19.

(9) See Le Corbusier, *La maison des hommes* (Paris, 1942).

(10) The essential ideas were developed during the 1920s and 1930s and were synthesized in his book *Propos d'urbanisme* (Paris, 1946).

(11) Le Corbusier *Propos* ...., p. 48.

(12) Le Corbusier and Pierre Jeanneret, *Oeuvre Complète 1910-1929* (Zürich, 1937), p. 23.

the *Weissenhofsiedlung* in Stuttgart (1927), was a residential neighbourhood, where a new image of life was concretized on the urban level. As a typical reflection of the Functionalist attitude, the new urbanism was as a rule presented in terms of three-dimensional projects. Even general principles were usually given a concrete interpretation, for instance in Le Corbusier's programmatic sketches.[9] Functionalism's interest in built forms rather than in abstract organization produced an aim that was urban design as opposed to mere planning. This concrete approach was both a strength and a weakness. Functionalist urbanism really represented an attempt to solve the problems, whereas recent planning often remains an abstract allocation of resources which makes us forget that man's environment in the end has to be built. But as they were presented in concrete terms, Functionalism's urban concepts were immediately understood by the totalitarian movements and the ruling taste of the period as a manifestation of new meanings, and hence were violently opposed.

Functionalism is most typically represented in the projects and theories of Le Corbusier.[10] His point of departure was a protest against the inhuman living conditions of the industrial cities of the nineteenth century, and the dream of a "green city," which was still understood as a concretization of the concept of open space. However, he did not wholly accept the garden city, and as an alternative introduced the "vertical garden city," that is, a very large *unité d'habitation* surrounded by free space, which in a new form preserved some of the properties and the identity of the traditional village, and at the same time restored "the essential joys": sunlight, space and greenness. The *unité* was conceived as a type, but it could be varied according to the local conditions, and Le Corbusier always planned his settlements in relation to landscape and nature in general. As a result his concept combines the general and the particular in a new and promising way.

However, Le Corbusier did not believe that large dwelling units freely placed in a green space of themselves constitute a city. "Towns are biological phenomena. They have hearts and organs indispensible to their spe-

cial functions."[11] Defining the basic urban functions as "living, working, cultivation of the body and the mind, and circulation," Le Corbusier introduced the civic centre as an urban element, as well as other, minor extensions of the dwelling. Of particular importance is his idea of differentiated traffic, which first of all implies the separation of motorized and pedestrian communication. The idea was not merely a practical one, but took as its point of departure the recognition that different velocities imply different rhythms, and hence require different kinds of space. Le Corbusier applied his general principles to three basic types of human settlement: the "unit of agricultural production," the "linear industrial town" and the "radio-concentric social city." All of these he conceived as structured places connected by routes. In addition, he worked out visionary plans for a series of existing cities, where the principles and the local circumstances interact in various ways. A particularly clear illustration of his ideas is offered by the project for Nemours on the North African coast (1934).

Unfortunately Le Corbusier did not get the opportunity to realize any of his projects. It was not until 1947–52 that he was able to build an *unité d'habitation,* in Marseilles, which, remaining an isolated element, does not give full justice to the concept of the city as a biological organism—nor does the German *Siedlungen* of the period, such as Gropius's *Siemensstadt* in Berlin (1929). This work is usually quoted as proof of the failure of Functionalist urbanism as, being excessively preoccupied with the relationship between sunlight and spacing of buildings, Gropius creates a rather sterile urban pattern consisting of parallel rows of apartment buildings. Nevertheless, Le Corbusier's principles and visions remain one of the truly great contributions to the development of a modern and human city.

Building

The Functionalist desire for principles and types also determines the buildings of the period. Already in 1914 Le Corbusier defined the basic concept of the free plan in con-

nection with his *Dom-ino* houses. "We have then produced a way of building—a bone structure—which is completely independent of the functional demands of the house plan . . . allowing for numerous combinations of internal disposition and every imaginable handling of light on the façade."[12] He thus recognized the natural relationship between skeleton construction and open space, and made generally possible something which so far had only been intuited by a few pioneers. Later he developed the general concept into his famous *5 points d'une architecture nouvelle* (1926). In these he listed the concrete advantages of the new approach, and thereby defined the general properties of Functionalist building. Stilts raise the building above the ground to allow for spatial continuity and free circulation, a roof garden gives us back the ground lost under the building and unites it with the surrounding landscape, a free plan makes the storeys independent of each other and allows for a meaningful and economic use of space, continuous windows make the spaces open and in contact with nature outside, and the free façade transforms the massive wall into a screen which may be opened or closed at will. Le Corbusier applied these principles in his main works of the late twenties, where they determine the general architectural character: the *Weissenhofsiedlung* (1927), Palais des Nations, Geneva (1927–28), Villa Savoye, Poissy, (1928–29), and the Pavillon Suisse, Paris (1930–32). Furthermore, he combined the definition of principles with the development of types. His Maison Citrohan ("not to say Citroen!") from 1921 formed the point of departure for a long research on the standard dwelling, which culminated with the *unité d'habitation* in Marseilles, where two double-height apartments are served by one corridor for every three floors. The desire for types is also illustrated by the spiral-shaped museum, a concept which appeared for the first time in 1929.

Mies van der Rohe, the other leading exponent of Functionalist architecture, even more than Le Corbusier centred his activity on the development of types and principles. Between 1919 and 1924 he produced five projects for office buildings and one-family houses. Each project represents a "typical"

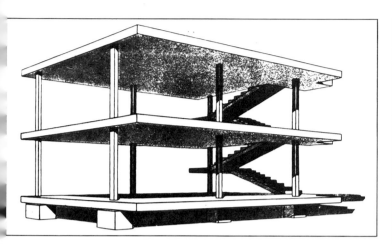

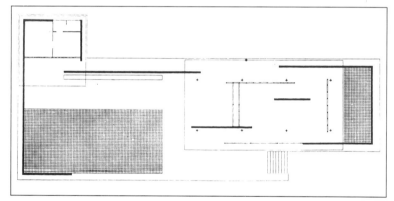

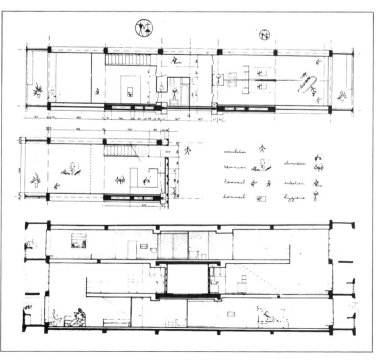

(13) L. Mies van der
Rohe, "Two Glass Sky-
scrapers," in P. John-
son, *Mies van der Rohe*
(New York, 1947), p. 182.

(14) C. Norberg-Schulz,
"Talks with Mies van der
Rohe," *L' architecture
d'aujourd'hui* 79, p. 100.

concept, and is worked out with the greatest possible economy of means. In general the attempt to define the essential properties of American prototypes. The two first projects are skyscrapers, and the third a horizontally directed building with continuous floor areas reminiscent of Sullivan's Carson-Pirie-Scott store. The two last ones are houses where the derivation from Wright's cross-shape plan is evident. (Later Mies also tackled the problem of the hall, and developed the court house as an original type.) In the two skyscrapers the building is reduced to a structural skeleton covered by a light curtain wall entirely of glass. Mies explained his intentions in 1922, which shows that his point of departure was the new technology, in particular skeleton construction in steel and glass: "Skyscrapers reveal their bold structural pattern during construction. . . . When the outer walls are put in place, the structural system which is the basis of all artistic design is hidden by a chaos of meaningless and trivial forms. . . . We can see the new structural principles most clearly when we use glass in place of the outer walls."[13] However, in the two projects for houses no skeleton is used, but instead attention is centred on the problem of spatial continuity. In the Brick House (1923) the long, directional walls after Wright are separated and juxtaposed to define a fluid space which nowhere comes to a full rest. In later works Mies developed his method into a systematic grammar of spatial articulation. The decisive step was taken with the Barcelona Pavilion (1929) where space-defining screens are combined with a regular steel skeleton which gives order to the free plan, achieving a synthesis of the two main innovations of the nineteenth century: the open, repetitive order of skeleton construction and the fluid, but articulate space of Frank Lloyd Wright. This synthesis was anticipated by Le Corbusier, and brought to its logical conclusion by Mies van der Rohe. Mies was fully aware of the importance of his achievement and said: "The free plan and a clear construction cannot be kept apart. The structure is the backbone of the whole and makes the free plan possible. Without that backbone the plan would not be free, but chaotic and therefore constipated."[14]

Articulation

Our discussion of the buildings by Le Corbusier and Mies van der Rohe indicate that Functionalist architecture posed radically new problems of formal articulation. Le Corbusier's *5 points* contains many references to articulation, and Mies's handling of space includes the treatment of corners, joints and other details as well as the choice of materials and textures: "The free plan is a new conception and has its own grammar, like a new language. A normal corner [for instance] gives an impression of massiveness which it is difficult to combine with the free plan. Many believe that the free plan means absolute liberty. That is a misunderstanding. The free plan asks for just as much discipline and understanding from the architect as the conventional plan."[15] In connection with the glass skyscrapers he also pointed out: "I discovered by working with actual glass models that the important thing is the play of reflections and not the effect of light and shadow as in ordinary buildings."[16]

However, the search for a new formal language was not confined to the solution of spatial problems. In fact, it started as a protest against the devalued motifs of historicism. In 1908 Adolf Loos wrote his famous article "Ornament and Crime," where he put forward the demand for a formal purge: "Cultural evolution means that we have to eliminate any ornament from our artifacts. It shows the greatness of our age that it is unable to produce a new ornament." In 1910 Loos built the ascetic Steiner House in Vienna, which illustrated the new purist ideal. Loos's attack upon ornament may be related to the contemporary wish for doing away with literary content in painting and sculpture and to transform them into "pure plastic arts," to use Piet Mondrian's term.[17] Purism well satisfied the aims of Functionalism, as it eliminated the traditional motif and prepared for the invention of new space-defining elements.

The new means of articulation were developed hand in hand with a growing consciousness of the spatial problems. The first step was to introduce the general property of transparency, inspired by the iron-and-glass buildings of the nineteenth century, and

(15) *Ibid.*, p. 100.

(16) Mies van der Rohe, *op. cit.*, p. 182.

(17) See P. Mondrian, *plastic art and pure plastic art*, New York, 1945.

(18) See Le Corbusier, *Towards a New Architecture*, p. 187.

404. Le Corbusier: project for a skyscraper, Algeria. 1942.
405. Theo van Doesburg: Aubette restaurant, Strasbourg. 1926. Interior.

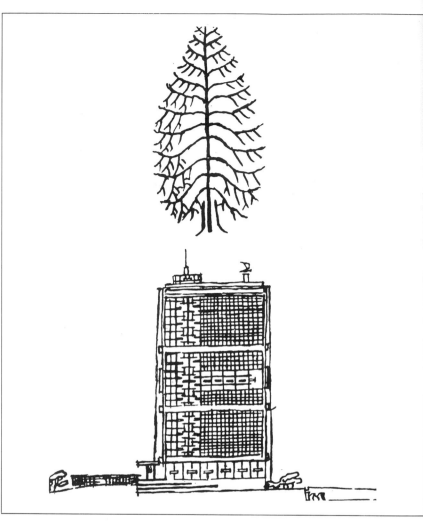

expressing a basic wish for openness and dynamism. In the Fagus factory by Gropius (1911) the wall is transformed into a light curtain of iron and glass, and the massive corner is eliminated. In Gropius's "model factory" for the Werkbund exhibition in Cologne (1914) the continuity of the glass curtain was emphasized, and incorporated the dynamic element of a transparent spiral staircase. The building also showed the influence of Wright's "destruction of the box" in its horizontal and vertical planes. The juxtaposition of separate planes was carried further by the Dutch *De Stijl* group, and culminated with Rietveld's Schröder House in Utrecht (1924). Transparency and juxtaposition of planes were furthermore inspired by other contemporary movements in the visual arts, starting with Cubism about 1910. Le Corbusier also showed an early interest in using proportion to give order and character to the free and asymmetrical compositions of the period.[18]

In general, early Functionalist architecture was characterized by abstract formal properties. Architects who were interested in topological organization and plastic articulation, such as Mendelsohn, Häring and Scharoun, remained outside the main development. They represented an "organic" current which only attained real importance after the Second World War. A desire for a more varied characterization, however, came to the fore in about 1930. Mies van der Rohe introduced walls of natural (although polished) materials, and showed a growing interest in the articulation of structural members and joints. Le Corbusier used rustic walls of stone and rough timber in the Maison de M. Errazuris (1930), and stone walls appeared again in his house for Mme. de Mandrot (1930–31) and the Pavillon Suisse. A decisive step towards a reintroduction of natural and regional characters was finally taken by Alvar Aalto towards the end of the thirties. About the same time Le Corbusier invented the strongly plastic *brise-soleil*. The more varied means of architectural articulation did not, however, interfere with the basic idea of open space, and thus suggested that a true pluralism of characters might be possible within the general universe of modern architecture.

406. *Walter Gropius: Bauhaus, Dessau. 1925-26. Aerial view.*
407. *Walter Gropius: Bauhaus, Dessau. Administration and workshop buildings.*
408. *Walter Gropius: Bauhaus, Dessau. Workshop building.*
409. *Walter Gropius: Bauhaus, Dessau. Students' dormitory.*

Bauhaus

The Bauhaus building is still standing in Dessau in East Germany. The school was closed by the Nazis in 1933, after Mies van der Rohe had taken over the directorship, its large surfaces of glass were walled up, and it was given a hipped roof, so clearly Functionalist architecture bore special meaning for its opponents as well as its adherents. The Bauhaus had a particular meaning. Since 1919 it had been the institution where modern architecture and design were taught, and where the image of a new way of life was being shaped. Under its director, Walter Gropius (1887–1970), it exercised an influence that can hardly be overestimated. "Bauhaus" simply became synonymous with "modern design," and the name still retains some of its old mystique.

The Bauhaus started its activities in Weimar, but in 1926 it was moved to a new and larger building in Dessau, designed by Gropius himself. Here Gropius not only created a practical frame for the activities of his school, but also sought to make the new image of man's architectural environment visually manifest.[19]

Functionally the Bauhaus consisted of three parts: the school proper, the workshops and the students' dormitory. Each of these was housed in its own wing, a plan which demonstrated a typical wish for functional differentiation, and at the same time created an active relationship between the building and its surroundings. The open and dynamic form of the Bauhaus was furthermore emphasized by connecting elements between the main wings. The school and the workshops were joined by means of a bridge spanning across the street of access, and this bridge contained the administration and the architectural department. The workshops were joined to the students' building by a lower wing containing the meeting hall and the dining room. As a result the building was in line with Gropius's statement: "The hollow sham of axial symmetry is giving place to the vital rhythmic equilibrium of free asymmetrical grouping."[20] The exterior wall treatment was varied to express the type of space behind, so the classroom wing and the administration had continuous window bands, the

(19) See W. Gropius, *Bauhausbauten Dessau* (Munich, 1930).

(20) Gropius, *The New Architecture and the Bauhaus*, p. 56.

(21) *Ibid.*, p. 37.

410. Le Corbusier: Villa Savoye, Poissy. 1928-31. Isometric drawing.
411, 412. Le Corbusier: Villa Savoye, Poissy. Plans of the ground floor and the upper floor with terrace (preliminary scheme).
413, 414. Le Corbusier: Villa Savoye, Poissy. Plans of the upper floor and solarium (final scheme).

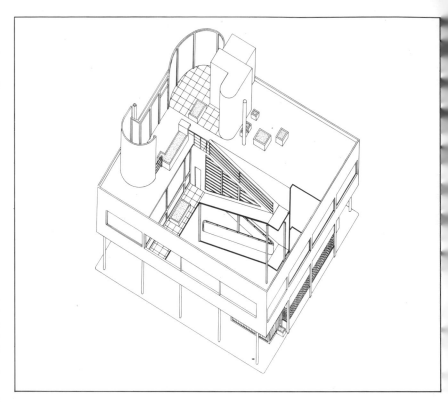

workshops an enveloping curtain wall of glass, and the students' building separate openings with projecting balconies. Everywhere the wall appeared as a thin membrane wrapped around the reinforced concrete skeleton. A fascinating effect of transparency and reflection was created by the great glass wall of the workshops. At night the whole building, lit from the inside, became a sort of large transparent light-modulator, which expressed the dynamism of open, but articulated space.

The educational philosophy of the Bauhaus sought a new synthesis of art and technology, that is, "to give the products of the machine a content of reality and significance."[21] To achieve this the Bauhaus simultaneously wanted to free the individual's power of self-expression and to develop an objective aesthetics, based on scientific knowledge. This idea places the Bauhaus in the tradition and spirit of the Enlightenment, and its singular success is due to the fact that it represented the fundamental spirit of the age. In two years, from 1926 until 1928, when Gropius left the school, the Bauhaus achieved more than other schools of architecture have done in two decades. To understand the Bauhaus, and Functionalist architecture in general, it is necessary to grasp its idea of freedom as well as its ideal of order. Gropius called an architect a "coordinator," rather than an artist in the traditional sense, as self-expression did not mean personal content and arbitrary caprice, but the power to use creatively the results of scientific investigation and technological development. Order meant primarily the establishment of standards capable of creative variation. Gropius did not like the word "style," but defined the Bauhaus idea as a method. It is often maintained that his method excluded the irrational as part of existence, but we should not forget that artists like Paul Klee and Vassily Kandinsky were leading teachers at the Bauhaus.

Villa Savoye

Since it was built in 1928–31, the Villa Savoye in Poissy has been a classic example of Functionalist architecture. Le Corbusier (1887–1965) illustrated here his *5 points* and

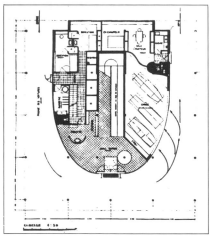

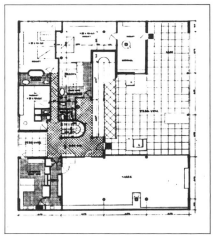

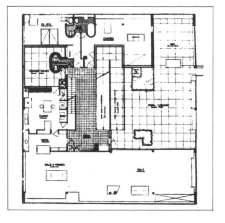

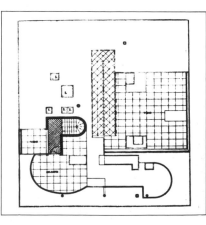

415. Le Corbusier: Villa Savoye, Poissy.
416,417. Le Corbusier: Villa Savoye, Poissy.
Transverse sections (preliminary scheme).
418. Le Corbusier: Villa Savoye, Poissy. Terrace with ramp and glass wall enclosing the living area.

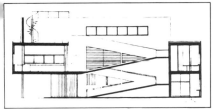
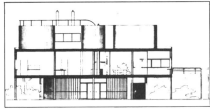

created a work of incomparable strength and poetic quality. The text that accompanies the presentation of the villa in his *Oeuvre Complète 1929–1934* shows that his ends and means were a deliberate choice.

In general, the design was determined by the architect's wish to combine structural rigour and spatial freedom, and by the particular conditions of the site, as well as access by car. To obtain a better view and to avoid the humidity of the ground, it was natural to raise the main floor on stilts. Thereby the ground floor could be utilized as a driveway around the entrance hall and the services. The simple movement of the car determined the general symmetry of the plan. The entrance is placed in the longitudinal axis in the middle of the curved glass wall which accompanies the driveway, indicating a certain representative character. This prepares for the splendid ramp which at the very centre of the building rises up to connect the three levels. Le Corbusier gives here a convincing modern interpretation of the function of arrival, and at the same time integrates the vertical dimension in the free plan.[22]

So far open space had been concretized as general transparency, or as free movement on the horizontal plane. In the Villa Savoye what is experienced is the occupation of three-dimensional space, that is, a new symbolic freedom. But this experience happens within the equally symbolic order of science and technology; we might say because of this order. Thus, Le Corbusier wrote: "In this house we are presented with a real architectural promenade, offering prospects which are constantly changing and unexpected, even astonishing. It is interesting that so much variety has been obtained when from a design point of view a rigorous scheme of pillars and beams has been adopted."[23] The ramp leads up to the main floor which is a masterly exercise in spatial adaptation to various functions, and from there on to the "solarium" on the roof, where curved walls represent a synthesis of informality, privacy and interaction with the surrounding landscape. A particularly significant detail is an opening in the wall which faces the visitor when entering the solarium. This means that the ramp not only leads to the roof, but into open space. It makes the architectural theme of the path a living reality.

(22) The design is obviously related to the entrances and staircases of Late Baroque palaces, although Le Corbusier denies that, and refers instead to "Arabian" architecture. See Le Corbusier, *Oeuvre complète 1929—1934* (Zürich, 1935), p. 24.

(23) *Ibid*. The scheme, however, is not entirely rigorous, as the central row of columns is split to give space for the ramp.

419. Ludwig Mies van der Rohe: Tugendhat House, Brno. 1930. View from the street.

420, 421. Ludwig Mies van der Rohe: Tugendhat House, Brno. Plans of the second and first floors.

(24) Le Corbusier, *Towards a New Architecture*, p. 31. In the English edition the French word "volumes" is translated misleadingly by "masses."

(25) R. Venturi, *Complexity and Contradiction in Architecture* (New York, 1966), p. 73.

(26) Ludwig Mies later added his mother's surname van der Rohe to his original name, and became Ludwig Mies van der Rohe. He is usually known as Mies.

The spatial richness and dynamism of the Villa Savoye is contained within an approximately square volume, which allows Le Corbusier to satisfy both of his basic intentions: the desire for spatial freedom and the desire for elementary form. Long, continuous openings indicate the free plan within, but the general exterior appearance is characterized by classical purity. In *Towards a New Architecture* he called cube, cone, sphere, cylinder and pyramid "the great primary forms," and said that "architecture is the masterly, correct and magnificent play of volumes brought together in light."[24] Villa Savoye thus represents the wish of enlightened man for a return to elementary truth. As archetypal abstractions the Platonic volumes refer to general natural properties, and their meaning is highly public. The simple main volume of the Villa Savoye serves to integrate the house in a wider natural and urban context, whereas the interior concretizes the topological relationships of the private domain. The meaning of the villa consists in the combination of these characters, as has been pointed out by Venturi: "Its severe, almost square exterior surrounds an intricate interior configuration glimpsed through openings and from protrusions above. . . . Its inside order accommodates the multiple functions of a house, domestic scale, and partial mystery inherent in a sense of privacy. Its outside order expresses the unity of the idea of house at an easy scale appropriate to the green field it dominated and possibly to the city it will one day be part of."[25]

Tugendhat House

What the Villa Savoye represents in the oeuvre of Le Corbusier, the Tugendhat House in Brno represents for Mies van der Rohe (1886–1969).[26] Whereas the two other early masterpieces by Mies, the Barcelona Pavilion and the House at the Berlin Building Exhibition in 1931, were theoretical studies, the Tugendhat House is the solution of a concrete building task, and shows how Mies's principles may be accommodated to the complex functions of a dwelling.

The house was built on a sloping site, with

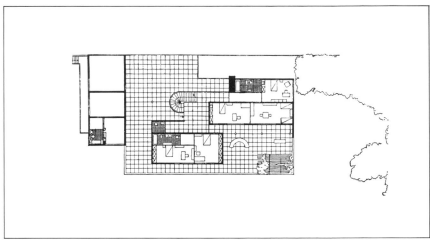

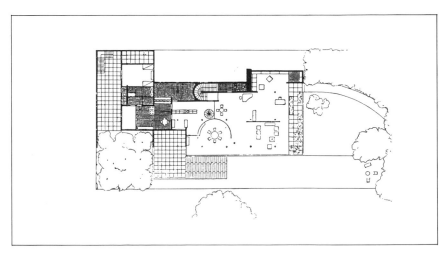

422. *Ludwig Mies Van der Rohe, Tugendhat house, Brno, view from the garden. The original windows have been filled in with small panes.*

423. *Ludwig Mies Van der Rohe, Tugendhat house, Brno, view from the living room.*

its entrance on the level of the upper floor, which contains the bedrooms. A staircase leads down to the living room which is connected with the garden below by means of a terrace and a wide flight of stairs. The layout is complex and in important respects differs from what is supposed to be Mies's ideal: a simple rectangular glass box placed on a horizontal podium. The Tugendhat House has therefore been characterized as a "compromise,"[27] but this judgement is unacceptable. Instead the house should be considered a particularly rich exercise in spatial articulation, which illustrates the possibilities inherent in Mies's method.

From the street the house appears as a low, horizontally extended building. Basically the upper floor consists of three, spatially separate volumes. One contains the owners' bedrooms, one the children's rooms, and one the garage and chauffeur's suite. The volumes are treated as boxes, with windows placed like holes in the walls, expressing the relatively enclosed and private character of the functions they contain. They are juxtaposed, however, in such a way that they overlap and indicate a fluid space between them. The boxes therefore have a spatial function analogous to that of the freestanding walls in the Barcelona Pavilion, only here the walls have become thick and hollow.[28] In the Tugendhat House the space between the boxes leads from the entrance to a terrace. It is half covered by a roof which connects the boxes, and which partially rests on steel columns which represent a continuation of the structural system of the main floor. To enter the house, one has to go along a curved glass wall, which causes outside and inside space to fuse at the point where they are functionally connected.

The main floor consists of a very large openly planned area for living, and a more enclosed kitchen section. The living area is articulated by means of a straight wall of onyx and a curved wall of Macassar ebony which define four subordinate domains: living room, dining room, study and hall. The study is located in the inmost point of the area, and has the character of a semienclosed pocket, but the living and dining areas open up on the landscape through continuous glass walls, which at the press of a but-

(27) V. Scully, *Modern Architecture* (New York, 1971), p. 28.

(28) The relevance of this interpretation is proved by Mies's study of a basically similar design in the project for the first Ulrich Lange House in Krefeld (1935). See P. Johnson, *op. cit.*, p. 114. The idea of using juxtaposed boxes to articulate fluid space prefigures the site planning of the Illinois Institute of Technology (1939 *ff.*).

(29) For a more precise definition of Mies's method see C. Norberg-Schulz *Intentions in Architecture* (Oslo and London, 1963), fig. 60. For a further study of the problem, Mies's *Hubbe House* (1935) may be recommended. See. P. Johnson, *op. cit.*, p. 118.

(30) The project has not been given the attention it deserves in the literature on Mies's work. See J. Joedike and C. Plath, *Die Weissenhofsiedlung* (Stuttgart, 1968). p. 11.

424. *Ludwig Mies van der Rohe: apartment house at the Weissenhofsiedlung, Stuttgart. 1927.*
425. *Ludwig Mies van der Rohe: general plan of the Weissenhofsiedlung, Stuttgart.*
426. *Ludwig Mies van der Rohe: Weissenhofsiedlung, Stuttgart. Aerial view.*

ton could slide into the floor. Along the side, the glass wall is double, and the intermediate space contains a conservatory which provides greenery the whole year round. The enclosure and subdivision of the main area could be regulated by means of movable curtains. To understand Mies's spatial articulation it is important to study how the different types of walls are joined together, for all joints and details are a function of the spatial composition and express the general underlying concept of open space.[29] The space-defining elements are also carefully related to the structural skeleton which forms a regular rhythm throughout the main floor. Cross-shaped chromium columns express the precision and general openness of the system. They thus prove Mies's dictum that a "clear" structure makes the free plan possible, that is, meaningful.

In the house for the Berlin Building Exhibition in 1931, Mies gave a particularly convincing demonstration of the combination of clear structure and free plan, and in his courthouses from the thirties applied the principle to generally enclosed organisms on relatively small urban building sites. His later houses from the postwar period show an increased preoccupation with the problem of articulated structure (Farnsworth House 1946 *ff.*), but the basic concept remains the same.

Weissenhofsiedlung

In 1927 the German *Werkbund* organized an exhibition in Stuttgart called The Dwelling. This exhibition was conceived as a group of houses which should visualize the new environment imagined by the modern movement. The vice-president of the *Werkbund*, Mies van der Rohe, was chosen as general director of the project. He first produced a fascinating plan (1926) which combined the intimate variety of a Mediterranean village with the fluid space of modern architecture.[30] As the houses had to be sold after the close of the exhibition, the design was later modified to make each element more independent. Mies invited many of the leading exponents of the modern movement to participate: Le Corbusier, Gropius, Oud, Stam, the brothers Taut, Scharoun, Frank, Rading, Döcker, Hil-

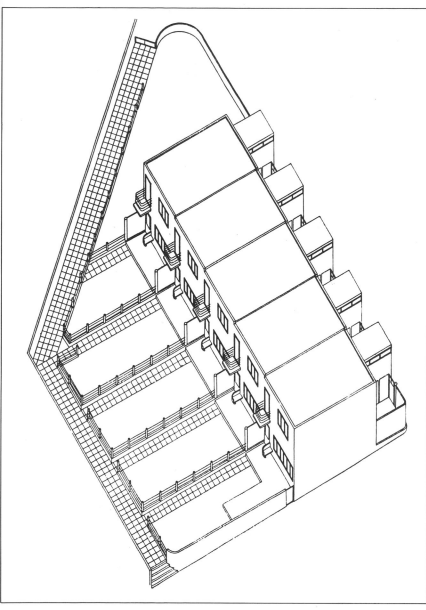

427. J .J. P. Oud: row of houses at the Weissenhofsiedlung, Stuttgart. Isometric drawing.
428. Le Corbusier: house at the Weissenhofsiedlung, Stuttgart. Isometric drawing.
429. Mart Stam: house at the Weissenhofsiedlung, Stuttgart. Isometric drawing.

berseimer, Bourgeois, Schneck, as well as the pioneers Behrens and Poelzig, so the exhibition really became the manifestation of a new style, and Philip Johnson in 1947 rightly called the *Siedlung* "the most important group of buildings in the history of modern architecture."[31] The *Weissenhofsiedlung* was considerably damaged during the war, but the general environmental character has been preserved, and except for Gropius's houses, the most interesting buildings are still standing, that is, those by Mies, Le Corbusier, Oud, Stam and Scharoun.

Functionalist housing developments are today often criticized for being sterile and devoid of true environmental quality. It is therefore somewhat surprising to experience the varied intimacy and human scale of the *Weissenhofsiedlung*. Although there is a noticeable wish for a common formal language, the architectural character varies considerably: from the calculated elegance of Mies to the restrained simplicity of Oud and Stam, and the dynamic volumes of Scharoun. From this it is apparent that the Functionalist approach did not exclude the environmental quality as such, which today is so much lacking.

The smaller units of the *Siedlung* form a varied milieu, given its backbone by a large apartment building by Mies van der Rohe. Although it appears as a unified volume, the construction is a regular steel skeleton which allowed for a new revolutionary freedom of interior planning. None of the twelve apartments is alike; all of them were adapted to different needs by means of secondary partitions. The intention was "to give the user the possibility of subdividing his space according to his needs," and "the industry has to produce technically satisfactory walls for this purpose," as pointed out by Giedion in a description of Mies's building.[32] A still more open type of planning was introduced in the larger of Le Corbusier's two houses. In general, the design follows his *5 points*, but the main storey is here conceived as a continuous space, where shallow alcoves for sleeping may be created at will. Le Corbusier explains the design as follows: "The large room is made by dispensing with the movable partitions which are only used at night so as to turn the house into a sort of sleeping-car. . . . A little corridor the exact width of those

(31) P. Johnson, *op. cit.*, p. 42.

(32) S. Giedion, *Bauen in Frankreich, Eisen, Eisenbeton* (Leipzig, 1928), p. 47.

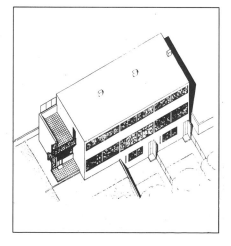

(33) Le Corbusier, *Oeuvre complète 1910—1929*, p. 150.

(34) See. F. R. S. Yorke, *The Modern House* (London, 1946), p. 206.

(35) Le Corbusier's term *"plan libre"* is sometimes translated "open plan." I prefer to use "free plan" to express the basic aim of attaining "freedom," and to distinguish the articulation of the plan from the more general concept of "open space."

(36) The problem was felt already by the Functionalists themselves. Gropius wrote: "The movement must be purged from within if its original aims are to be saved from the strait-jacket of materialism and false slogans inspired by plagiarism or misconception." Gropius, *The New Architecture and the Bauhaus*, p. 19.

(37) See H. Berndt. A. Lorenzer, K. Horn, *Architektur als Ideologie* (Frankfurt-am-Main, 1968), p. 51.

(38) S. Giedion, *Walter Gropius* (Teufen and St. Gallen, 1954), p. 63.

(39) The idea was prefigured in Öskar Strnad's project for a theatre with ring stage (1918-20). See Otto Niedermoser *Oskar Strnad* (Vienna, 1965).

(40) P. Klee, *Das bildnerische Denken* (Basel and Stuttgart, 1964).

(41) See A. Schönberg, "Composition with Twelve Tones," in *Style and Idea* (London, 1951).

(42) Bertrand Russell's Introduction to L. Wittgenstein's *Tractatus Logico-Philosophicus* (New York and London, 1922).

in the coaches of the Compagnie Internationale des Wagons-Lits acts as a passage solely at night."[33] Only the study is separated from the common area and is placed on the same level as the roof terrace. The other house by Le Corbusier is based on the Citrohan model. It has a double-height living room and anticipates the typical dwelling of Le Corbusier's *unités d'habitation.*

So it can be seen that both Mies and Le Corbusier used the Weissenhof exhibition to demonstrate some of their basic ideas. The same was the case with Gropius, who built a technically ingenious house where a light and closely spaced steel frame carried an insulation of cork slabs, and exterior and interior covering of asbestos cement and Celotex sheets respectively.[34] The dry-mounting process introduced here represented an important contribution to the industrialization of building.

From the general urban layout, and the planning of dwellings for a modern form of life, to the solution of problems of technology and economy, the *Weissenhofsiedlung* represented a great collective achievement, and immediately became a goal of architectural pilgrimage.

Space Conception and Development

Our discussion of the ideas and works of leading Functionalist architects has demonstrated the general search for principles, characteristic of the period between the two world wars. But it has also shown that the implied scientific approach did not impede the creation of rich and meaningful works of architecture. This was first of all a result of the growing ability to articulate open space. Two main endeavours determined Functionalist articulation: the establishment of a unity of form and function, and the recovery of essential meanings. The first aim was satisfied by the free plan,[35] which was made possible by use of the independent, regular skeleton structure. The second aim led to a preference for elementary stereometric volumes, and the avoidance of traditional motifs and ornament. Functionalism thereby led on the process of phenomenization initiated during the Mannerist and Baroque periods, and regained some of the archetypal abstractions of primitive architecture. We have also seen that the desire for truth also determined the concept of the green city, as demonstrated by Le Corbusier's return to the "essential joys."

In general, the Functionalist approach led to a pronounced differentiation of functions and forms. To define the functions and determine their formal consequences, Functionalism isolated them and reduced them to their measurable aspects. Functionalist architecture therefore easily degenerated into a machinelike juxtaposition of separate parts. This weakness is less strongly felt in the works of the truly creative architects of the period than in the works of those who had not fully understood the integrating power of the concept of open space.[36] One class of spatial organization, however, is almost entirely lacking in Functionalist architecture: topological organization. Topological properties are obviously closely related to meanings such as elementary enclosure, palpableness, environmental warmth, and the more general "variations on a theme." In the past these meanings were concretized in terms of urban squares and streets, bordered by continuous rows of related but varied buildings, and by intimate interior spaces. It should also be realized that the spatial aspect of many important human activities have a topological structure. Early Functionalism, therefore, did not fully satisfy its dictum "design for life." This does not, however, justify the criticism that sees Functionalism as a failure and finds in it a "sacrifice of architecture," as do Lorenzer and other writers.[37] Early Functionalism represented an important and necessary step towards the creation of fully satisfactory human environment, and it is important to point out that the further development towards this goal has grown out of Functionalism.

The human aims and potential richness of Functionalist architecture may be illustrated by one of the most fascinating projects of the period, Gropius's *Totaltheater* of 1927. In the total theatre actor and spectator are no longer separated as they had been since the Renaissance. Gropius's aim was to "pull the spectator into the very centre of the dramatic action."[38] He achieved this by making a part of the auditorium mobile, so that the stage could be surrounded by the spectators, and by his intention to use film projections on the wall surfaces to "build with light." A more radical innovation yet was the introduction of a "ring stage" engirdling the whole space. By opening the surrounding walls the spectators may experience being placed in the middle of the action.[39] In its overall effect the *Totaltheater* is a symbolic expression of man's new existential situation as a participant in a "total' dynamic world of incessantly self-changing energies. In other words, it gives human content and meaning to the concept of open space.

The theatre was made for Erwin Piscator, one of the pioneers of the modern theatre. In 1927 Marcel Breuer furnished Piscator's apartment in Berlin as a complement to the imaginative milieu of the theatre. He made it a "machine for living," containing a minimum of practical equipment. It illustrated the Functionalist belief that participation in the modern world calls for individuals who have become free of preconceived ideas and sentimental attachments.

Meaning and Architecture

The Functionalist search for essentials was felt in all fields of human activity after the First World War. In art it became manifest as different purist currents, the most important being the "pure plastic art" of Piet Mondrian and other members of the Dutch *De Stijl* group, the Constructivism of Pevsner, Gabo and Malevich, the purism proper of Le Corbusier and Ozenfant, and the sculpture of the great Constantin Brancusi. Brancusi's works are true archetypes; his *Bird* in a simple synthetic form expresses all the aspects of the bird's conquest of the vertical. Brancusi dealt with only a limited number of themes, but in each case he made several replicas producing ever more perfect definitions of the essential character. Even the profoundly irrational Paul Klee tried to work out a systematic *Gestaltungslehre*.[40] In music Arnold Schönberg developed his method between 1912 and 1923. It was the first truly open organization of symbolic forms, and in many ways is the most important theoretical achievement of the whole period.[41] In philosophy the search for essentials and the desire for a logical method was most significantly manifested in Ludwig Wittgenstein's *Tractatus Logico-Philosophicus* (1921) and Rudolf Carnap's *Der logische Aufbau der Welt* (1928). Bertrand Russell points to the basic intentions of the new philosophy in his introduction to the English edition of Wittgenstein's *Tractatus:* "Wittgenstein is concerned with the conditions for *accurate* symbolism, i.e., for symbolism in which a sentence "means" something quite definite. . . . In order that a certain sentence should assert a certain fact, there must, however the language may be constructed, be something in common between the structure of the sentence and the structure of the fact. This is perhaps the most fundamental thesis in Mr. Wittgenstein's theory."[42] And, we may add, this is nothing but the thesis of Functionalism.

Our historical survey of architectural symbolism has demonstrated that the archetypal symbols of early civilizations were abstractions in line with Wittgenstein's demand for similarity of structure between symbol and fact. Later the symbols became conventional elements in a language of forms. When the elements were combined to solve a complex task, the rule of structural similarity was still valid, as shown for instance by the expressive compositions of Mannerist architecture.[43] A decline occurred during the nineteenth century when true symbolism gave way to a superficial play with historical clichés. Functionalists wanted to do away with this situation, and aimed at a return to a true correspondence between form and content. To solve this problem in an open world, a closed system of symbols is insufficient. It would only allow for a certain range of meanings and exclude the democratic pluralism represented by the *Totaltheater.* That is why Gropius did not accept the word "style," but preferred the more general term "method." However, to start with, the Functionalist method could not be truly open. During the 1920s, thus, forms such as holes in the wall, closed corners, frames around doors and windows, arches and sloping roofs were proscribed, not only because they reminded one

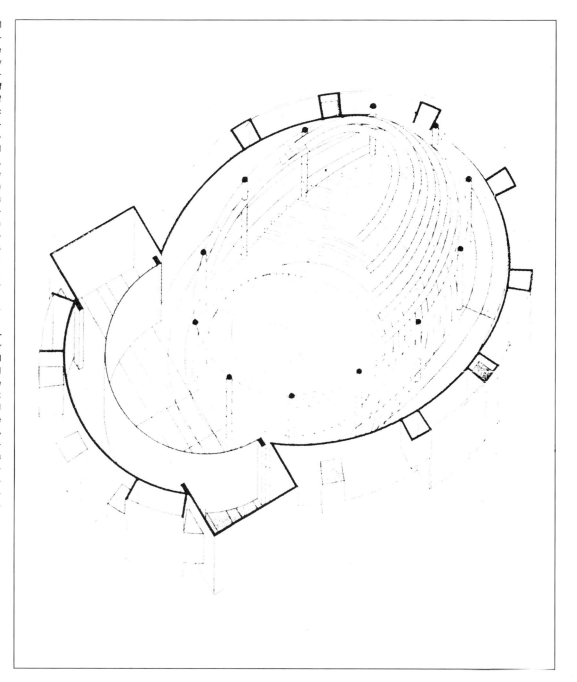

(43)   For a discussion of symbolism and structural similarity see C. Norberg-Schulz, *Intentions in Architecture* (London, 1963; Cambridge, Mass., 1968), pp. 71 ff. and 167 ff.

(44)   Analogously Schönberg forbade all references to the closed tonal system of the past.

of the past, but because their use might have closed the system.[44] Paradoxically, as a result Functionalist architecture became an "architecture of exclusion," that is, a style which could not account for all aspects of human existence. But the International Style was not the goal of the modern movement, but only a transitory stage. With an increasing understanding of the principles of open symbolism, even the more particular forms of the past could become part of the pluralism of formal structures which developed after the Second World War.

From what is said above, it follows that it is a misunderstanding to believe that Functionalism was only interested in efficiency. Like any great historical movement, it was first of all concerned with meanings, that is, with the problem of giving man an existential foothold.

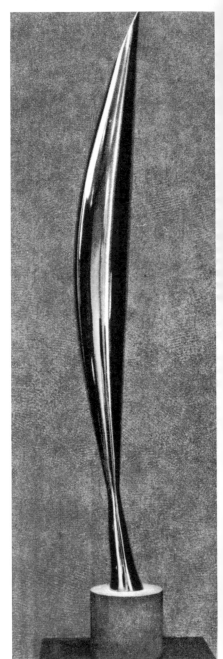

431.   Constantin Brancusi: Bird in Space. *1919. Museum of Modern Art, New York.*

12. Pluralism

Introduction

In contrast to the period between the wars, which was stylistically characterized by a similarity of ends and means, the architecture of the last decades shows an ever-growing diversity. The whole architectural scene seems to have exploded, and the resulting multitude of scattered parts is usually described as "visual chaos." When order is encountered, it consists mostly of a monotonous repetition of unarticulated elements. At hardly any time before has man's environment been more problematic and his sense of existential foothold less secure. However, some positive phenomena are also present. There is a growing awareness of the importance of the environmental problem, and there are also reasons for presuming that architecture today is in a position to solve the problem. For during the last decades Functionalism has developed into that flexible tool which was intended, but not realized, between the wars.

The new diversity became evident soon after the Second World War. Some of the leading exponents of the modern movement aimed at a further systematization of Functionalist architecture. The most influential was Mies van der Rohe, who in his American buildings followed a sensitive and meaningful articulation of skeleton construction. To some extent his treatment of these made the somewhat insubstantial buildings of early Functionalism less abstract. More fruitful, however, was the "organic" current, which took a new interpretation of the concept of function as its point of departure. Its exponents wanted the building to be what Hugo Häring, an early pioneer of the organic trend, called *organhaft*. The most influential exponent during the first decade after the war was Alvar Aalto (b. 1898), who had suggested an organic approach in his Functionalist buildings from the early 1930s. Aalto was one of the first to reintroduce natural materials and topological forms as, for example, in the Finnish Pavilion at the New York World's Fair in 1939.[1] The organic movement was also inspired by the later works of Frank Lloyd Wright, such as Taliesen West (1938) and the Guggenheim Museum in New York (1946). To conceive the building as an organ,

(1) The first to recognize the importance of Aalto was Sigfried Giedion. See the chapter on Aalto in *Space, Time and Architecture*, 5th ed. (Cambridge, Mass., 1967), entitled "Irrationality and Standardization."

(2) See S. Cauman, *The Living Museum* (New York, 1958), p. 173.

433. *Le Corbusier: Chandigarh. 1950-56. General plan.*
(1) Capitol (2) commercial center (3) reception buildings (4) museum and stadium (5) university (6) market (7) green zone with recreation facilities (8) commercial streets.
434. *Jörn Utzon: residential project for Birkehöj. 1960.*

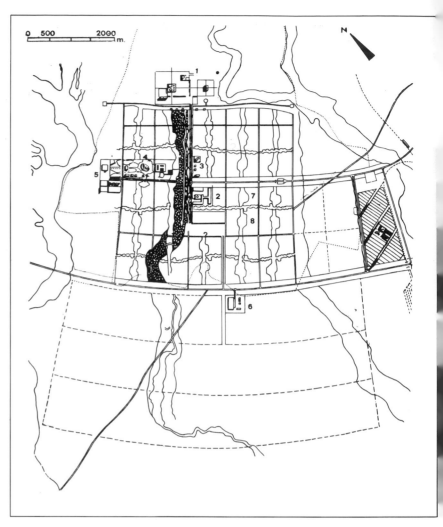

however, implied a certain danger of a return to a closed, self-sufficient form. The present writer, therefore, in 1957 formulated a demand for a synthesis of the "technological" and "organic" trends.[2] And, in fact, such a synthesis has proved to represent the right path towards an open, varied and organic architecture. During the last two decades, accordingly, a pluralism of technically founded formal structures has developed, starting in the 1950s with the *ultima maniera* of Le Corbusier and the first great works of Louis Kahn.

The basic aim of the pluralist approach to architectural form is to obtain individual characterization of buildings and places, an intention which stems from a reaction to the rather scarce variations in character permitted by early Functionalism. At the same time this integration marks a wish to take differences in regional character into consideration—regional character not only in the sense of geographical factors, but also the implied way of life and historical and cultural background. These factors had been forgotten during the first phases of modern development, when the new global situation made people leave their places physically and psychologically to participate in the conquest of open space. Today, in reaction to this, there is a predominant, if latent, wish to "return home," although it is important that this return should happen without losing the freedom which forms the basis of modern existence. Neither the homeless nor the isolationist can contribute to the creation of a common meaningful world, so in pluralist architecture the concepts of place, path and domain regain their fundamental importance; the problem of spatial identity again comes to the fore. The *genius loci* constitutes the content of pluralist architecture—not as an isolated character, but, in Louis Kahn's words, as "a world within a world."

Landscape and Settlement

In 1950 Le Corbusier was finally given the opportunity to put his theories on city planning into practice when he was asked to direct the development of Chandigarh, the capital of the Punjab in India. Although a

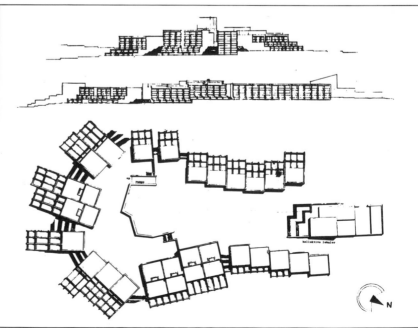

A project for the Berlin Centre competition by Alison and Peter Smithson and Peter Sigmund Wonke. Key: 1 ministries 2 bus station 3 S.-bahn. 4 Platz der Republic 5 Brandenburg gate 6 technical centre 7 fashion centre 8 city administration 9 Casbah 10 reception 11 Chinese wall of offices 12 cinema 13 Friedrichstrasse 14 printing. This project was awarded...

general plan had already been worked out by Matthew Nowicki, Le Corbusier succeeded in transforming it in accordance with his basic principles. His master plan shows a characteristic Functionalist differentiation of activities, related to form a meaningful whole. Each urban element is given its own identity and character. Le Corbusier divided the approximately square area into neighbourhoods by roads for through traffic. The neighbourhoods are given inner identity by means of continuous bands of parkland running from the north to the south, and transverse bazaar streets. A main avenue accompanied by a "valley of leisure" runs north-south, dividing the urban area into two halves. It is crossed by another east-west axis, and the main commercial centre is at their intersection. Where the main avenue ends to the north the "Capitol" stands, on the border between city and nature (like a Baroque residence). The Capitol is deliberately related to the Himalayas behind, creating an interaction of the man-made forms and nature which had never been achieved before in modern architecture.[3] In general, Chandigarh unifies basic themes of past and present city planning, and represents a most convincing synthesis of order and freedom. However, there is one basic quality lacking: the intimate interiority of past settlements, for the general image of open space is still concretized as a flowing continuum which does not accept a true inside. The flow is only broken at the northern fringe of the Capitol where there is a small *Fosse de la considération* sunk into the ground as a contained space, and open to the sky. From the *Fosse* rises a powerfully expressive great symbol of an open hand.

The major problem of how to create an urban inside without giving up the general idea of open space has been approached by various architects during the last two decades, and a solution has now been formulated. In general, it consists of conceiving the urban structure as several patterns of open growth. This implies a return to topological principles of composition such as clustering and plastic continuity. Words such as "identity," "patterns of growth," "cluster" and "infrastructure" were introduced into architectural thinking by Alison and Peter Smithson during the 1950s, and illustrated

(3) For a perceptive analysis of this relationship, see V. Scully, *Modern Architecture* (New York, 1961), p. 47.

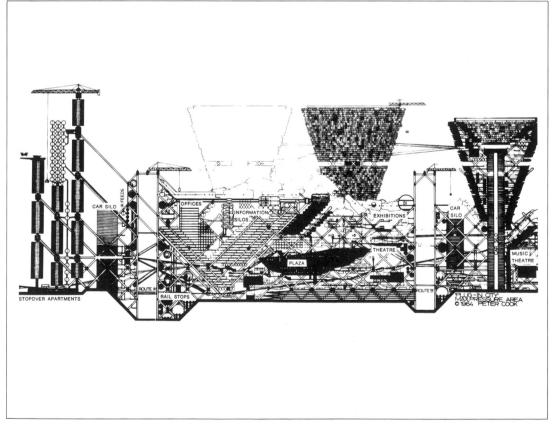

in several projects, notably in the plan for *Hauptstadt Berlin* (1958).[4] Here functions and circulation are still differentiated in a way which is evidently derived from Le Corbusier's works, but the idea of a "pedestrian net" of urban spaces represents an important step towards a renaissance of the city as a system of places. During the 1960s the problem of identity of place was approached in several smaller works. Well known is the dense, but basically open cluster of *Siedlung Halen* near Berne by Atelier 5 (1961). Of note also are residential layouts by Jörn Utzon, especially the project for Birkehöj (1960), and the project for a new civic centre in Liverpool by Colin Wilson (started in 1966). In all these works spatial identity is combined with formal variation and openness. Louis Kahn's Richards Medical Research Building in Philadelphia (1958–60) illustrates particularly finely the urban milieu which may result when buildings are conceived as patterns of growth.

The idea of open growth has been taken as far as it can go in numerous utopian projects from the last decade. In these the city is conceived as an extendable three-dimensional infrastructure, where prefabricated or self-made dwellings may be "plugged-in" at will and dissected and discarded when obsolete (Peter Cook *Plug-in City* 1964).[5] It is doubtful, however, whether a city of this kind would provide the necessary existential foothold. Urban space may of course contain mobile elements, and its substructures may offer varying degrees of freedom, but it cannot be characterized by a general mobility. If things change too quickly, history becomes impossible. In other words, man needs a relatively stable system of places to develop himself, social life and culture in general. And he also needs the assurance of that plastic presence which is the distinguishing property of Le Corbusier's buildings at Chandigarh.

Building

It is a paradox of architectural development that Wright's "destruction of the box" led to the Functionalist principle of separating the technical structure from the functionally

441. Ludwig Mies van der Rohe: National Gallery, Berlin. Plans of the ground floor and lower level.

442. Ludwig Mies van der Rohe: National Gallery, Berlin.

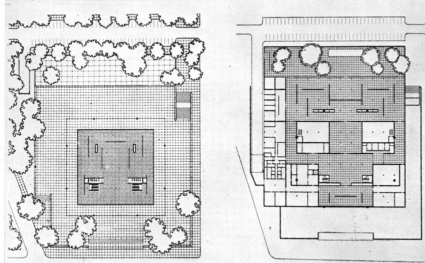

determined space-defining elements, which produced a general tendency to envisage buildings as simple boxes again. There is, however, a basic difference between the boxes before and after Wright in that the former were static entities containing an addition of separate rooms, whereas the new kind of box contains a free plan.

The most enthusiastic study of the modern box was made by Mies van der Rohe, who defined his aims as follows: "The purposes the building serves are always changing, but we cannot afford to pull buildings down. Therefore we put Sullivan's slogan 'form follows function' upside down, and construct a practical and economical space into which we fit the functions."[6] His postwar works show incessant efforts to give the boxes character by means of an articulate structure, a process which culminated with the National Gallery in Berlin (1962–68). Here a "total" space, surrounded by glass walls, is covered by a square roof carried on eight cross-shaped steel columns which are placed along the perimeter, but which leave the corners free. The museum represents a magnificent conclusion to Mies's work, but his general concept of building hardly satisfies the environmental needs of our day, even though a juxtaposition of boxes may constitute a kind of "urban free plan," as indicated by the layout of the Illinois Institute of Technology (started in 1940).

Le Corbusier also gave primary importance to a simple main form, but from the outset he showed a stronger desire for plastic articulation than his contemporaries. In his postwar works he succeeded in creating a true modern monumentality, that is, buildings which through their plastic presence symbolizes characters that give identity to the society for which they are built. This is just as much the case in the Dominican monastery of Sainte Marie de la Tourette (1956–59), as in the great public buildings of Chandigarh. His Legislative Assembly building (1956) shows a rhythmic interaction of several systems of spatial organization, and therefore particularly well illustrates Le Corbusier's prophetic power. In general, his later works may be considered the most important achievement in twentieth-century architecture.

The intention to make of a building some-

(4) See "Alison and Peter Smithson" in *Uppercase 3* (London, 1960).

(5) See P. Cook, *Architecture: Action and Plan* (London and New York, 1967).

(6) See C. Norberg-Schulz, "Talks with Mies van der Rohe," *L'architecture d'aujourd'hui* 79, p. 100.

443. *Alvar Aalto: Baker House, dormitory at Massachusetts Institute of Technology (MIT), Cambridge. 1947-48. Ground plan.*

444, 445. *Alvar Aalto: Baker House.*

446. *Le Corbusier: monastery of Sainte-Marie de la Tourette, Eveux. 1956-59. Ground plan.*

447. *Le Corbusier: monastery of Sainte-Maries de la Tourette, Eveux.*

448. *Le Corbusier: monastery of Sainte Marie de la Tourette, Eveux.*

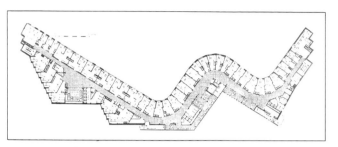

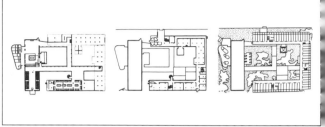

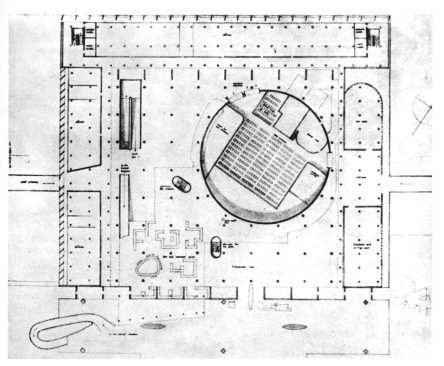

449. *Le Corbusier: Legislative Assembly Building, Chandigarh. 1956-59. Ground plan.*

450, 451. *Le Corbusier: Legislative Assembly Building, Chandigarh.*

(7)   V. Scully, *Louis I. Kahn* (New York and London, 1962), p. 25.

(8)   See *Alvar Aalto* (Zürich, 1963).

thing more than a functional container also distinguishes the works of Louis Kahn. Although less dynamic than Le Corbusier, Kahn convincingly succeeds in creating buildings which are based on a strong and expressive theme. Scully writes of him: "The impression becomes inescapable that in Kahn, as once in Wright, architecture began anew."[7] Kahn's basic dictum is that a building must be what it "wants to be." In practice that means the invention of a theme which may be varied or constitute the point of departure for a pattern of growth. This holds true both for simple buildings like the Hurva Synagogue in Jerusalem (1965) and large-scale projects, like those in Dacca and Ahmedabad (started in 1962).

The fourth great protagonist of postwar architecture, Alvar Aalto, also operates with themes which generate spatial patterns. His themes are mainly functionally determined in the "organic" sense. The undulating shape of his M.I.T. Senior Dormitory (1947–48) was determined by the intention to give each room a diagonal view across the Charles River, whereas the fanlike layout of the Neue Vahr apartments in Bremen (1958) stems from a desire to let the rooms broaden out towards the light. His church in Vouksennika, finally, was given a pattern that resembles a series of waves, for acoustical reasons (1956).[8] Aalto's method, clearly expressed in his sketches, is to take a general vision of the fundamental theme as his point of departure. In this he resembles Filippo Juvarra, the great eighteenth-century pioneer of pluralist architecture.

In the works of the younger generation of modern architects, the wish for individual characterization based on a pluralism of patterns of spatial organization is ever more felt. We may therefore conclude that modern architecture has liberated itself from the fetters of general types and basic principles, and is in the process of realizing a true synthesis of freedom and order.

Articulation

We have already suggested that the desire for individual characterization of buildings and places implies an articulation which

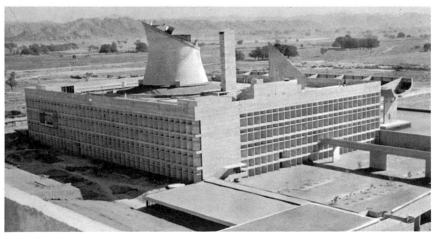

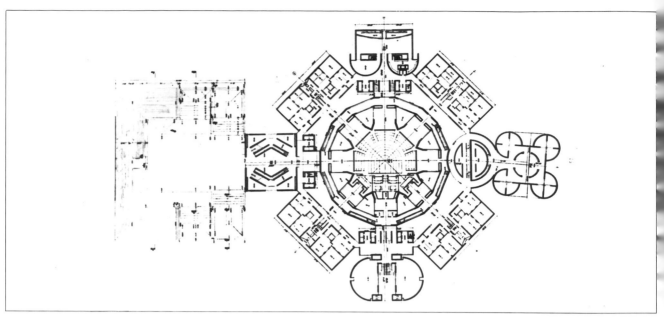

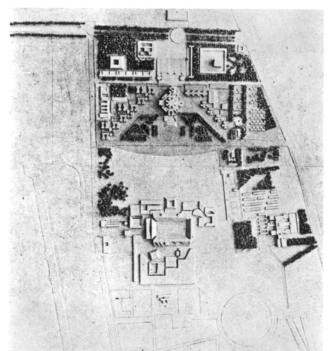

452. *Louis Kahn: National Assembly Building, Dacca. Begun 1962. Ground plan.*

453. *Louis Kahn: Dacca. Begun 1962. Model of general layout.*

454. *Louis Kahn: National Assembly Building, Dacca. Model.*

455, 456. *Le Corbusier: Unité d'habitation, Marseilles. 1947-52.*

457. *Pier Luigi Nervi: Diagrams of columns.*

458. *Eero Saarinen: TWA Terminal, Kennedy Airport, New York, 1956-62. Detail.*

offers more possibilities of variation than the ascetic and somewhat insubstantial forms of early Functionalism. The most important experiments of the 1950s took the structural and plastic possibilities of reinforced concrete as their point of departure. In the *unité d'habitation* at Marseilles (1947–52) Le Corbusier used rough concrete to give the building a general physical presence. The slender *pilotis* of the thirties became here massive and powerful, and the abstract skin has been replaced by a *brise-soleil* which characterizes the building as a sculptural body. "It thus stands upon its muscular legs as an image of human uprightness and dignifies all its individual units within a single embodiment of the monumental human force which makes them possible."[9] (Less convincing is Le Corbusier's *modulor,* a proportional system which should bring order into the new and rich world of forms.)

An imaginative use of reinforced concrete also distinguishes the works of Pier Luigi Nervi (b. 1891). Nervi's buildings are entirely structural, and illustrate Mies van der Rohe's dictum: "Wherever technology reaches its real fulfilment, it transcends into architecture." Nervi "builds" the forces inherent in a structure, transforming a covering vault or floor slab into a fascinating net of ribs. His columns similarly express their structural role and become plastic members whose section varies according to the static context. A chart showing Nervi's columns would represent a new universe of expressive orders. His intentions are particularly well illustrated by his *Palazzetto dello Sport* (1957) and *Palazzo dello Sport* (1958–60), both in Rome.[10]

In Kahn's works the situation becomes more complex. Here the problem of physical presence is combined with the problem of light, for Kahn has reestablished light as an architectural factor. He defines it as "the giver of all presences," and goes on to say, "To make a square room, is to give it the light which reveals the square in its infinite moods."[11] To control how the light enters the building, Kahn usually surrounds his main spaces with an "in-between" zone, which may be compared to historical double-shell structures. The image of open space is thus given a new and highly fascinating interpretation.

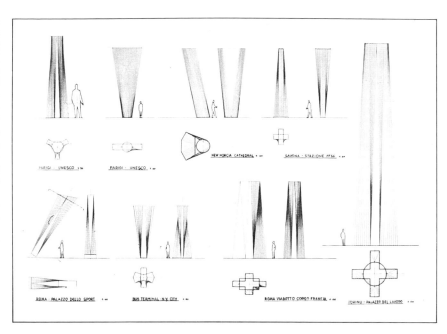

(9) Scully, *Modern Architecture,* p. 44.

(10) See P. L. Nervi, *New Structures* (London, 1963).

(11) L. Kahn, "Space and Inspirations," *L'architecture d'aujourd'hui* 152, p. 13.

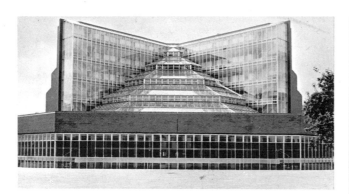

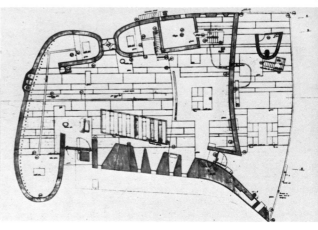

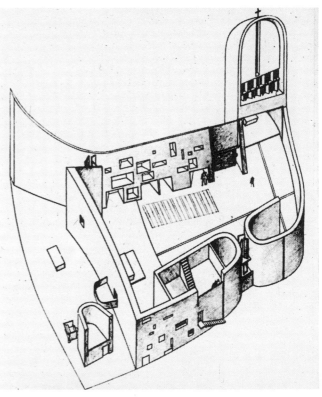

459. James Stirling: library, Cambridge. 1964-66.

460. Robert Venturi: house of the architect, Philadelphia. 1962.

461. Paolo Portoghesi: Casa Baldi, Rome. 1959-62.

462. Louis Kahn: National Assembly Building, Dacca. Begun 1962.

463. Le Corbusier: Notre Dame du Haut, Ronchamp. 1953-55. Ground plan.

464. Le Corbusier: Notre Dame du Haut, Ronchamp. Isometric drawing.

465. Le Corbusier: Notre Dame du Haut, Ronchamp.

Whereas Le Corbusier, Nervi and Kahn are concerned with general possibilities of articulation and characterization, Eero Saarinen (1910–61) aimed at a dramatic characterization of the individual building task. Each of his buildings is entirely different, and hardly seems to be designed by the same architect. The approach is interesting, but unfortunately the buildings have a somewhat superficial and rhetorical character, with the exception of his dynamic expression of flight in the TWA Terminal at Kennedy Airport (1956–62).

Among the younger generation there is a growing desire for regional characterization. Aalto is here followed by his "Finnish" pupil Reima Pietilä, who concentrates on topological forms and natural materials. The metal-and-glass buildings of James Stirling, in contrast, are truly "English," and the sophisticated elegance of Paolo Portoghesi unmistakably "Italian." The tamed dynamism of Jörn Utzon is certainly "Danish," and the "melting-pot" architecture of Robert Venturi eminently "American." Venturi's works are of particular interest as they indicate that a new relationship to the past is coming to the fore. He restores conventional elements such as arches and string-courses, and claims: "Familiar things seen in an unfamiliar context become perceptually new as well as old."[12] He thus adds a new psychological dimension to architecture, the dimension of memory and association, and represents a new fundamental step towards an architecture which expresses the "richness and ambiguity of modern experience."[13]

Ronchamp

When the project for Le Corbusier's pilgrimage church Notre Dame du Haut at Ronchamp was published in 1953, it came as a disconcerting surprise to most adherents of the modern movement. Suddenly all the "proscribed" forms reappeared: the plastic mass, the hole in the wall, the expressive curve and the cavelike interior. But those who visited the church after its completion in 1955 forgot their worries and recognized that a new dimension had been given to modern architecture. At the same time the church marks a rebirth of a truly significant

religious architecture. During the two hundred years which had passed since the construction of the last Baroque churches hardly any ecclesiastical building of importance had been conceived, so the appearance of Ronchamp is a symptom of renewed interest in basic existential meanings.

As indicated by the name Notre Dame du Haut, the church is located in a high place. Since time immemorial it had been a place of prayer, and Le Corbusier accordingly aimed at creating "a vessel of intense concentration and meditation."[14] As a high place it is integrally related to the surrounding landscape, and it is known that Le Corbusier took the "four horizons" as his starting point. An outdoor altar serving for the pilgrims' mass indicates the symbolic relationship between the place and its environment. The building itself is simultaneously a refuge and an open, embracing form which receives the visitor. Within its heavy, protecting walls it seems that a "secret" is kept, which is symbolically offered to the surroundings by the extended, curved roof. The interior also has a vertical reference, thanks to the three towers which rise up to receive light. The synthesis of enclosure and openness not only satisfies the task of making a church, but creates a true "centre of meaning" where man may experience a return to his origins. The symbolic ambiguity inherent in the simultaneous protection and extension which characterize the building implies that all the forms have a double nature or seem to undergo a constant metamorphosis. A great sloping wall to the south is both fortress and a sign of an intense wish for communication, as it rises up and bends to mark the point of contact between the outdoor sanctuary and the interior. The hanging roof is both a heavy weight which concentrates the interior and reminds man of his precarious situation on earth, and a light "heavenly" veil which floats over the walls, separated from their physical presence by a narrow slit where light enters the room. The tower chapels are the innermost places in the church, as well as the places where divine light is more strongly felt.

Although the plan does not follow the traditional disposition of churches, Le Corbusier has succeeded in recovering the basic properties of the Christian sanctuary. His

building is receptacle and giver, fortress and poetic vision of otherness. Above all he has managed to re-create the interiority of the early churches with means which are simultaneously new and old, making the interior in Ronchamp a space which simultaneously protects and liberates. It is a cave, open to the essential meanings of human existence, and supporting Heidegger's equation that "on Earth" means "under the Heavens."

Ronchamp's importance in the history of architectural form can hardly be overestimated. The church demonstrates the importance of physical presence, and is a lesson in how to treat plastic mass in a new and old way. The numerous windows of the south wall, for instance, would have destroyed the sculptural unity of the building if they had been larger and more regularly placed. In general, Ronchamp shows that archetypal and cultural values may be combined with the modern idea of open space provided they are properly understood. Ronchamp thus represents a return to historical values in a new and more profound sense, and offers to man the possibility of a foothold which is not only spatial, but temporal as well. In fact, true spatial identity without integrating the dimension of time is an impossibility. To integrate time is a problem of architectural character and articulation.

Philharmonie

In the Philharmonie in Berlin by Hans Scharoun (1893–1972) the architect has also grasped the problem of creating meaningful space. The building was finished in 1963, but the basic idea was already defined in 1956 in Scharoun's entry for a competition held to choose the design. Basically the Philharmonie is a "container of music," and resembles a kind of large instrument where the outer walls appear as the thin membranes of a sound box. "Music in the centre, that is the simple idea, which determined the new concert hall of the Berlin Philharmonie Orchestra. The whole building has to be understood in relation to this idea," Scharoun wrote to explain his design.[15] His buildings return to the basic notion that human actions "take place," and that the character of the

(12) R. Venturi, Complexity and Contradiction in Architecture (New York, 1966), p. 50.

(13) Ibid. p. 22.

(14) Le Corbusier, Oeuvre complète 1946—1952 (Zürich, 1961), p. 72.

(15) Hans Scharoun, Akademie der Künste, Berlin 1967, p. 95.

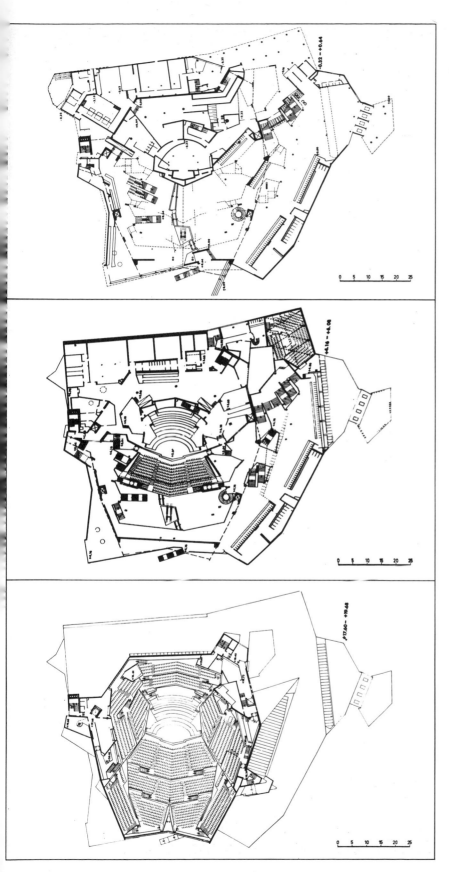

466. Le Corbusier: Notre Dame du Haut, Ronchamp. Interior detail.

467. Hans Scharoun: Philharmonie, Berlin. 1956-63. Ground plan of the foyer.

468, 469. Hans Scharoun: Philharmonie, Berlin. Plans of the mezzanine and hall.

place and the meaning of the action have a reciprocal relationship. His basic method was always to generate a work of architecture from a meaningful centre, and his buildings were conceived as an "organ" for the functions represented by the centre.

In the Philharmonie the concept of "music in the centre" means that the audience surround the orchestra. Arranged in groups, 2,218 seats are placed on rising series of steps which Scharoun likened to wine terraces. In the artificial landscape which is created the individual may identify himself with the whole, while at the same time he belongs to a smaller, easily comprehensible "domain." The result is an extraordinary combination of unity and intimacy. Whereas on photographs the space may seem confusing, it is in reality quiet and assuring, and offers an ideal environment for listening to music. From a purely practical point of view it has been doubted whether it is visually and acoustically satisfactory to surround a "directional" function such as a musical performance, but in fact the acoustics are excellent, and the feeling of participation is much stronger than in conventional concert halls. Moreover, Scharoun has taken the directional aspect of the function into consideration by introducing a longitudinal axis which gives the space an important sense of general order.

The main hall is surrounded by a lobby of extraordinary shape and character. Functionally it serves to distribute the visitors to the cloakrooms and to the different sections of the concert hall, and as an "organ" of circulation it functions better than most regular spaces. Beyond this practical purpose, however, the lobby creates a meaningful expectation in the visitor. Like music itself, it is a fairy-tale world full of secrets, which are discovered through movement in space and time, leading on to the illuminating experience of the inner core. At the same time the lobby prepares the visitor for the busy, urban world outside—it is already like a city, grand and intimate, and infinitely varied.

The Philharmonie is a masterpiece of organic architecture showing that man's environment as a whole becomes meaningful when a multitude of elements are related to a meaningful centre. Here the concept of

470. *Hans Scharoun: Philharmonie, Berlin. Interior.*

471. *Hans Scharoun: Philharmonie, Berlin.*

472. *Hans Scharoun: Philharmonie, Berlin. Interior of the foyer.*

(16) *Ibid.*, p. 7.

(17) Scully, *Louis I. Kahn*, p. 44.

organic form is not limited to the natural environment which was the point of departure for a basically "rural" architect like Aalto. In the Philharmonie the urban environment has been treated organically, and the image of a city consisting of live organs and their extensions comes to mind. It is a possible model for urban building; after seeing the Philharmonie, the Dutch architect and planner Bakema remarked, "That is how we ought to build our cities."[16] But to build such cities we need the spiritual forces represented by the meaningful centres. Only then can the environment take shape around the places of significant action.

Richards Medical Research Building

Louis Kahn's development (1901–74) is one of the most extraordinary phenomena in the history of modern architecture. After spending much of his life theorizing and teaching, he suddenly came to creative maturity and realized a growing series of buildings, which for a whole generation of (younger) architects has restored belief in architecture as an art, capable of expressing essential existential values. His development and importance have been characterized by Vincent Scully: "how slow the growth of this tree, like an olive, bearing for the generations to come."[17]

Kahn's work initiates a new age of true architectural pluralism; he neither reduces pluralism to theatrical statements like Saarinen, nor is he the victim of a personally determined uniformity of character like Scharoun. In his works the basic intentions of modern architecture are united to form a singular synthesis. All his designs seem to be determined by a generating principle, like the buildings of the organic movement, but they also possess the structural regularity and articulation of Mies van der Rohe, as well as the presence and power of the later works by Le Corbusier. They also contain obvious references to architectural history, without ever becoming a pastiche. In Kahn's work architecture is reborn, not only as a general method, but as a concrete fact in every single work. Every design fol-

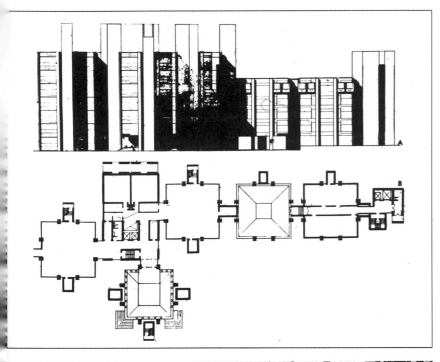

473.   *Louis Kahn: Richards Medical Research Building, Philadelphia. 1958-60. Ground plan and elevation.*

474.   *Louis Kahn: Richards Medical Research Building, Philadelphia.*

475.   *Louis Kahn: Richards Medical Research Building, Philadelphia. Structural system.*

lows his dictum: "In the nature of space is the spirit and the will to exist in a certain way."[18]

Few works of architecture from the last two decades have been more influential than Kahn's Richards Medical Research Building at the University of Pennsylvania in Philadelphia (1958–60). Its basic ideas resulted from two crucial facts: that scientists work alone or in groups, although they form a kind of collectivity, and that the dangerous exhaust air produced by the research activities should not interfere with the work spaces. With these determinants, the logical and natural form for the building to take was a cluster of relatively small main spaces, served by separate elements for air intake and outlet. As the building site was of limited extent, the final design consists of three laboratory towers with entirely open floor areas, a more enclosed service tower, and a series of slender stacks containing staircases and ducts. (Later two more main towers and a service tower, for the Biology School, were added.) The resulting cluster of towers bears a certain resemblance to the eminently urban clusters of medieval towns, and at the same time represents a fundamentally new pattern of open growth. It is important to stress, however, that this pattern is the product of the specific needs of a Medical Research Building in Philadelphia, and does not represent a general type. Hence it is against the spirit of pluralist architecture when imitators employ Kahn's pattern of towers for entirely different purposes. Kahn himself said, "A stripe-painted horse is not a zebra."[19]

Each laboratory tower has a primary skeleton of precast concrete, with eight perimeter columns placed at the points a third and two thirds along each side. Structurally articulate two-way trusses give the system a powerful and dignified appearance. The corners are cantilevered, and are filled in with panels of brick and glass. Particularly successful is the diagonally oriented entrance, where the structure itself becomes a projecting canopy. Between the columns, entirely independent of the main structure, brick stacks are placed. These are higher than the main towers, and thus prevent the complex from becoming a visually compact mass. In general the Richards Medical Research Building

(18)   *Ibid.*, p. 113.

(19)   *Ibid.*, p. 113.

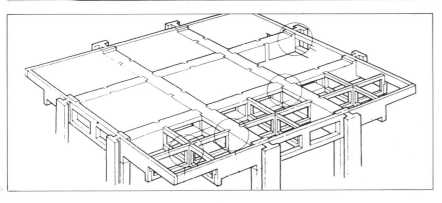

(20) The term "the third generation" is due to S. Giedion (*Space, Time and Architecture, op. cit.*, p. 668 ff.), who calls the pioneers (Le Corbusier, Mies, Gropius) the "first generation" of modern architects.

(21) R. Pietilä, "Dipoli;" *Arkkitekti*, no. 9, 1967.

(22) In *Existence, Space and Architecture* I have used the works of Paolo Portoghesi and Vittorio Gigliotti to illustrate a fundamentally similar approach.

(23) Venturi, *op. cit.*, pp. 46, 23.

(24) Venturi has opened our eyes to a whole set of environmental characters which were so far ignored or regarded as purely negative. See R. Venturi, D. Scott Brown, S. Izenour, *Learning from Las Vegas* (Cambridge, Mass., 1972).

concretizes the concept of open form, which is one of the truly basic principles of modern architecture, and which had already been suggested by Paxton, but later forgotten under the pressure of the classicist idea that a building must have a simple, general form. In Kahn's works, classicism is replaced by a more profound sense of order—a distinction Kahn makes when he says: "With order I do not mean orderliness."

Dipoli

The third generation of modern architects has produced several fine talents who have shown a keen interest in the problems of spatial identity and characterization, and who have contributed to the development of the concept of form as open growth.[20] It is not possible to give here more than a representative example from all their work. The Finnish Students' Union Building at Otaniemi by Reima Pietilä suits this purpose particularly well. "Dipoli" was built between 1965 and 1967. Pietilä had won an architectural competition in 1961 with a somewhat different project, but the principal idea has been preserved throughout the design process. Pietilä gave the background with these words: "There are two kinds of caves, caves of stone and caves of wood. The caves of wood are the dream of the people of the forest." Dipoli is a building for the cult of the *genius loci*. "A cult is a function. The duty of a cult is to implant. The duty of a cult is to produce a local character," that is, "to be something that does not exist elsewhere."[21]

To gain his end, Pietilä turned his back on the accepted forms of the twentieth century, and invented a new vocabulary, which seems old and universal as well. The corners and the edges of the building melt together and resemble the forms of the Finnish rocks. A wide overhang in dark copper stretches between the trees, and the windows follow the rhythm of the tree trunks. Natural materials unify the floor to the surrounding rocks. All these features combine to make the building an integral part of the site. Exterior space enters the building and gradually becomes interior. A wide, rising and falling roof embraces the whole space, with light entering through it. Differences of height and the play of light particularize each place.

However, Dipoli is more than the concretization of a particular "spirit of place." It also gives the actions which take place spatial identity. Being situated between the students' dormitories and the school buildings, the building is penetrated by a dynamic "path" on ground-floor level, which forms the backbone of the functional pattern. By means of this path the building is furthermore actively integrated with its surroundings. Thus the building also becomes a "nonbuilding," that is, a place which forms part of a larger context. Where the path enters the interior, the walls swing back to create concave spaces of transition. The diagonal path separates the main functional domains from each other—to the north the orthogonally organized services, which appear like an efficient machine, and to the south the topologically shaped common rooms. (On the level of the upper floor the path is naturally omitted, and the two zones meet directly.) The image of a "cave of wood" is fully realized in the common rooms. Here an elementary sense of protection and belonging can be experienced, simultaneous with the excitement of mystery and discovery offered by a continuous spatial variation. As in the Richards Medical Research Building there is a synthesis between "being somewhere" and symbolic openness, which constitutes the essence of the character of the place. But being is no longer concretized by the presence of a regular technical structure, and openness is not indicated by visual transparency. Instead both qualities are inherent in the same spatial form which is both new and old.

Although Dipoli primarily concretizes a regional character, the use of a functionally determined pluralism of spatial patterns is of universal importance. Here Dipoli manifests the same basic approach as many other works by members of the third generation.[22] The number of basic patterns at the architect's disposal are limited by the principles of topological and geometrical organization, but their possible combinations and metamorphoses are numberless, and so it becomes possible to "accommodate the circumstantial contradictions of a complex reality" and to create "the difficult unity of inclusion."[23]

Space Conception and Development

The examples discussed above have substantiated our tenet that a new architecture of pluralism is in the course of development. As this architecture does not concentrate its attention on fixed types or basic principles, but aims at understanding the total character of each task, it is a method rather than a style. Pluralist architecture is generated rather than designed, and as a result the milieu becomes a dynamic totality of interacting organs. Pluralism is not at odds with Functionalism, but extends the concept of function beyond its physical aspects. Meaning and character again receive primary importance, and the building is no longer a mere container, but becomes an expressive presence active in the environment. Character in relation to space means place in the sense of an individual "here," which helps man to gain existential foothold. However, a place is a product of many forces: natural, social and historical, so while the architecture of pluralism is new, it takes account of the old. It looks towards the future, but is rooted in the past, and its present makes clearer man's position in space and time.

In contrast to the sterile and monotonous environment of the purist architecture of exclusion, the pluralist architecture of inclusion carries with it the danger of environmental chaos if it is superficially interpreted. This danger can only be evaded if the concepts of "character" and "spatial structure" are properly understood. So far, the problem of character has hardly been studied, and the convincing concretizations mentioned above are due to the intuition of individual architects of genius. Granted that the role of intuitive creation is important, an awareness of environmental characters has to be developed through education.[24] Kahn's question, "What does the building want to be?," offers a general solution. The problem of spatial structure is better understood, probably because it is more abstract, and more easily open to scientific investigation. Study of

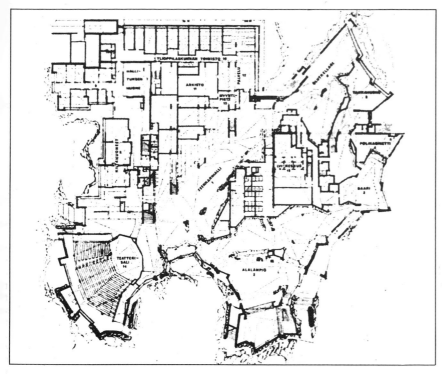

476. Reima Pietilä: "Dipoli" student union, School of Engineering at Otaniemi, Helsinki. 1961-67. Ground plan.
477. Reima Pietilä: "Dipoli" student union, Helsinki. Interior.
478. Reima Pietilä: "Dipoli" student union, Helsinki.

Gestalt psychology and systems theory has made us aware of the various types of spatial structure, and some architects have utilized the knowledge with much success.[25]

However, there is still the danger that the use of spatial structures degenerates into a mere exercise in three-dimensional geometry, as has happened in some cases.[26] Spatial structure is not a goal in itself, but is only relevant if it concretizes the spatial implications of a character by means of structural similarity, and thus establishes a meaningful definition of places, paths and domains. The concepts of character and spatial structure are brought together in the inclusive concept of *genius loci,* but to avoid misunderstandings it has to be stressed that the concept of *genius loci* comprises circumstantially determined meanings, as well as the general symbolizations of a cultural tradition.

Pluralism, usually called "modern architecture," forms the natural conclusion to the development which was initiated by the architecture of the Enlightenment and carried on by Functionalism. Pluralism does not imply a return to a multitude of closed worlds, but means that each solution should interpret openness in its own characteristic way. In pluralist architecture the basic notion of open space has been transformed into the concept of open growth or open form. Every work of architecture is thoroughly individual, at the same time as expressing that it forms part of a general field of interacting forces. Thus the image of open space is truly concretized and integrated in our daily life.

The basic aim of pluralism is a new synthesis of freedom and order. In the pluralist interpretation of open form, form is not something that is imposed from outside as it still was in Paxton's Crystal Palace, but an order which is inherent in each task, and which determines the generation and growth of the solution. Kahn has said that "form precedes design." Freedom means that the solution is free to shape itself, as a product of inner and outer forces. Thus it does not imply arbitrary caprice, but the conditioned freedom of organic growth. In other words, the open world intuited at the outset of the modern development has become alive.

(25) We may in this context again refer to the works of Portoghesi and Gigliotti.

(26) See C. Norberg-Schulz, *Existence, Space and Architecture* (London and New York, 1971), p. 13.

(27)   See M. Heidegger, *Unterwegs zur Sprache* (Pfullingen, 1959); also H. Jaeger, *Heidegger und die Sprache* (Bern, 1971).

(28)   The first was certainly Le Corbusier. Already in *Vers une architecture* he stressed the need for character and talked about the "standards of the human heart." He was also fully aware of the fact that architectural character is related to the natural site.

Meaning and Architecture

The word "pluralism" suggests that man has lost his belief in global solutions, and hence in an "international style." Evidently a great number of people still maintain an absolutist attitude, but for two centuries absolutism has been spiritually dead. The modern movement has been the only living architectural force since the end of the Baroque epoch, and the modern movement has from the very beginning tended towards pluralism. That is implicit in Voltaire's refusal of *a priori* principles, and explicit in the description of the Paris World's Fair in 1867: "All peoples are represented: enemies live in peace side by side." This does not mean, however, that man should not make a choice and have a belief. It only means that he has to recognize the fact that life can be lived in different ways. But the different ways ought to be based on education to become significant and to allow for meaningful social interaction, "education" in this context implying the development of man's sensibility to environmental characters.

Our survey of architectural history has shown that the characters have been discovered in the process of time, and since their discovery they have remained at our disposal as "existential possibilities." However, under the pressure of absolutism many fundamental meanings have been forgotten or proscribed. It is the aim of pluralism to make the totality of significant human experiences potentially available again, with the result that history becomes a dimension of fundamental importance in the pluralistic world. The new attitude to history is already manifest in many fields. A characteristic example is Heidegger's philosophy, where language is used as the main source of information about men and existence in general.[27] By studying the history of words, such as "thing," "building," and "dwelling," Heidegger has brought fundamental meanings back to life, and has given us a more concrete basis for the understanding of the relationship between ourselves and our environment. When approaching the problem of language he does not say, "Man speaks," but, "Language speaks." Man is present in language, just like nature and God. But architecture too is a language. If we study architecture as the history of meaningful forms, we will also discover man, nature and God. Thus we will learn who we are, and be helped to take a stand, and thus architecture becomes a mode of existence.

Many contemporary architects have interpreted and practised architecture in this way, and have so contributed to a more concrete understanding of the environmental problem.[28] It was, in fact, the weakness of the *esprit systématique* that it tended to separate man from the concrete, meaningful object. "Phenomenization" meant a necessary liberation from the abstract world of totalitarian systems, but as a substitute it could only offer another kind of abstraction, the world of atomism in the general sense of the word. The rediscovery of the total, concrete character is the most important contribution of the last phase of modern architecture. The need for meaning was certainly also the driving force behind the Functionalist search for essentials, but it was not yet the time for an interpretation of the concept of "essential" in terms of meanings. The rediscovery of the total, concrete character not only enables us to make our new environment meaningful, but it also brings past environments to life again. Thus the place may become a true expression of man's identity as part of the general historical process, and it can be seen that the spirit of pluralism has a wider scope than the *esprit systématique*. Without giving up the freedom of Enlightenment, it is deeply concerned with meaning. It recognizes the fact that meaning is the basic human need, and that the purpose of architecture is to make meanings manifest as a concrete system of places, paths and domains.

479.   Louis Kahn: Hurva Synagogue, Jerusalem. 1965. Model.

480.   Le Corbusier: sketch of the "Open Hand" monument, Chandigarh. Built 1951 (conceived 1948).

Existence, Meaning and Symbolism

It is essential to bear in mind some elementary facts concerning man and his position in the world, facts which are too easily forgotten or insufficiently understood. The first is man's indeterminate nature. Whereas animals are functionally and organically specialized, man is characterized by adaptability. In animals specialization has led to rigidity of structure and function, and an animal always remains at the level of its species. Man, instead, has remained flexible, and at the same time capable of further developing his functions. This human freedom, however, implies demands and responsibilities. Whereas learning plays a secondary role in animals, the newborn child comes into the world helpless, and is equipped with a few inborn reflexes and instincts only. With the aid of others and through personal action, the child slowly gains existential foothold. To a high degree, therefore, man is free to shape his own destiny.

By what means, then, does man gain the foothold and identity which are not offered him by nature? In general, he succeeds because of his ability to reach beyond the individual situation, that is, because of his ability to abstract and generalize. This means that man is capable of recognizing similarities and relationships between phenomena and discovering the laws which govern natural and human processes. What he abstracts from the continuous flow of phenomena constitutes his existential meanings. This implies that the meaning of any phenomenon is the context in which it appears, and that any man *is* the interrelationships or meanings which are accessible to him. The faculty of abstraction and generalization, or induction, is therefore the basic distinction of man, and the experience of *meaning* his basic need. To grow up signifies to become aware of meanings.

Induction operates on different levels, from simple sensory-motor behaviour to complex intelligence, and although the basic capacity may be considered inborn, its different applications are developed during the growth of the individual as well as through the history of mankind. At about one year of

(1) J. Piaget, *Genetic Epistomology* (New York and London, 1970), p. 43.

(2) H. Werner, *Comparative Psychology of Mental Development* (New York, 1965) (1948), p. 26.

(3) M. Eliade, *Patterns in Comparative Religion*.

(4) C. Norberg-Schulz, *Intentions in Architecture* (London, 1963; Cambridge, Mass., 1968), pp. 63 ff.

age, the child already possesses notions of the permanence of objects and their movement in space.[1] About six months later language is mastered well enough to make true abstraction possible; that is, the experienced generalizations are brought to a level of representation rather than existing only at the level of action. By means of language the experienced generalizations necessary to man may be talked about, described and conserved. Only language makes possible the transmission of experiences from one generation to another. It follows from what is said above, that words do not designate a particular phenomenon, but a class of similarities between phenomena. It is, in fact, the basic purpose of any kind of symbol to conserve the inductions of man, and the symbolic function forms a necessary complement to man's faculty of abstraction and generalization.

It is through symbolization that man becomes able to transcend the individual situation and thereby to live a social and purposive life. Symbolization, however, is not confined to spoken or written language; it also comprises gestures and other kinds of expressive behaviour, symbolic objects such as pictures, as well as more abstract concepts. Any human product may be considered a symbol or tool which serves the purpose of bringing order (meaning) into certain relations between man and his environment, and nonverbal behaviour is just as dependent upon structured symbol systems as verbal behaviour. Whether we employ gestures, other kinds of actions, images or sounds, these have to be ordered and connected to form a system to allow for the necessary conservation and transmittance of experienced meanings. Taken together the symbol systems constitute the common order we call culture. Participation in a culture means that one knows how to use its symbols through perception (experience) and representation (expression).

Symbolic behaviour develops during the growth of the individual, and in a general sense through the history of mankind. As meaning is a social phenomenon, the development of individual symbolism naturally does not proceed beyond the actual stage reached by mankind in general. But the child does not arrive at this general level without first going through a development which is similar to the historical process at large.[2] This parallelism between individual and cultural development is most significant as it indicates a natural course in the development of human understanding, and as it shows that culture and mentality are interdependent aspects of the same totality, that is, existence. "Human freedom" therefore does not mean that man can do anything; rather he is free to choose between culturally determined possibilities, and to a certain extent he can make creative contributions to a given culture. This means that any individual is born into a system of meanings which he comes to know through its symbolic manifestations.

The growth of man's mental faculties proceeds from initial diffuse perceptions characterized by the grasping of "total" qualities, into more articulate experiences where the parts and the interrelationships within the totality are understood. Similarly, the function of representation moves through a course of development from a syncretic symbolism to one that is pure and detached. The perceptions and representations of children and of primitive man are tied to concrete actions, or rather interactions between the subject and the environment, as primitive mental life is characterized by a relatively limited differentiation of subject and object. The things perceived at this level appear animate; nature seems alive throughout and everything is understood to behave dynamically. In the world of primitive man things have meaning in so far as they are integral parts of the concrete context in which they function. The animals painted in the Magdalenian caves were not intended as pure images, but as live realities which made the practice of homeopathic or imitative magic possible. By killing the image, Magdalenian man hoped to bring about a successful hunting trip, as he believed that an operation performed on the image of a real being would produce the same effect on the being itself. Primitive action, thus, is intimately tied to the concrete situation, but it already contains the element of generalization, as when the enacted situation represents a real one.

In advanced forms of mental activity symbolizations are found which are quite detached from concrete perception and sensory-motor behaviour. They are based on a more articulate structuring of the perceptual field and on more complex conceptual classifications, and gradually open up a world of pure possibility, of "as if." In this way conscious choice and planned action become possible, and man becomes able to move freely from one level of reality to another. In general, then, mental development implies a simultaneous increase in differentiation and systematic integration, and therefore implies the mastery of increasingly difficult situations. Whereas primitive perception and conception fuse meanings which would be conflicting to logical thought, rational thinking aims at the representation of specific and unambiguous truths. The cost of the knowledge thereby obtained is a relative loss of the ability to experience existence spontaneously as a meaningful whole. As it is the aim of symbolism "to abolish the limits of the 'fragment' man is within society and the cosmos . . . and making him one with the rhythms of nature,"[3] the development of the symbolic function here seems partly to work against its own purpose.

This apparent contradiction is resolved by differentiating between symbol systems. As the primitive world is a dynamic whole characterized by a relative lack of differentiation in so far as the single spheres of reality are concerned, the modes of symbolization are also unified in the syncretic categories of magic and myth. A purely cognitive understanding of the situation is unknown; instead good and bad forces are associated with the things. This, of course, does not happen accidentally, but reflects the fact that the environment really may be said to consist of hostile and friendly objects. Later development produces a differentiation of symbol systems, which in general can be classified as descriptive and nondescriptive (expressive) symbol systems. The main descriptive systems are science and philosophy, and the most important nondescriptive art and religion.[4] Whereas the former aim at a cognitive and instrumental understanding through advanced and systematic abstraction and generalization, the latter work with generalizations of a more concrete kind in an attempt to grasp the totalities and processes which seem directly given or inherent in nature and human life. The work of art concretizes an experienced or possible life-situation where several levels of reality are interacting. In this sense, nondescriptive symbolism conserves something of the syncretic character of the primitive symbolism, with one basic difference. Whereas primitive symbolism is relatively diffuse, advanced nondescriptive symbol systems are highly articulate. Rather than serving specific and unambiguous meaning, artistic articulation therefore may express the complexities and contradictions inherent in life.[5]

Art and religion have common roots and together serve the purpose of making man aware of existential meanings. The further development of artistic and religious symbolism during the history of mankind does not alter this basic function for this development consists mainly of a differentiation and systematic integration of the symbol systems in question, to make them capable of expressing any shade of existential relationships.

It must be emphasized that existential meanings are not something which is arbitrarily added to man's daily life. Such meanings are inherent in daily life, consisting of the relationships between natural and human properties, processes and actions. They therefore contain components possessing some degree of invariance in space and time. But, if meanings are inherent in daily life, why do we have to worry about "making life meaningful?" Firstly, it is necessary to become sensitive to meanings; the faculty of perception has to be developed to allow for an adequate "intentional depth."[6] Secondly, meanings have to be made clearly manifest to make a socially valid perception possible. Hence the importance of symbolism.

The purpose of the work of art is to conserve and communicate experienced existential meanings. In perceiving an articulate symbol, a man experiences an act of identification which gives his individual existence meaning by relating it to a complex of natural and human dimensions. Identification presupposes a choice, or, we might say, an act of orientation, and orientation implies that any meaning is experienced as forming part of a

comprehensive spatio-temporal order. That is, any meaning is necessarily revealed in a particular *place*, and the character of the place is determined by this revelation. In other words, the experienced meanings constitute from the very outset an *existential space*, which forms a framework of man's actions. This existential space is not identical with geographic space, as defined in purely physical terms, but is determined by experienced properties, processes and interrelations. It is therefore usually not homogeneous and neutral, but has a qualitative and live character. As the spatial order is of particular importance in our context, it is necessary to discuss it in more detail.

Space, Character and Architecture

The concept of existential space is based on the fact that any human action has a spatial aspect.[7] Actions *take place* and need a more or less precisely defined spatial frame to take place. The concept has a double meaning: It denotes the objectively describable spatial aspects of an intersubjective form of life as well as the single person's image of the spatial relations which form part of his existence. We may therefore talk about "public" and "private" existential spaces. The private existential space is constituted during mental development through interaction between the individual and his environment. As a result an image is formed which consists of three-dimensional relations between meaningful objects. This image does not correspond to immediate perceptual space. Whereas perceptual space varies continuously, existential space has a relatively stable structure which serves as a frame of reference for the transitory perceptions and turns them into experiences. For example, my image of the town where I live gives meaning to its elements, be it buildings, streets or squares. A public existential space is constituted by the most stable, common properties belonging to a large number of private existential spaces. It has the character of a cultural tradition which undergoes a relatively slow process of change and development. Participation in a society, among other

things, means that one's private existential space has certain properties in common with the public existential space. It thereby becomes possible for the individual to use the environment in a meaningful way.

Beyond the analysis of various private and public existential spaces, it is also possible to describe some basic structural properties which are common to all existential spaces. These properties are related to the archetypal relations of primitive symbolism and constitute the point of departure for any further development of spatial images and concepts. Again there are close parallels between children and primitive people. Piaget, in findings in agreement with Gestalt psychology, demonstrates that the infant's space can be described as a collection of separate spaces, each centred on a single activity.[8] The first relations which go beyond this original centralization are topological in that topology does not deal with permanent distances, angles and areas, but is based on relations such as proximity, separation, succession, continuity, and closure (Inside-outside). In order to interpret these basic results of perception psychology in more general terms, it may be said that elementary organization comprises the establishment of centres or places (proximity), directions or paths (continuity), and areas or domains (closure).[9] To orient himself, man needs above all to grasp such relations, whereas geometrical structures develop much later, to serve more advanced purposes. The importance of the spatial dimension is such that children born blind show a considerable delay in developing the symbolic function.[10]

The study of early civilizations and their symbolism confirms these findings. The notion of centre may be considered the basic element of primitive existential space. Every place where a meaning becomes manifest is, in fact, a centre. "According to many traditions, the creation of the world was begun in a centre and for this reason the building of towns must also develop round a centre." The city walls were a magic symbol long before they became military erections, "for they marked out from the midst of a chaotic space, peopled with demons and phantoms, an enclosure, a place that was organized, made cosmic, in other words, provided with

(5) R. Venturi, *Complexity and Contradiction in Architecture* (New York, 1967).

(6) Norberg-Schulz, *op. cit.*, p. 31.

(7) C. Norberg-Schulz, *Existence, Space and Architecture* (London and New York, 1971).

(8) J. Piaget and B. Inhelder, *The Child's Conception of Space* (London, 1956; New York, 1967).

(9) K. Lynch, *The Image of the City* (Cambridge, Mass., 1960).

(10) Piaget, *Genetic Psychology on Mental Development*, p. 46.

(11) Eliade, op. cit., pp. 371 ff.

(12) Werner, op. cit., p. 168.

(13) As early as in Vers une architecture (1923) Le Corbusier recognized the importance of the path, writing: "An axis is perhaps the first human manifestation; it is the means of every human act. The toddling child moves along an axis, the man striving in the tempest of life traces for himself an axis." (English edition, London 1924, p. 173.)

(14) Norberg-Schulz, Existence, Space and Architecture, p. 27.

(15) Lynch, op. cit.

(16) M. Heidegger "Bauen Wohnen Denken," Vorträge und Aufsätze II (Pfullingen, 1954), pp. 32 ff.

a 'centre'."[11] If the concept of "centre of the world" designates an ideal, public goal, the word "home" simply tells us that any man's personal world has its centre. From the beginning the centre represents to man what is known in contrast to the unknown and frightening world around. The places are goals or foci where we experience the meaningful events of our existence, but they are also points of departure from which we orient ourselves and take possession of the environment. The place is therefore experienced as an inside in contrast to the surrounding outside, and has to be relatively small to offer psychological security. The limited size of known places naturally goes together with a centralized form. A place, therefore, is basically round.

The fact that the concept of place implies an inside and an outside makes it clear that the place is situated within a larger context and cannot be understood in isolation. Any place, in fact, contains directions and openings. Primitive terms for spatial relations suggest that the body itself, with its personal dimensions of above-below, before-behind, and right-left, is the source of a psychophysical system of coordinates.[12] These directions are also related to natural phenomena, such as gravitation and the cardinal points, and therefore represent different characters. The vertical direction represents a rising-up or falling-down, and has since remote times been considered the sacred dimension of space. It represents a path towards a reality which is higher or lower than daily life. The vertical axis, the axis mundi, is therefore an archetypal symbol of a passage from one cosmic region to another. If verticality has something surreal about it, the horizontal directions represent man's concrete world of action. In a certain sense, all horizontal directions are equal and constitute a plane of infinite extension. The simplest model of man's existential space is then a horizontal plane pierced by a vertical axis. On the plane man chooses and creates paths which give his existential space a more particular structure. Sometimes the paths lead to known goals, but often they only indicate a direction which gradually dissolves into the unknown distance. In all cases the path represents a basic property of human existence, and is

one of the great original symbols.[13]

Paths divide man's environment into areas which are more or less well-known, and which I have called "domains." In a certain sense domains are places, because they are defined by closure or by proximity and similarity of the constituent elements. Domains have a unifying function in existential space for they form a relatively unstructured ground on which places and paths appear as more pronounced figures. By structuring the world into domains by natural directions, ancient man gained an existential foothold. He no longer felt lost and helpless, and even the blank spots on his personal map could be placed within a general all-embracing scheme.

Places, paths and domains are the constituent elements of existential space. Like other symbolic forms they are determined by an interaction between man and his environment.

The elements of existential space are made manifest on different environmental levels.[14] The most comprehensive level relevant to this discussion is landscape, then follows the urban dimension of human settlements, and finally single buildings and parts of these.

The level of landscape has generally been that of a ground on which the configurations of existential space have become manifest. Its domains, therefore, are of primary importance, but it also offers areas where the development of places is particularly favoured, and it indicates natural paths. In general, it has a certain capacity determined by its structural properties. The capacity is not only related to physical-practical conditions, but also to the meanings indicated by the landscape forms. As nature is not man-made, it keeps us at a certain distance and offers great but relatively undifferentiated experiences. Correspondingly, the formal structures of the landscape consists of topological relationships. The history of garden and landscape architecture illustrates man's attempts to make the forms of his landscape more precise, or transform them to fit his environmental image.

On the urban level the structures are mostly determined by man's own actions, and on this level the basic form is what could

be called "our place." In his development the individual discovers a structured whole which he shares with others and which more than anything else gives him a feeling of identity. For most of history the town was a civitas, the known and safe world where man's foothold was secure amidst unknown surroundings. Its primary qualities are singleness and identifiability—qualities for which the settlement ought to have figural character in relation to the landscape. The urban structure also comprises an interior organization, as has been studied by Kevin Lynch.[15] According to Lynch, man needs an urban environment which facilitates his image-making: he needs districts which have a particular character, paths which lead somewhere and nodes which are "distinct and unforgettable places."

Within the urban level is the smaller unit of the building or the house. The house really brings us inside and represents the basic need for "being somewhere." This is the essential function of dwelling, and the house remains the central place of human existence, the place where the child comes to understand his being in the world and the place from which man departs and to which he returns. Heidegger points out that the German words for "building," "dwelling" and "being" have common roots, and says: "Only when we are capable of dwelling, can we build. . . . Dwelling is the basic property of existence."[16] The structure of the house is accordingly primarily that of an enclosed place, but as such it also contains an interior structure of subordinate foci and connecting paths. The fireplace, for instance, has since ancient times been the very centre of the dwelling, and the table was the place where the family came together. The bed may represent the centre even more convincingly, being the place where man starts his day, and to which he returns in the evening. In bed the circle of the day, and of life, is closed.

However, to take into consideration only the function of orientation and to describe the spatial structure in terms of places, paths and domains as abstract relations do not give sufficient understanding of the full meaning of the environment. "To be somewhere" implies more than location; it involves primarily identification with the particular *character* of the places, paths and domains in question. Here we return to the existential meanings proper. As has been maintained, any meaning is revealed in a particular place, and the character of the place is determined by this revelation, so existential meanings manifest themselves as "characters."[17] The word "character" indicates an unmistakable totality, or *Gestalt*, where each single part has a relevant function within the whole. When, for instance, we say that a person has "strength of character," we imply a certain moral and behavioural integrity. In my book *Intentions in Architecture* I have analysed the totalities which I here designate with the word "character" in terms of physical, social and cultural objects. Such an analysis may be theoretically correct and useful, but it does not grasp the character as such. The totality, in fact, can only be symbolized by means of nondescriptive concretization, but it may be indicated by what I have called "qualitative concepts."[18] Such concepts usually comprise all the basic dimensions of objects, and simultaneously refer to meanings and their physical manifestations. The best way of arriving at relevant qualitative concepts is through a study of the history of nondescriptive symbolism. Three fundamental categories of characters have been subject to architectural concretization throughout the course of time, and may be indicated by the adjectives "natural," "human" and "spiritual."

The natural characters comprise the qualities of things and materials, such as weight and hardness, but also large-scale phenomena such as the cardinal points and the course of the sun. They also comprise the individual properties of places, as well as natural processes. The human characters comprise such elementary categories as masculine and feminine, personality types and correlated traits, as well as human actions and interactions. Finally, the spiritual characters refer to beliefs and values which cannot be understood as abstractions from natural and human phenomena. The natural, human and spiritual characters are related to the concepts of physical, social and cultural objects, but they cannot be reduced to

these. As manifestations of meanings, the characters are syncretic categories. This is beautifully expressed by Heidegger when analysing a jug: "In the poured water dwells the source. In the source dwells the rock, and the dark slumber of the earth, which receives the rain and the dew of the sky. In the water of the source dwells the wedding of sky and earth. The gift of the pouring is the jugness of the jug. In the character of the jug sky and earth are present."[19]

As is well known, the categories of characters are interrelated by structural similarities, and therefore may represent each other. For example, the "human" characters of the Greek gods also represented related natural properties, and the gods were accordingly worshipped in places with a corresponding character. There is nothing mysterious about this psychophysical isomorphism; it simply indicates that man chooses those places in his environment which satisfy his physical needs. As the character of a natural or artificial place is determined by its formal articulation, character is described by means of concepts such as "closure," "openness," "width," "narrowness," "sombreness," "luminosity," etc., that is, qualities which depend upon plastic modelling, proportion, rhythm, scale, dimension, material texture and colour. Particularly important among the determinants of architectural character is the "play of forces" expressed by a real or fictitious construction.

Through the concept of character, the concepts of the environmental levels of landscape, settlement and house have been made more concrete. These characters constitute the true subject matter of architecture, and the task of the architect is to create places with a particular, meaningful character, for without the dimension of character all the levels would remain mere abstractions, like a country or a town we only know from a map. When we concretize a character by means of formal articulation, we bring the work "close," we make the existential meanings manifest as palpable *things*. Thus Heidegger says: "Close at hand are what we usually call things. When we take care of things as things, we dwell in this place."[20] In other words, man only gains existential foothold if he manages to give his place a

concrete character. Since ancient times the environmental character has been recognized as *genius loci* or "spirit of place," and even today Lawrence Durrell may write: "As you get to know Europe slowly, tasting the wines, cheeses and characters of the different countries you begin to realize that the important determinant of any culture is, after all—the spirit of place."[21] For architectural theory it is important to understand space in such concrete terms, rather than as an abstract system of semiological relations.

From what has been said above, it appears that existential space may be understood as a hierarchy of interrelated characters. Whereas "existential space" denotes the environmental *image*, "architecture" comprises the concrete *forms* which determine or result from this image. Architecture, thus, may be defined as a concretization of existential space. As such, architecture is a symbol system expressing the characters and spatial relations which constitute the totality—man-environment. However, the interaction man-environment hardly produces a finished, complete image. Usually it will contain contradictions, and parts will be missing. As a result existential space comprises wishes and dreams, and to satisfy these wishes, man tries to change his environment. Man's relationship to the environment hence consists in adaptation as well as a wish for change, and an interpretation of works of architecture must take both aspects into consideration.

A work of architecture is always related to a specific situation, but it also has to transcend this situation and make it appear as part of a more comprehensive, meaningful totality. Even at the earliest stage of building, the choice of a fitting, natural site implies an evaluation of alternatives, that is, a recognition of similarities, differences and relationships. The choice is made to satisfy human needs, and is thus related to human actions and intentions. In vernacular architecture, in fact, sites are carefully chosen for different functions, and these functions are satisfied by specific building types. The existential meanings which constitute a "form of life" are thus accompanied by corresponding, systematically organized environmental symbols.

The process of abstraction which leads to the formation of other concepts therefore

(17) H. Sedlmayr, *Epochen und Werke* I (Vienna, 1959), p. 9.

(18) Norberg-Schulz, *Intentions in Architecture*, pp. 89 ff., p. 182.

(19) M. Heidegger, "Das Ding," *Vorträge und Aufsätze* II.

(20) *Ibid.*, pp. 38, 54.

(21) L. Durrell, *Spirit of Place* (London and New York, 1969), p. 156.

(22) A. Rapoport,
House Form and Culture
(Englewood Cliffs, N.J.
and London, 1969), pp.
47 ff.

(23) K. Popper, *The
Poverty of Historicism*
(London and New York,
1957).

also holds good for architecture. It is reasonable to maintain that architecture comes into being when man transcends the specific environmental situation and recognizes principles which may serve to solve other (related) tasks. From a set of specific situations man abstracts meaningful forms and principles of organization which make a more general planning possible. Some of these forms may be called archetypal, as they represent the meanings of man's most original experiences. Rudimentary architectural symbol systems are found in primitive and early civilizations, but the first truly integrated and developable system belongs to ancient Egypt, which therefore plays a particularly important role among the ancestors of Western culture.

The abstraction of symbolic forms also implies that a specific meaning is no longer tied to a particular geographic location. Meanings are transported when similar buildings are erected in different places, just as language allows for flexible communication. In this way the diffusion of culture becomes possible. When the archetypal solution is not directly or totally determined by the particular site, this produces a man-made or artificial milieu, although the forms employed originally might stem from the experience of natural phenomena. The architectural symbol system, thus, allows man to experience a meaningful environment, wherever he might be on earth, and in this way helps him to find an existential foothold. This is the true purpose of architecture, to help make human existence meaningful; all other functions, such as the satisfaction of mere physical needs, can be satisfied without architecture.

The History of Architecture

The history of architecture describes the development and use of the architectural symbol systems. It therefore forms part of the history of culture, which in general can be defined as the history of meaningful or symbolic forms. Thereby it also becomes a history of existential possibilities.

The two terms "development" and "use" are employed because history itself proves that forms developed are not necessarily used. There are two parallel histories: the factual history of building and use, and the ideal history of possible symbolizations. Whereas the former shows an unsteady course where "primitive" and "sophisticated" solutions alternate according to the situation, the latter illustrates a general growth of knowledge and possibilities. On the basis of the theory of architecture as a concretization of existential space, it becomes possible to understand the contribution of an individual work to the general development of culture, and to understand that cultural development does not mean that the world gets better or human beings happier, but certainly that man's possibilities of choice are augmented. History, thus, may be defined as a growth of accessible meanings.

It might seem that to take existential space as the dimension of comparison for a history of architecture is to overlook a series of determinants, such as physical needs, climate, topography, building technique, production and economy. To a certain extent these factors are included in the concept of existential space, as man's image of the environment is certainly influenced by all of them and by their different manifestations. But, as Amos Rapoport maintained, none of these factors may alone explain the properties of human settlements, and no single factor may be considered primary in relation to the others. Instead Rapoport gives decisive importance to "the vision that people have of an ideal life," and says: "Buildings and settlements are the visible expression of the relative importance attached to different aspects of life and the varying ways of perceiving reality. . . . Creation of an ideal environment is expressed through the specific organization of space."[22] It is important to note that Rapoport's conclusions are based on a study of vernacular architecture.

Insight into a field of studies means a grasp of its structure. This happens most easily when we manage to define a few primary properties which illuminate extensive relationships, according to Goethe's dictum: "The value of an idea is proved by its power to organize the subject matter." I have introduced the concept of existential space to serve this purpose, and may point to the successful employment of related concepts by Kevin Lynch and others. Naturally any method is selective, as an historical investigation cannot as a matter of principle be complete,[23] but the Goethe quotation suggests that a presentation which manages to structure the field may be characterized as particularly prolific. The method of study followed in this book, based on the theory of architecture as a concretization of existential space, centres on the spatial properties of the work or group of works in question and offers a structural analysis of the various environmental levels, indicating the pattern of places, paths and domains, as well as the interaction of the levels. Structural analysis has also had to include an investigation of the formal articulation and its importance for the general character. The aim of this inquiry has been to conclude with an interpretation of the architectural form as a concretization of a particular set of existential meanings, which is ultimately defined in terms of cultural, social and physical objects, and to evaluate architecture in relation to the historical situation and cultural tradition.

Our study of the history of architecture based on this method has been intended to provide a definition and an understanding of basic symbolizations and to describe how such elements are related to form an architectural language on a higher level of abstraction. Such a language does not only consist of a set of interrelated motifs, but also comprises characteristic modes of spatial organization. It has already been pointed out that the basic symbolic forms usually possess a pronounced Gestalt quality, and that the basic modes of organization are related to the so-called Gestalt laws (similarity, proximity, continuity, closure). Examples from any farm or village from any part of the world demonstrates this, and show that vernacular architecture is not a direct reflection of physical conditions and needs, but possesses the distinguishing properties of symbol systems. As vernacular architecture and the monumental buildings of the grand-design tradition have common roots and serve the same symbolic function, both express the meanings, values and needs inherent in a public form of life. Any distinction of basic human purpose is therefore artificial and forms a block to a true understanding of our total environment.[24] The real difference is that monumental architecture represents a higher level of abstraction than vernacular architecture. Whereas vernacular buildings conserve a strong attachment to the specific character of a limited situation, monumental buildings stress the general, systematic and interhuman aspects of symbolization, and contribute to the constitution of architectural languages which form an important part of cultural development. Monumental architecture therefore usually comprises public tasks such as buildings for worship and government, and hence it is not a mere convention when histories of architecture give such buildings pride of place.

In general, architectural history shows a development from an initial concretization of diffuse totalities to a precise symbolization of natural and human characters. This development took place mainly in antiquity and was accompanied by the introduction of geometrical means of organization which possess a higher capacity than the topological forms of primitive symbolization. Here architectural history parallels the psychological development of the individual. During the Middle Ages a new "spiritual" dimension came to the fore, whereas the humanist architecture of the Renaissance and the Baroque aimed at a synthesis of natural, human and spiritual characters.

Today we experience a pluralism of manifest characters. All the existential possibilities experienced during history are at our disposal, but either we are blind to them or we select one narrow set of meanings, believing that we have discovered absolute truth. Existential security certainly depends upon a choice between values, but the choice ought to be made on the basis of real insight, and in such a way that it respects the choice of others.

A meaningful environment forms a necessary and essential part of a meaningful existence. As meaning is a psychological problem, which cannot be solved through control of production and economy alone, architecture, in the true sense of the word, ought to be a primary concern for modern man. The problem of meaning in architecture, however, is hardly understood, and there is much research to be done. Architectural research can only make use of laboratory experiments to a very limited extent, and theoretical insight above all has to be based on an analysis of already existing environments. Architectural history describes how man found "spatial foothold" under different conditions, and may therefore help us to reeducate our sensibility to environmental characters, and to improve our understanding of the relationship between man and his environment.

(24) Rapoport, *op. cit.*, p. 2 makes this fundamental error.

Selected Bibliography

1. Egyptian Architecture

Badawy, Alexander. *A History of Egyptian Architecture*. 3 vols. Berkeley, Los Angeles, and London, 1965.

Baldwin Smith, E. *Egyptian Architecture as Cultural Expression*. New York and London, 1938. Reprint: Watkins Glen, N.Y., 1968.

Edwards, I. E. S. *The Pyramids of Egypt*. Rev. ed. Harmondsworth and Baltimore, 1961.

Giedion, Sigfried. *The Beginnings of Architecture*. New York, 1964.

Hölscher, Uvo. *The Excavation of Medinet Habu*. London and Chicago, 1934–51.

Kaschnitz von Weinberg, Guido. *Mittelmeerische Kunst*. Berlin, 1965.

Smith, William Stevenson. *The Art and Architecture of Ancient Egypt*. Pelican History of Art. Harmondsworth and Baltimore, 1958.

2. Greek Architecture

Berve, Helmut, and Gruben, Gottfried. *Greek Temples, Theatres, and Shrines*. New York and London, 1963.

Dinsmoor, William B. *The Architecture of Ancient Greece*. New York and London, 1950.

Gerkan, Armin von. *Griechischen Städteanlagen*. Berlin and Leipzig, 1924.

Kähler, Heinz. *Der griechische Tempel*. Berlin, 1964.

Krauss, Friedrich. *Die Tempel von Paestum*. Berlin, 1959.

Lawrence, Arnold W. *Greek Architecture*. Pelican History of Art. Harmondsworth and Baltimore, 1957.

Martin, Roland. *L'urbanisme dans la Grèce antique*. Paris, 1956.

Robertson, Donald S. *Greek and Roman Architecture*. Cambridge, 1964. 2d ed., 1969.

Schede, Martin. *Die Ruinen von Priene*. Berlin, 1964.

Scully, Vincent J. *The Earth, the Temple and the Gods: Greek Sacred Architecture*. New Haven, Conn., and London, 1962. Rev. ed. New York, 1969.

3. Roman Architecture

Baldwin Smith, E. *Architectural Symbolism of Imperial Rome and the Middle Ages*. Princeton, N.J., 1956.

Boëthius, Axel, and Ward-Perkins, J. B. *Etruscan and Roman Architecture*. Pelican History of Art. Harmondsworth and Baltimore, 1970.

Crema, Luigi. *L'architettura romana*. Vol. 1. Enciclopedia classica, 12 vols. Turin, 1959.

Kähler, Heinz. *Der römische Tempel*. Berlin, 1970.

Kaschnitz von Weinberg, Guido. *Römische Kunst*. 4 vols. Hamburg, 1961–63.

L'Orange, H. P. *Art Forms and Civic Life in the Late Roman Empire*. Princeton, N.J., 1965; London, 1966.

Müller, Werner. *Die heilige Stadt*. Stuttgart, 1961.

Vitruvius, Pollio. *De architectura. Vitruvius, On Architecture*. 10 vols. Frank Granger, ed. and trans. London, 1931–34; Cambridge, Mass., 1955–56.

4. Early Christian Architecture

Conant, Kenneth John. *Early Medieval Church Architecture*. Baltimore, 1942.

Deichmann, Friedrich Wilhelm. *Frühchristliche Kirchen in Rom*. Basel, 1948.

Demus, Otto. *Byzantine Mosaic Decoration: Aspects of Monumental Art in Byzantium*. London, 1953.

Kähler, Heinz. *Hagia Sophia*. New York and London, 1967.

——. *Die frühe Kirche*. Berlin, 1972.

Krautheimer, Richard. *Early Christian and Byzantine Architecture*. Pelican History of Art. Harmondsworth and Baltimore, 1965.

Mango, Cyril. *Architettura bizantina*. Milan, 1974.

Sherrard, Philip. *Constantinople: Image of a Holy City*. London, New York, and Toronto, 1965.

5. Romanesque Architecture

Braunfels, Wolfgang. *Die abendländische Klosterbaukunst*. Cologne, 1969.

Conant, Kenneth John. *Carolingian and Romanesque Architecture, 800–1200*. Pelican History of Art. Harmondsworth and Baltimore,1959. 2d ed., 1966.

——. *Cluny: Les églises et la maison du chef d'ordre*. Cambridge, Mass., 1968.

Eschapasse, Maurice. *L'architecture bénédictine en Europe*. Paris, 1963.

Frankl, Paul. *Die frühmittelalterliche und romanische Baukunst*. Potsdam, 1926.

Hell, Vera, and Hell, Hellmut. *The Great Pilgrimage of the Middle Ages: The Road to St. James of Compostela*. New York and London, 1966.

Kubach, E. *Architettura romanica*. Milan, 1973.

Webb, Geoffrey. *Architecture in Britain: The Middle Ages*. Pelican History of Art. Harmondsworth and Baltimore, 1956.

6. Gothic Architecture

Branner, Robert. *Burgundian Gothic Architecture*. London, 1960.

Braunfels, Wolfgang. *Mittelalterliche Stadtbaukunst in der Toskana*. Berlin, 1953.

Clasen, Karl Heinz. *Deutsche Gewolbe der Spätgotik*. Berlin, 1958.

Fitchen, John. *The Construction of Gothic Cathedrals: A Study of Medieval Vault Erection*. Oxford, 1961.

Frankl, Paul. *Gothic Architecture*. Pelican History of Art. Harmondsworth and Baltimore, 1962.

Jantzen, Hans. *Die Gotik des Abendlandes*. Cologne, 1962.

Panofsky, Erwin. *Gothic Architecture and Scholasticism*. Latrobe, Pa., 1951.

Sedlmayr, Hans. *Die Entstehung der Kathedrale*. Zurich, 1950.

Simson, Otto von. *The Gothic Cathedral: Origins of Gothic Architecture and the Medieval Concept of Order*. 2d rev. ed. New York and London, 1962.

7. Renaissance Architecture

Alberti, Leone Battista. *De re aedificatoria*. 1485. *Ten Books on Architecture*. London, 1955.

Bruschi, Arnaldo. *Bramante architetto*. Bari, 1969.

Förster, Otto Helmut. *Bramante*. Vienna, 1956.

Heydenreich, Ludwig Heinrich. *Die Sakralbau-Studien Leonardo da Vincis*. Munich, 1971.

Heydenreich, Ludwig Heinrich, and Lotz, W. *Architecture in Italy: 1400–1600*. Harmondsworth and Baltimore, 1974.

Klotz, Heinrich. *Die Frühwerke Brunelleschis und die mittelalterliche Tradition*. Berlin, 1970.

Luporini, Eugenio. *Brunelleschi*. Milan, 1964.

Murray, Peter. *The Architecture of the Ancient Renaissance*. London, 1969. New and enl. ed. New York, 1971.

Sanpaolesi, Piero. *Brunelleschi*. Milan, 1962.

Wittkower, Rudolf. *Architectural Principles in the Age of Humanism.* 3d ed. rev. London, 1962; New York, 1965.

Zevi, Bruno. *Biagio Rossetti.* Turin, 1960.

8. Mannerist Architecture

Ackerman, James S. *The Architecture of Michelangelo.* 2 vols. New York and London, 1961.

Forssman, Erik. *Dorisch, Jonisch, Korintisch.* Uppsala, 1961.

Giovannoni, Gustavo. *Antonio da Sangallo il giovane.* Rome, 1959.

Palladio, Andrea. *I quattro libri dell'architettura.* 1570. *The Four Books of Architecture.* New York and London, 1965.

Pane, Roberto. *Andrea Palladio.* Turin, 1961.

Portoghesi, Paolo, and Zevi, Bruno. *Michelangiolo architetto.* Turin, 1964.

Puppi, Lionello. *Michele Sanmicheli, architetto di Verona.* Padua, 1971.

Serlio, Sebastiano. *Tutte l'opere d'architettura.* 1537–51. Ridgewood, N.J., 1964.

Tafuri, Manfredo. *L'architettura del Manierismo.* Rome, 1966.

9. Baroque Architecture

Argan, Giulio Carlo. *The Europe of the Capitals, 1600–1700.* Cleveland and Geneva, 1964.

Blunt, Sir Anthony. *Art and Architecture in France, 1500–1700.* Pelican History of Art. Harmondsworth and Baltimore, 1957.

Boscarino, Salvatore. *Juvarra architetto.* Rome, 1973.

Franz, Heinrich Gerhard. *Bauten und Baumeister der Barockzeit in Böhmen.* Leipzig, 1962.

Grimschitz, Bruno. *Johann Lucas von Hildebrandt.* Vienna, 1959.

Hager, W. *Barock Architektur.* Baden-Baden, 1968.

Hibbard, Howard. *Bernini.* Harmondsworth and Baltimore, 1965.

———. *Carlo Maderno and Roman Architecture, 1580–1630.* Studies in Architecture, vol. 10. University Park, Pa., 1971; London, 1972.

Lieb, N. *Barockkirchen zwischen Donau und Alpen.* Munich, 1953.

Norberg-Schulz, Christian. *Kilian Ignaz Dientzenhofer e il barocco boemo.* Rome, 1968.

———. *Baroque Architecture.* New York, 1971.

———. *Late Baroque and Rococo Architecture.* New York, 1972.

Passanti, Mario. *Nel mondo magico di Guarino Guarini.* Turin, 1963.

Portoghesi, Paolo. *Bernardo Vittone.* Rome, 1966.

———. *Borromini.* London, 1968.

———. *Roma barocca: The History of an Architectonic Culture.* Cambridge, Mass., and London, 1970.

Reuther, Hans. *Die Kirchenbauten Balthasar Neumanns.* Berlin, 1960.

Sedlmayr, Hans. *Die Architektur Borrominis.* Berlin, 1930.

———. *Johann Bernhard Fischer von Erlach.* 2d ed. Vienna, 1956.

Summerson, John N. *Architecture in Britain, 1530–1830.* Pelican History of Art. Harmondsworth and Baltimore, 1953. 5th rev. ed. (Harmondsworth), 1969.

Wittkower, Rudolf. *Art and Architecture in Italy, 1600–1750.* Pelican History of Art. Harmondsworth and Baltimore, 1958. 2d rev. ed., 1965.

10. Enlightenment

Chadwick, George F. *The Works of Sir Joseph Paxton.* London, 1961.

Christ, Yvan. *Projets et divagations de Claude-Nicolas Ledoux.* New York, 1961.

Condit, Carl W. *The Chicago School of Architecture: A History of Commercial and Public Building in the Chicago Area, 1875–1925.* Chicago and London, 1964.

Giedion, Sigfried. *Bauen in Frankreich, Eisen, Eisenbeton.* Leipzig, 1928.

Hermann, W. *Laugier and Eighteenth-Century French Theory.* London, 1972.

Hitchcock, Henry-Russell. *In the Nature of Materials, 1887–1941: The Buildings of Frank Lloyd Wright.* New York and London, 1942.

———. *Architecture: Nineteenth and Twentieth Centuries.* Pelican History of Art. Harmondsworth and Baltimore, 1958. 3d ed. (Harmondsworth), 1968.

Kaufmann, Edgar, and Raeburn, Ben, eds. *Frank Lloyd Wright: Writings and Buildings.* New York, 1960.

Manson, Grant C. *Frank Lloyd Wright to 1910: The First Golden Age.* New York, 1958.

Morrison, Hugh. *Louis Sullivan: Prophet of Modern Architecture.* New York, 1935. New ed., 1952.

Portoghesi, Paolo, and Borsi, F. *Victor Horta.* Rome, 1969.

Scully, Vincent J. *Frank Lloyd Wright.* New York, 1960.

———. *American Architecture and Urbanism.* New York and London, 1969.

Sedlmayr, Hans. *Verlust der Mitte.* Salzburg, 1948.

Sullivan, Louis. *The Autobiography of an Idea.* New York, 1924. Reprint: New York, 1956.

———. *Kindergarten Chats and Other Writings.* New York, 1947.

Sweeney, James Johnson, and Sert, José Luís. *Antonio Gaudi.* New York and London, 1960.

Wright, Frank Lloyd. *The Natural House.* New York, 1954; London, 1972.

11. Functionalism

Argan, Giulio Carlo. *Walter Gropius e la Bauhaus.* Turin, 1951.

Banham, Reyner. *Theory and Design in the First Machine Age.* New York and London, 1960.

Conrads, Ulrich. *Programme und Manifeste zur Architektur des 20. Jahrhunderts.* Berlin, 1964.

Giedion, Sigfried. *Space, Time and Architecture: The Growth of a New Tradition.* 1941. 5th ed., enl. Cambridge, Mass., 1967; London, 1968.

Gropius, Walter. *The New Architecture and the Bauhaus.* London, 1935. Reprint: London, 1956.

Hitchcock, Henry-Russell, and Johnson, Philip. *The International Style: Architecture Since 1922.* New York, 1932. New ed. New York, 1966.

Joedicke, Jürgen, and Plath, Christian. *Die Weissenhofsiedlung.* Stuttgart, 1968.

Johnson, Philip. *Mies van der Rohe.* New York, 1947. 2d rev. ed., 1953.

Le Corbusier. *Vers une architecture.* Paris, 1923. Translated as *Towards a New Architecture.* London, 1927. New York and London, 1960.

———. *Oeuvre complète, 1910–1965.* 7 vols. Zurich, 1937–57.

Moos, Stanislaus von. *Le Corbusier.* Frauenfeld, 1968.

Münz, L., and Künstel, G. *Der Architekt Adolf Loos.* Vienna, 1964.

Index

Pevsner, Nikolaus. *Pioneers of Modern Design from William Morris to Walter Gropius.* 2d ed. New York, 1949. Rev. ed. 1960.

Scully, Vincent J. *Modern Architecture: The Architecture of Democracy, c. 1789–1960.* New York, 1961; London, 1968. New ed. 1971.

Wingler, Hans Maria. *Das Bauhaus, 1919–33.* Weimar, Dessau, and Berlin, 1962.

12. Pluralism

Aalto, Alvar. *Gesamtwerk. Oeuvres complètes. Complete Works.* 2 vols. Zurich, 1970–71.

Drew, Philip. *Third Generation: The Changing Meaning of Architecture.* New York and London, 1972.

Joedicke, Jürgen, and Lauterbach, H. *Hugo Häring.* Stuttgart, 1965.

Nervi, Pier Luigi. *Aesthetics and Technology in Building.* Cambridge, Mass., 1965; London, 1966.

Scully, Vincent J. *Louis I. Kahn.* New York and London, 1962.

Venturi, Robert. *Complexity and Contradiction in Architecture.* New York, 1966; London, 1968.

Picture Credits